BEYOND CHINATOWN

NIAS STUDIES IN ASIAN TOPICS

20 M. C. Hoadley & C. Gunnarsson (eds) *The Village Concept in the Transformation of Rural S.E. Asia. Studies from Indonesia, Malaysia and Thailand*
21 Lisbeth Littrup (ed.) *Identity in Asian Literature*
22 O. Bruun & O. Odgaard (eds) *Mongolia in Transition. Old Patterns, New Challenges*
23 S. Tønnesson & H. Antlöv (eds) *Asian Forms of the Nation*
24 Vibeke Børdahl (ed.) *The Eternal Storyteller. Oral Literature in Modern China*
25 I. Reader & M. Söderberg (eds) *Japanese Influences and Presences in Asia*
26 Leif Manger (ed.) *Muslim Diversity. Local Islam in Global Contexts*
27 J. Koning, M. Nolten, J. Rodenburg & R. Saptari (eds) *Women and Households in Indonesia. Cultural Notions and Social Practices*
28 S. Sparkes & S. Howell (eds)*The House in Southeast Asia. A Changing Social, Economic and Political Domain*
29 P. P. Masina (ed.) *Rethinking Development in East Asia. From Illusory Miracle to Economic Crisis*
30 L. Manderson & P. Liamputtong (eds) *Coming of Age in South and Southeast Asia Youth, Courtship and Sexuality*
31 Li Narangoa & R. Cribb (eds) *Imperial Japan and National Identities in Asia, 1895–1945*
32 C. E. Goscha & S. Ivarsson (eds) *Contesting Visions of the Lao Past. Lao Historiography at the Crossroads*
33 M. Beresford & Ngoc Angie (eds) *Reaching for the Dream. Challenges of Sustainable Development in Vietnam*
34 O. Bruun & Li Narangoa (eds) *Mongols from Country to City. Floating Boundaries, Pastoralism and City Life in the Mongol Lands*
35 V. Børdahl, Fei Li & Huang Ying (eds) *Four Masters of Chinese Storytelling. Full-length Repertoires of Yangzhou Storytelling on Video*
36 C. Derichs & T. Heberer (eds) *The Power of Ideas. Intellectual Input and Political Change in East and Southeast Asia*
37 B. Sellato & P. Sercombe (eds) *Beyond the Green Myth. Borneo's Hunter-Gatherers in the 21st Century*
38 M. Janowski & F. Kerlogue (eds) *Kinship and Food in Southeast Asia*
39 M. Gravers (ed.) *Exploring Ethnic Diversity in Burma*
40 G. Helgesen & S. Risbjerg Thomsen (eds) *Politics, Culture and Self: East Asian and North European Attitudes*
41 M. Thunø (ed.) *Beyond Chinatown*
42 G. Bankoff & S. Swart *Breeds of Empire. The 'Invention' of the Horse in Southeast Asia and Southern Africa 1500–1950*

Beyond Chinatown

New Chinese Migration and the Global Expansion of China

Edited by Mette Thunø

NIAS Studies in Asian Topics Series, 41

First published in 2007 by NIAS Press
Reprinted in 2012
NIAS – Nordic Institute of Asian Studies
Leifsgade 33, DK-2300 Copenhagen S, Denmark
tel (+45) 3532 9501 • fax (+45) 3532 9549
email: books@nias.ku.dk • website: www.nias.press.dk

© NIAS – Nordic Institute of Asian Studies 2007
While copyright in the volume as a whole is vested in the Nordic Institute of Asian Studies, copyright in the individual chapters belongs to their authors. No chapter may be reproduced in whole or in part without the express permission of the author or publisher.

British Library Cataloguing in Publication Data

Beyond Chinatown : new Chinese migration and the global expansion of China. - (NIAS studies in Asian topics ; 41)
1.Chinese - Foreign countries 2.Chinese - Foreign countries - Ethnic identity 3.China - Emigration and immigration
I.Thunø, Mette
909'.04951083

ISBN 978-87-7694-000-3

Typeset by NIAS Press
Printed in the United Kingdom by Marston Digital

Publication of this work was supported by generous grants from the Chiang-Ching-kuo Foundation and the Danish Research Council for the Humanities.

CONTENTS

Preface	vii
Contibutors	ix
1. *Mette Thunø* Introduction. Beyond 'Chinatown': Contemporary Chinese Migration	1

PART I CONTEMPORARY CHINESE MIGRATION: ORDINARY AND DISTINCT

2. *Ronald Skeldon* The Chinese Overseas: The End of Exceptionalism?	35
3. *Cheng Xi* The 'Distinctiveness' of the Overseas Chinese as Perceived in the People's Republic of China	49

PART II CONTEMPORARY CHINESE MIGRATION: CHANGING ECONOMIC IMPACT AND HOST-COUNTRY RESPONSES?

4. *Zhang Xiuming* Remittances, Donations and Investments in Qingtian County since 1978	67
5. *Yow Cheun Hoe* Detraditionalized and Renewed. *Qiaoxiang* Areas: Case Studies of Panyu and Wenzhou in the Reform Period since 1978	83
6. *Antonella Ceccagno* The Chinese in Italy at a Crossroads: The Economic Crisis	115
7. *Teresita Ang See* Influx of New Chinese Immigrants to the Philippines: Problems and Challenges	137

PART II: CHINA'S RISE AS A GLOBAL POWER AND TRANSNATIONAL ISSUES

8. *Wang Gungwu* *Liuxue* and *Yimin*: From Study To Migranthood	165
9. *Wang Cangbai and Wong Siu-lun* Home as a Circular Process: The Indonesian-Chinese in Hong Kong	182
10. *Maggi W.H. Leung* Rethinking 'Home' in Diaspora. A Family Transnationalized? A Place of Nostalgia? A Commodity for Sale?	210
11. *Live Yu-Sion* The Sinwa of Reunion: Searching for a Chinese Identity in a Multicultural World	234

12. *Peta Stephenson* Altered States: Indigenous Australian
and Chinese Diasporic Alliances   254

Index   275

TABLES

2.1. Manufacturing trade and the relative importance of immigration, 2000	38
2.2. Relative importance of trade in services, 2000	39
2.3. Fertility decline, China and selected other areas, 1965–2000	40
2.4. Increase in China-born in selected destinations, various years	43
4.1. Qingtian people migrating abroad	70
4.2. Distribution of Qingtian migrants	70
4.3. Qingtian associations in Europe	73
5.1. Demographic profiles of Panyu (1997) and Wenzhou municipality (2001)	90
5.2. *Qiaoshu* enterprises in Wenzhou municipality, 1985–1998	96
5.3. *Sanzi* enterprises in Wenzhou municipality, 1984–1999	97
6.1. Businesses headed by Chinese (PRC) in Italy, September 2004	119
6.2. Businesses headed by Chinese (PRC) in selected Italian regions, September 2004	119
6.3. Selected commercial activities of the Chinese in Italy and in some Italian regions, September 2004	131
11.1. Number of Chinese in Reunion (1902–1941)	238

MAPS

5.1. Major *qiaoxiang* areas in Guangdong	87
5.2. Wenzhou in Zhejiang Province	89

FIGURES

2.1. Population pyramid summary for China, 2025	42
12.1. Zhou Xiaoping, 'Land', 1998	260
12.2. Photographer unknown, 'Jimmy Pike and Zhou Xiaoping in China', 1996	262
12.3. Zhou Xiaoping and Jimmy Pike, 'Drew each other' (1 and 2), 1995	263

Preface

Originally, the chapters included in this book were presented at the Fifth Conference for the International Society for the Study of Chinese Overseas (ISSCO) held in Copenhagen in May 2004. The conference was jointly sponsored by the Chiang Ching-kuo Foundation, the Danish Research Council for the Humanities, Daloon Foundation, Knud Højgaards Fund, Asia House Foundation, International Institute of Asian Studies (IIAS), Nordic Institute of Asian Studies and the University of Copenhagen. Its purpose was to bring together scholars from all continents and across academic disciplines to discuss the significance of contemporary Chinese migration compared with Chinese historical migration and migration in general. The selection criteria for the contributions included in this volume encompassed the presentation of new theories and novel empirical data related to the overall theme of contemporary Chinese migration and ethnic Chinese identity constructions associated with the rise of China as an economic and cultural power.

    I am grateful to all the contributors and the staff at NIAS Press for their eagerness to complete this volume and for their patience with several rounds of revisions. I also wish to acknowledge the contributions of participants at the conference whose presentations are not included in this volume, but whose engagement and comments during the conference have added positively to the final outcome of this book. Finally, I sincerely thank the abovementioned sponsors of the conference for funding the conference and several participants' travel costs. Without this support the conference and this volume would not have been realised.

Mette Thunø

Contributors

Ang See, Teresita is President of ISSCO (International Society for the Studies of Chinese Overseas), Executive Trustee and founding president of Kaisa Heritage Center and a visiting lecturer at the Ateneo de Manila University. She has authored, co-authored and edited a dozen books on the Chinese in the Philippines and other countries among these she is the author of a three-volume *Chinese in the Philippines: Problems and Perspectives* (1990; 1997; 2004). A multi-awarded social activist, Ang See speaks up on behalf of the ethnic Chinese in the Philippines against all forms of harassments, prejudices, and discrimination. She is one of the key persons responsible for the establishment of the Kaisa Heritage Center that houses the Museum of the Chinese in Philippine life – a repository of the historical and cultural legacy of the Chinese in all aspects of Philippine life.

Ceccagno, Antonella is Research Director of Centre for Immigration Research and Services in Prato, Italy. For several years, she has assisted local authorities in formulating immigration policies and carried out research in relation to the socio-economic integration of Chinese migrants in Italy and Europe. Ceccagno is also Associate Professor of Chinese language and cultural studies at the University of Bologna, Italy. She has published extensively within the field of Chinese migration to Europe including articles in *Journal of Ethnic Migration Studies* and is the co-author (together with Frank Pieke, Pal Nyìrì and Mette Thunø) of *Transnational Chinese. Fujianese Migrants in Europe* (2004).

Cheng, Xi is Associate Professor at the Chinese Institute for Overseas Chinese History Studies, Beijing, China. Her major research interest is the study of Chinese students abroad and Chinese migration since 1978 with special emphasis on the relationship between China and Chinese migrants.

Cheng Xi has published numerous articles in Chinese journals such as *Huaqiao huaren lishi yanjiu* [Overseas Chinese history studies]. Among her most recent books is *Qiaowu yu waijiao guanxi yanjiu: Zhongguo fangqi shuangchong guoji de huigu yu fansi* [Overseas Chinese affairs and national diplomacy: review and thoughts on China's abandonment of dual nationality] (2005).

Leung, Maggi is a geographer, born and raised in Hong Kong. She received her MA Degree (1996) from the University of Minnesota and her Ph.D. degree from the University of Bremen (2002). She has spent more than three years conducting research on the ethnic Chinese migrants in Germany and published her results in *Chinese Migration in Germany: Making Home in Transnational Space* (2004). This book earned her the Young Researcher Award (2004) from the Chinese University of Hong Kong where she worked from 2002 to 2006. She has recently received a fellowship from the Alexander von Humboldt Foundation and is presently affiliated to the Department of Geography, University of Bonn, Germany. Other areas of emphasis in her teaching and research are tourism, cultural heritage, sustainable development and gender-related issues.

Live, Yu-Sion is Professor of Sociology in the Department of Anthropology at the University of Reunion, France. He received his Ph.D in Sociology from the École des Hautes Études en Sciences Sociales (Paris) in 1991. He is the co-author with J. Costa-Lascoux of *Paris XIIIe, lumières d'Asie* (1995). Live's research areas include the Chinese diaspora in France and in the Indian Ocean islands; cross-cultural studies in Creole societies. His most recent work include several articles in E. Deroo and P. Blanchard (eds) *Paris Asie* (2004) and 'Phénotypes et métissage culturel à La Réunion' in *Revi Kiltir Kreol* (2005).

Skeldon, Ronald is Professorial Fellow in Geography at the University of Sussex in the United Kingdom and previously was on the faculty of the University of Hong Kong. Currently, he is working on skilled migration and on linkages between internal and international migration as part of the research at the Development Research Centre on Migration, Globalization and Poverty at the University of Sussex funded by the UK Government's Department for International Development. He has published widely on migration and development and particularly on migration in and from Asia.

Stephenson, Peta is Postdoctoral Research Fellow in the Australian Studies Centre at the University of Queensland. She specialises in the study of cross-cultural alliances between non-white migrant and Indigenous peoples and is the author of *The Outsiders Within: Telling Australia's Indigenous-Asian Story* (2007). Her book discusses the varying ways in which Indigenous-Asian histories and identities are being creatively explored in cross-cultural artistic and theatrical production. Her current project explores why an increasing number of Indigenous Australians are identifying with Islam and will forge new ways of understanding the long but largely unknown history of Islamisation in Indigenous communities.

Thunø, Mette is Pro-Dean for Research of the Faculty of Humanities at the University of Copenhagen. She holds a Ph.D. in Chinese studies from the University of Copenhagen and she has for several years been engaged in research on Chinese migration to Europe and on the policies of the People's Republic of China towards migration. Her studies have appeared in journals such as *The China Quarterly* and *The International Migration Review*. Thunø's most recent book (co-authored with Frank Pieke, Pal Nyìrì and Antonella Ceccagno) was *Transnational Chinese. Fujianese Migrants in Europe* (2004). Currently, she is working on a project based on multisited fieldwork on the implications of cultural investments from ethnic Chinese in Southeast Asia in Chinese migration villages.

Wang, Cangbai is Post-Doctoral Fellow, Centre of Asian Studies of the University of Hong Kong. He obtained his Ph.D. degree from the University of Hong Kong in 2003. From 1990 to 1995, he was a researcher in Research Department, Office of Overseas Chinese Affairs of the State Council of the PRC. His research interests include the study of diasporic Chinese, China and overseas Chinese communities, Hong Kong society and its population polices. His most recent publication include '*Haigui*: A New Area in China's Policy towards Chinese Diaspora?' in *Journal of Chinese Overseas* (2006) (co-authored with Wong Siu-lun and Sun Wenbin) and *Huo zai biechu: xianggang yinni huaren koushu lishi* [Life is elsewhere: life stories of the Indonesian Chinese in Hong Kong] (2006).

Wang, Gungwu is the Director of the East Asian Institute, National University of Singapore. BA Hons. and MA (Malaya); Ph.D. (London). Wang has taught at the University of Malaya (1957-1968) and Australian National University (1968-1986). From 1986 to 1995, he was Vice-Chancellor of the University of Hong Kong. Among his most recent books in English are *The Chinese Overseas: From Earthbound China to the Quest for Autonomy* (2000); *Don't Leave Home: Migration and the Chinese* (2001); *Bind Us in Time: Nation and Civilization in Asia* (2002); *Anglo-Chinese Encounters Since 1800: war, trade, science and governance* (2003); *Diasporic Chinese Ventures* (2004). He recently also edited a volume of essays, *Nation-building: Five Southeast Asian Histories* (2005).

Wong, Siu-lun is Professor of Sociology and Director of the Centre of Asian Studies of University of Hong Kong. He obtained his BA of Social Sciences degree at the University of Hong Kong in 1971, his M.Phil. degree at the Chinese University of Hong Kong, and his B.Litt. and D.Phil. degrees at the University of Oxford. His research interests include the study of entrepreneurship, business networks, migration, social indicators and the development of sociology in China. He is the author of *Emigrant Entrepreneurs: Shanghai Industrialists in Hong Kong* (1988), co-editor of *Hong Kong's Transition: A Decade After the Deal* (1995) and *Hong Kong in the Asia-Pacific Region: Rising to the New Challenges* (1997) and editor of *Chinese and Indian Diaspora: Comparative Perspectives* (2004).

Yow, Cheun Hoe is Research Fellow at the Centre for Chinese Language and Culture, Nanyang University of Singapore. His main academic interests include Chinese overseas and their relations with China. His most recent article 'Weakening Ties with the Ancestral Homeland in China: The Case Studies of Contemporary Singapore and Malaysian Chinese' was published in *Modern Asian Studies* (2005). Currently he is working on Chinese education in Southeast Asia.

Zhang, Xiuming is the Chief Editor of *Huaqiao huaren lishi yanjiu* [Overseas Chinese history studies]. She holds a MA degree in History. Her main research area is recent Chinese migrants and comparative studies of international migration. Zhang has published articles on Chinese students studying abroad, cultural identity of ethnic Chinese of Southeast Asia and comparative studies of the influence of Chinese and Indian migrants on sending countries.

Chapter 1

Introduction

Beyond 'Chinatown': Contemporary Chinese Migration

Mette Thunø

The emergence of the People's Republic of China (PRC) as an economic superpower has become a significant topic in popular media and scholarship around the world. The simultaneous soaring rates of Chinese migration, on the other hand, have been much less analysed. In international media reports, Chinese migration has most commonly been associated with irregular migration related to human smuggling and trafficking from particular localities in China. Academic estimates of the number of Chinese irregular migrants range from several tens of thousands (Skeldon 2000: 12-14) to some hundred thousands (Smith 1997: x), but regular Chinese migration is actually more prevalent.[1] Since the beginning of the 1980s when emigration from the PRC was officially decriminalized, regular migration has amounted to at least two million Chinese migrants (Liu 2005: 295; Guowuyuan Qiaoban Qiaowu Ganbu Xuexiao 2005: 11).[2]

All calculations of both regular and irregular Chinese migration should of course be treated with caution given the difficulties of defining who constitutes a migrant; the difficulties of systematically collecting official data on human mobility and the general lack of cumulative studies on contemporary Chinese migration numbers in receiving countries. Available data, however, reflect a novel situation of renewed Chinese migratory movements in the last three decades after a hiatus of more than 30 years. The novelty of this phenomenon lies not simply in the re-establishment of a long migration history out of China, but in the present features of contemporary Chinese migration which differ in several ways from the period prior to 1949. Contemporary Chinese migratory developments are, it is argued below, characteristic of other current migratory movements and thus belong to a larger world migration system. However, they simultaneously display distinctive features that need to be incorporated into general migration studies.

The scope of recent Chinese migration is limited in relation both to overall global migration, the population of China (Skeldon 1997: 44) and in comparison with the estimated 16 million Chinese who migrated between 1840 and 1949 (IOM 2005: 126). As such, the most significant feature of Chinese migration is not the reintroduction of high numbers of Chinese on the move in the present period, but Chinese migration experiences that are shaped in new ways by global capitalism, globalization and the rising economic significance of China. As the research in this book demonstrates, Chinese migration no longer primarily consists of male contract labourers having to live in isolated or secluded areas in destination countries. Unlike the colonial era when Chinese indentured or contract workers went to Southeast Asia and settled in designated Chinatowns or remote plantation and mining areas, present-day migration from China is directed to developing, industrialized and post-industrialized countries alike. Manual labour migrants are accompanied by students, entrepreneurs, traders, highly skilled professionals and political refugees of both sexes. The estimated 30–35 million ethnic Chinese already living outside China, in addition to the number of potential migrants in China, also suggest that Chinese migration today differs in some respects from the Chinese migration history of the late nineteenth and early twentieth centuries. Rather, contemporary Chinese migration is comparable to the present situation of other countries with large contingents of migrants. Finally, unlike the Chinese imperial state of the nineteenth century, the present Chinese party-state actively supports migration through various political decisions, organizations and activities and keenly liaises with migrants abroad in a manner similar to other governments of migrant-sending countries (Thunø 2001).

The chapters in this book address various issues related to contemporary Chinese migration and patterns of adaptation, demonstrating that Chinese migration no longer constitutes an exceptional migration case. Migrant entrepreneurship and trading, migrant-sending communities and remittances, irregular migrants, ethnic identity and 'home' constructions and inter-ethnic co-operation are all features comparable to the migration experiences of migrants from other countries of origin. These Chinese features just need to be integrated more into general academic understandings and general conceptualizations of contemporary human migration.

CONTEMPORARY CHINESE MIGRATION: ANYTHING NEW?

The following chapters were originally presented at the Fifth Conference for the International Society for the Study of Chinese Overseas (ISSCO) held in Copenhagen in May 2004. The conference theme 'New Chinese migrants' was inspired by a relatively new notion among PRC migration scholars, government related organizations working within the field of Chinese migration and popular media.[3] Instead of referring to Chinese migrants either as 'overseas Chinese' [huaqiao] or 'ethnic Chinese' [huaren],[4] 'new migrants' appears to be used most often to encompass Chinese who, since the early 1980s, left China to settle elsewhere regardless of their purpose, legal status and citizenship. Moreover, the (re)-import of the Japanese word for 'migrant' [yimin] to typify international mobility from China suggests a preference for terminology corresponding more closely to the international language applied to human mobility issues. It also reflects an attempt to encompass a broader conception of those persons leaving China than the existing discourse which refers to Chinese migrants primarily within the frame of reference of legal citizenship.

Nevertheless, the old distinction between the 'Overseas Chinese', appealing and referring to Chinese citizens, and 'ethnic Chinese', encompassing non-Chinese citizens living outside China, is still maintained in central official discourse. 'New migrants' is very rarely used in the official mouthpiece of the Chinese Communist Party, the *People's Daily* (*Renmin ribao*) and a newly published book on Chinese migration to be used as an official curriculum for cadres who will be working with Chinese migrants exclusively employs the terms *huaqiao/huaren* with reference to all matters concerning Chinese migration (Guowuyuan Qiaoban Qiaowu Ganbu Xuexiao 2005). This central official commitment to terminology related to migrants' citizenship status, even in discussions of more general Chinese migration issues, reflects more than anything else the politically sensitive issue of dual Chinese citizenship.

In response to the anxieties in South-east Asia caused by large numbers of Chinese migrants, the PRC agreed to abolish dual citizenship in 1955. This policy was reaffirmed with the passage of the Chinese Nationality Law of 1980 (Thunø 2001). The reintroduction of dual citizenship was recently suggested in discussions by members of the advisory body of the Chinese People's Political Consultative Conference (Yuan 2005).[5] Notwithstanding some official suggestions that the PRC emulate India's bestowal of dual citizenship on Indian migrant investors, the official Chinese position still seems firmly opposed to the notion of dual citizenship.[6]

Despite the unwillingness of Chinese central authorities to accept and make use of the concept of 'new migrants', its existence and popular usage indicate a need to be able to distinguish recent migrants from the Chinese contract labour migrants of the nineteenth and twentieth centuries (who were hired to toil in mines and plantations in European colonies or semi-colonies mainly in South-east Asia).[7] In fact, the origins, destinations and constitutions of contemporary migrants from China are markedly different from earlier contingents of migrants, as are the reasons for migratory movements.

Demographically, Chinese migration has shifted from being typically young, male, 'coolie' pioneers from the Chinese countryside in south-eastern China to migrants of both sexes coming also from urban areas (Guowuyuan renkou pucha bangongshi and Guojia tongjiju renkou he shehui keji tongjisi 2002: 10–13; Zai and Morooka 2004: 153; Zhao Hongying 2000). In 1990, 34 per cent of all registered Chinese living outside China were female migrants (Guowuyuan renkou pucha bangongshi and Guojia tongjiju renkou tongjisi 1993: 7), and this figure increased to 38 per cent in 2000 (Guowuyuan renkou pucha bangongshi and Guojia tongjiju renkou he shehui keji tongjisi 2002: 10–11). Contemporary Chinese female migrants have entered the present migrant population as students, spouses or single migrants and are vastly different from their poorly educated predecessors who mostly followed their husbands abroad.

In the same way that migration from other parts of the world first originates in areas affected by the penetration of capitalist markets – rather than poor areas disconnected from world markets (Massey et al. 1998) – we find that international mobility from China was initiated in the 1980s from the large cities of Beijing, Shanghai and Guangzhou (Canton) as well as from the provinces of Guangdong and Fujian. These provinces were selected as the pioneers in economic development and both were areas with long migration histories.⁸ Beijing and Shanghai urbanites migrated as part of family re-unification schemes with relatives in Asia, North America and Europe or as students and professionals extending their stays overseas to become migrants.

Students from urban China who initially went abroad to study but who stayed on in their receiving countries have also added significantly to the number of urban Chinese migrants in industrialized countries. According to official Chinese data, since 1949 China has sent 900,000 students abroad, of whom only one quarter has returned to China (see also Cheng 2003; Zhang 2003: 74; Zweig et al. 2004).⁹ Recently, an increasing number of students are officially reported to have returned to China from their overseas studies (20,000 students returned in 2003)¹⁰ but, with a record high of 115,000 students studying abroad in 2004, China also became the number one exporter of students in the world.¹¹

This large student cohort of contemporary Chinese migrant streams may also be considered as novel and a significant trait of contemporary Chinese migration flows. Chinese students also went overseas in the beginning of the twentieth century, when young Chinese went to Japan to study between 1898 and 1911 (Bailey 1998a: 335; Huang 1982), some went to the United States (Bieler 2004; Ye 2001) and others went to Europe (including Russia) (Bailey 1998b: 318), but only a fraction settled as migrants.¹² These pioneer Chinese students were self-financed or studied on Chinese and foreign government scholarships (this being the case into the late twentieth century), but compared to this early period contemporary Chinese student migration is now responding to the commercialized educational sectors in many industrialized countries. As a result of education having changed into a profitable service industry, and thus opening up new channels of entry into developed countries, Chinese student migration has increased numerically, as has the number of those who stay to become migrants or settlers.

As market reforms and global capitalism spread in China from the originally designated economic areas along the eastern coast into the north (and in the 1990s to inland provinces), more people were displaced from their traditional livelihoods and prompted to migrate to secure the survival of their households. In 2000, migration from urban centres in the three north-eastern provinces of Liaoning, Jilin and Heilongjiang increased significantly to constitute 17 per cent of all registered Chinese migrants in that year (Guowuyuan renkou pucha bangongshi and Guojia tongjiju renkou he shehui keji tongjisi 2002: 10–11). These migrants were typically laid off from state-owned enterprises that were closed down or restructured as a result of economic market reforms. The displacement of Chinese industrial workers and the lack of a well-functioning social security system triggered migration especially to neighbouring Russia and, subsequently, into Europe.

In the 1990s, urban migration from municipalities was gradually supplemented and then taken over by rural migration. Rural migrants from Fujian, Zhejiang and Yunnan officially made up 54 per cent of all registered Chinese migrants, while registered migrants from Beijing and Shanghai constituted only 14 per cent (Guowuyuan renkou pucha bangongshi and Guojia tongjiju renkou tongjisi 1993: 7; Guowuyuan renkou pucha bangongshi and Guojia tongjiju renkou he shehui keji tongjisi 2002: 10–13). In addition, several reports point to undocumented migration also stemming from specific localities in these provinces (Pieke et al. 2004).

This development during the 1980s and 1990s of the changing local origin of Chinese migration illustrates the causal link between economic development and migration. Chinese migration, like international mobility from other countries, stems from China's integration into the global market economy and not from lack of economic development. The poorest provinces in western and central China, with the least economic integration into world markets, are rarely sending migrants to join the international labour markets. Conversely, some of the richest areas in China, including the large cities of Beijing, Shanghai and Guangzhou (Canton), have reached a standard of living and social security that has seen a decreasing number of their inhabitants needing to pursue overseas strategies. In contrast, in rural localities in Fujian, Zhejiang and Yunnan provinces, as well as in north-eastern China where economic development has produced extensive unemployment and economic insecurity, we find economic, political, social and cultural transformations that have changed specific localities into major migration areas (see Li Minghuan et al. 2003; Pieke et al. 2004; Thunø and Pieke 2005).

In terms of migrant destinations, rural and urban Chinese migration has become multidirectional and multidimensional, with a clear preference for global cities in the Americas, Australasia (including Japan) and Europe, rather than traditional destinations in South-east Asia. In this respect, contemporary modern Chinese migration follows the general trend of the late twentieth century of migration to (largely, though not exclusively) metropolitan areas in high income migration societies (Skeldon 1997: 78–80;

84–85). But Chinese entrepreneurial and trading migration is also uniquely directed to transformation societies all over the world (see below).

In the new receiving countries and localities, Chinese migrants no longer encounter nineteenth-century targeted Chinese racial exclusion[13] or discriminating anti-Chinese legislation forcing them into secluded occupational niches and living quarters such as Chinatowns (Wong 1988). Rather, contemporary Chinese migrants (like other migrants) are met with general immigration restrictions in the major receiving countries of the US and Canada. Despite immigration regulations and other political measures to curb migration to the Americas, Australasia and Europe, mobility to post-industrialized countries appeals to both Chinese migrants and other migrants alike. Chinese migrants are also comparable to other migrants who make use of a range of different means in their pursuit to enter destination countries in the Americas, Australasia and Europe. In the process many become part of the large contingent of irregular or undocumented migrants entering these destination countries.

Chinese migration to the Americas, Australasia and Europe, and more specifically to the global cities of New York, Chicago, Los Angeles, Toronto, Vancouver, London, Paris, Frankfurt, Milan, Rome, Tokyo, Osaka and Sydney, follows general international migration flows that are the result of capital accumulation and a strong demand for the services of unskilled workers as well as highly skilled professionals in these urban capital strongholds (Castells 1989; Sassen 1991, 1998). In this way, contemporary Chinese migration may be regarded as part of a larger world migration system thus general migration theories of migration networks, migration institutions and cumulative causation are also relevant and applicable to the Chinese case (Massey et al 1993: 448–454).

In Chapter 2, Ronald Skeldon considers whether contemporary Chinese migration is an exceptional case or similar to other migration flows and processes in the larger global migration system. He argues that prior to China's integration into the global economy in the 1980s, migration from China was significantly different from migration from Europe to North America. Europeans moved into virgin land that was taken over and controlled by migrants themselves, whereas Chinese migrants in Southeast Asia and North America were marginalized and excluded by European colonial powers and European settlers. In the 1980s and 1990s, as China started experiencing rapid economic growth, migration out of China accelerated. This was also the case in the late nineteenth century when economic development in North America saw increased migration from Europe.

Skeldon also emphasizes the constitution of the new Chinese migrants who originate from rural areas, urban students and contract labourers. In contrast to the early phase of Chinese migration to colonial South-east Asia, these newer Chinese migrants encounter opportunities and constraints in receiving societies that are comparable to those faced by migrants from other source countries. As such, it is argued that China and Chinese migrants have become ordinary players in the global migration system. Nevertheless, China's territorial and demographic size, the large number of ethnic Chinese residing in South-east Asia and other continents, as well as a long history of migration, are all factors suggesting that Chinese migration holds some distinct features.

'Universal' contra 'distinct' qualities of recent Chinese migration have also become a significant topic of research among Chinese researchers studying the characteristics of new Chinese migrants. In Chapter 3, Cheng Xi accounts for the vivid re-emergence of PRC academic scholarship on new Chinese migration following a regained recognition of Chinese migrants in the early 1980s and the increasing research investments within the field of migration made by the Chinese government (see also Gao and Shi 2002; Zhou 2001). Prior to the economic reforms in China, the 'overseas Chinese' had been a politically sensitive topic to conduct research on, but by the turn of the twenty-first century the central role attributed to the ethnic Chinese, and Chinese migrants in China's economic reforms, has fundamentally changed PRC academic possibilities and interests. As China's economic power has strengthened globally, national research investments and research institutes on diverse aspects of Chinese migration have also increased considerably and stimulated varied research approaches. Lately, discussions about establishing a particular academic discipline [xueke] called 'Overseas and Ethnic Chinese Studies' [huaqiao huaren xue] have also resounded among PRC researchers (see Gao Weinong 2004; Guo Liang 2003; Liang Zhiming 2002, 2003).

Cheng Xi argues that anxieties among non-Chinese researchers and popular media in relation to the volume of Chinese migrants are based on erroneous data interpretations. Likewise, concern with Chinese scholarship on Chinese migrants' cultural attachments to China is unfounded given the various research approaches presently existing in China. Instead, Cheng holds that distinctive features of contemporary migrants encompass

Chinese migrants' financial contributions to and investments in China, the PRC government's extensive administrative system for liaising with ethnic Chinese and new Chinese migrants, as well as the key position of contemporary migrants in China's pursuit for Great Power status. Although these features may be regarded as particular to contemporary Chinese migrants, new migration from China has also become part of international flows of migrants and needs to be conceptualized and studied as a component of the larger global migration system.

CONTEMPORARY CHINESE MIGRATION: CHANGING ECONOMIC IMPACT AND HOST-COUNTRY RESPONSES

The significance of contemporary Chinese migrants' transfer of financial resources to China does not constitute a significant break with China's past migration history. As early as the end of the nineteenth and beginning of the twentieth century, the Chinese government mobilized Chinese migrants on the basis of cultural loyalty towards localities of origin and political allegiance to the new nation-state for political and economic purposes. As a result, remittances were transferred back to China, albeit only a fraction was used on productive investments (Chen 1940; Douw et al. 1999: 35).

Contemporary Chinese migration differs from the earlier periods in terms of migrants' donations, remittances and investments in China in at least two ways: the total sum of financial investments and remittances appears to surpass earlier practices and financial investments are made in production, rather than being spent primarily in individual households. In fact, China is now among the top receiving countries in the world of remittances[14] and industrial investments from Chinese migrants or ethnic Chinese. In contrast to many Latin American labour sending countries (Massey et al. 1998: 239–253), China has been able to attract overseas resources from ethnic Chinese to achieve long-term economic development. This success story of a significant part of foreign direct investments (FDI) originating from Chinese migrants or persons of Chinese descent[15] is to some extent similar to other Asian countries such as India, where migrant investments are also pursued by various means (Basch et al. 1994: 258, 278; Russell 1986), however, China may even seem more successful in attracting remittances and investments as a result of its long migration history. The tremendous overseas capital investments are thus achieved by reconsolidating and reinvigorating China's transnational ties to the descendants of the centuries-old Chinese merchant migrants in South-east Asia (Bolt 1996; 2000; Lever-Tracy et al. 1996; Zhuang Guotu 2001).

The effects of migrant remittances and investments at the micro and macro levels in various countries have been studied extensively (see e.g. Russell 1992). Many labour-exporting countries have confidence in migration and subsequent remittances as a viable development model, but a number of empirical studies have so far been disappointing in their conclusions regarding reliance on migration for economic development. Investments in productive activities in many countries with strong out-migration have not proven to be easily converted into national economic development, as the cases of Turkey and countries in the Middle East demonstrate (Massey et al. 1998: 222–253). In the PRC, local Chinese officials in areas affected by contemporary migration similarly consider remittances as vital for local development and anticipate that investments from first-generation migrants will boost local economic growth, but frequently they experience migration as a difficult development strategy. Zhang Xiuming's study of remittances, investments and donations in Qingtian county, Zhejiang province, provides an example of weak local economic development, despite the availability of migrant resources (Chapter 4).

Qingtian is situated immediately to the west of Wenzhou municipality and a salient feature of this area is a specialization in migration, since the late nineteenth century, to Europe. Zhang shows how the first generation of Qingtian migrants of the 1980s and 1990s by way of remittances, donations, and investments supported and strengthened their home communities in terms of economic, social and educational development. Like earlier migrants from Qingtian who remitted their savings to relatives in Qingtian, contemporary migrants from the early 1980s onwards have also started to send remittances. During the 1980s and 1990s, remittances only increased slowly, but in Qingtian County in 2001 private foreign currency savings reached more than US$300 million for the first time.

Such personal money flows not only raise the living standard of individual households and families, they also significantly contribute to the retransformation of cultural and social practices as well as altering the physical features of many migrant villages (Levitt 2001; Thunø and Pieke 2005). In Qingtian County, Zhang suggests that remittances and other types of individual transnational practices have had similar effects, such as the construction of new ostentatious houses and international telephone connections, changing consumption practices and providing a more global outlook generally (see also Li Minghuan et al. 1999). Similarly, philanthropic activities by donations for local projects in the fields of communication, sanitation and education are argued by Zhang to raise the educational level in the county and improve infrastructure.

Although the effect of both remittances and donations in the case of Qingtian are profound and have contributed positively to local changes, investments in production bringing about new job opportunities have lagged behind. As with studies in other regions (Massey et al. 1998: 222–253), Zhang demonstrates that Qingtian's poor infrastructure (roads, communication, irrigation, education, investment policies and regulations) still discourages migrants from placing their savings in local productive investments. Despite remittances, donations and investments, Qingtian remained, in 2002, one of the least developed counties in all of Zhejiang province. Qingtian local government seems to have acknowledged this with a policy decision to regard migrant remittances and investments as only supportive, rather than a principal force for development.

In the future, similar studies of Chinese migrant communities will be able to complement the body of academic research investigating the impact of migrant remittances and investments on the development of local communities. China also offers the possibility of studying how typical historical migrant communities, owing to investments from ethnic Chinese outside the PRC during the last couple of decades have been economically transformed to the extent that migration has almost ceased. As mentioned above, such localities are, among other places, situated in coastal Guangdong province with a long history of extensive migration going back to the mid-nineteenth century and from where a majority of migrants in the United States originate. Southern coastal Fujian around the municipality of Xiamen, from where many migrants in South-east Asia originate, is another example of a restructured migrant locality resulting from the economic development linked to migration. In these areas, economic research has been conducted to understand the vast economic changes and dynamics taking place, but only occasionally from the perspective of transnational migrant relations.[16]

In Chapter 5, Yow Cheun Hoe compares two large migrant communities located in southern China, both characterized by long-term overseas migration, but with very different migration development trajectories during the last three decades. Panyu, located close to Hong Kong, and Wenzhou, located south of Shanghai, have both been typical areas of out-migration from the mid-nineteenth century to the establishment of the PRC in 1949. But during the Chinese era of economic reforms, migration from the for-mer did not resume, whereas international mobility from the latter has significantly accelerated. Yow argues that economic development in Panyu has benefited from the proximity of kin in Hong Kong who, with donations and investments, have transformed the area so successfully that the livelihoods of the inhabitants have been secured, thus reducing the incentive to leave for overseas destinations. Productive and industrial investments, however, are not based on sentiments of local attachments, so much as on pure business calculations. As a result, Panyu now attracts internal migrant workers from central China.

In Wenzhou, on the other hand, far-reaching economic transformations of local production into small-scale private businesses integrated into global market production have made linkages to migrants more important than investments in local production. In this locality, migrants facilitate the promotion of local products for global markets, and hence gain foreign exchange and know-how for Wenzhou's development, rather than large-scale investments into productive sites.

Yow's carefully selected case studies of the influence of migrant investments in shaping Chinese overseas migration areas offer a new perspective on migrant remittances, donations and investments and their significance for local economic development. Yow's study shows that in Panyu investments from migrants primarily living in neighbouring Hong Kong have generated the kind of conventionally sought after investments within the production sector that have enabled the area to transform, promote sustainable development and generate local employment opportunities. Wenzhou, on the other hand, has not achieved these kinds of extensive migrant investments in local production, because its developmental model relies heavily on migrants to trade in local garments, leather shoes, cigarette lighters, hardware and handicrafts manufactured for European markets. In Wenzhou, migration has thus increased.

The two case studies of Chinese migrant-sending communities offer a new perspective on the significance of considering both central and local policies in shaping source areas of migration and sustaining migration over time. In general, migration theories pay limited attention to the role of the state in endorsing, initiating and supporting migration as part of economic developmental strategies, but as demonstrated by Yow, Zhang and Cheng in this volume, the Chinese state's migration policies and the ensuing local implementation of these policies are paramount factors for our understanding of contemporary migration from China.[17] Yow argues that central economic reforms of decentralizing foreign trade facilitated the founding of many import–export companies by Wenzhou migrants living in Central and Eastern Europe. This calls attention to more closely incorporating the state – central and local – into migration theory as an independent factor determining the outcome of migration and migration processes. Exploring the causes of international mobility as merely the outcome of the global economy's penetration into developing countries and an increasing demand for migrant labour in advanced industrial societies as stipulated in segmented labour market (Piore 1979) and world system theories (Massey et al. 1998: 286) seems insufficient in light of the increasing interests and activities of developing states to develop and gain advantages from migration (see also Østergaard-Nielsen 2003).

Similarly, general theory building on migration pays insufficient attention to active local economic responses to global capitalism in sending states and the effect such reactions may have on initiating and sustaining migration. The Chinese state coined a special term for villages affected by emigration – *qiaoxiang* [sojourning or overseas Chinese township] – to identify such localities for preferential treatment and policies, although it is unclear what qualifying elements makes an area into a *qiaoxiang*. Yow's study points our attention to the diverse economic and political decisions made by local *qiaoxiang* governments, despite central attempts to assign these localities similar conditions of emigration and migrant involvement.

Chinese localities' responses to the global economy have not been limited to the passive acceptance of central migration policies, nor to the merely passive reception of international capital and the entry of multinational companies in China. Chinese economic policies have focused intensively on developing local manufacturing in small or medium-sized townships and village enterprises of inexpensive, low-quality consumer goods for domestic consumption and export (Saich 2004: 251–253). The growth of these rural enterprises has, despite or possibly because of the adaptation to global markets in the latter part of the 1990s, generated new commercial opportunities for Chinese migrants to go abroad to both developed as well as developing countries to import and trade in inexpensive products manufactured in China. In this respect, Chinese migration from such localities as Wenzhou offers an alternative to the African and Mexican cases and a new perspective on human mobility contingent on trading and business undertakings in destination countries and close commercial linkages to sending societies in China.

Obviously, the Chinese border-crossing trader-turned-migrant is a well-known historical phenomenon. Merchants from Fujian were among some of the earliest traders to become recognized as Chinese migrants when they established trading communities in Manila and Nagasaki in the 1570s (Wang Gungwu 1994: 80–99; Zhuang Guotu 2001). Later Chinese merchants expanded to the most important port cities in South-east Asia selling Chinese silk, tea and porcelain. The interest in Chinese silk commenced this trade, but with the arrival of European trans-continental shipping and colonial expansion into China and South-east Asia, a rising demand for labour was instead created, transforming Chinese migration from the nineteenth century into primarily labour or coolie migration.

Contemporary Chinese migration may be considered as an extension of this Chinese migration legacy related to international trading in Chinese products. Chinese traders or entrepreneurs have re-emerged among contemporary Chinese migrant flows, but the formerly coveted Chinese merchandise has been exchanged for more commonplace commodities such as clothes, shoes, toys and household necessities produced in China. The attraction is no longer products that are unique to China, but inexpensive and low-quality global products that can be vended at very competitive prices, in particular in transformation societies with weak links to global markets or loosely structured economies.

Business or entrepreneurship based on importing and selling low-priced goods from China has given rise to large migration flows from China to Europe, Africa and Latin America where only small numbers of Chinese migrants resided prior to the 1980s (see e.g. Bolt 1996; Nyíri 2003; Haugen and Carling 2005). The possibilities for Chinese migrants to engage in entrepreneurial activities such as wholesale or retailing manufactured goods in receiving societies have spurred migration. In other words, a new type of highly mobile commercial migrant relying mainly on China's new position in the global division of labour as the world's manufacturing house of inexpensive and low-quality goods has emerged as part of contemporary Chinese migration.

The dimensions and implications of this new type of migration are still not well known. Ethnographic studies of Chinese migrant traders in different destination countries such as those in this volume by Ceccagno and See are available, but findings and conclusions about this type of migration appear to be indefinite at the moment, given the limited scope of local studies in different national contexts. Nevertheless, as the two studies on Chinese trading migrants in Italy and the Philippines illustrate, globalization creates new opportunities for Chinese to migrate by opening up international consumer markets. The Chinese trading migrants may contribute to diversifying industries and making markets more competitive and viable as Ceccagno argues in the case of Chinese migrants in Italy, but as agents of globalization, Chinese migrants also face many constraints and abuses in host societies.

Chapters 6 and 7 by Antonella Ceccagno and Teresita Ang See on recent Chinese migration and entrepreneurship, as well as trading in Italy and the Philippines respectively, present two different types of studies focusing on new issues relating to the interplay between the causes of migration and the novel possibilities of migrant trading and entrepreneurship in the wake of significant economic growth in China. Ceccagno's study of Chinese garment entrepreneurs and import traders in Italy indicates that global capitalist development in China prompts increasing Chinese migration to Italy, since the global economic integration of China not only disrupts local Chinese economies, but because this type of economic development has also given rise to new opportunities for translocal manufacturing and trading to Chinese migrants or potential migrants.

In the case study of Italy, new Chinese migrants of the 1980s and early 1990s initially worked in garment workshops performing contract work (sewing and hemming) for Italian manufacturers that later developed into the local manufacture of shoes and the production of furniture and home appliances. Recently, this typical ethnic niche production has changed into transnational business activities of trade in imported competitive goods produced in China. Chinese migrants' trading in imported wholesale goods such as garments and shoes has turned Italy and more specifically Piazza Vittorio in Rome into one of the principal European wholesale centres for manufactured Chinese goods, comparable to the similar Chinese import centres in Budapest and Moscow (Nyíri 2003: 242; Pieke et al. 2004: 29–36; 135–143) and on a lesser scale in Madrid and Barcelona in Spain (Nieto 2003).

Ceccagno's detailed study of the Chinese in Italy elucidates the development and transformation from the earlier periods of Chinese migrants' economic engagement in a socially and economically isolated ethnic garment and leather niche into transnational entrepreneuship based on importing and selling manufactured goods from China. The early types of ethnic niche activities by migrants are, however, the suject of most available studies on migrant entrepreneurship, conceived as migrants' economic activities in receiving countries and the impact of these economic practices on receiving societies (Aldrich and Waldinger 1990; Light 1984; Portes et al. 1986; Portes et al. 2002). Ceccagno's study contributes to a new understanding of contemporary migrant entrepreneurship as closely linked to sending countries and highly contingent on the political and economic developments in both sending and receiving countries.

In Chapter 7, political activist Teresita Ang See discusses the phenomenon of Chinese migrant traders arriving as irregular migrants in the Philippines. Empirical studies suggest that irregular and undocumented migration has primarily been perceived as a problem for industrialized countries and irregular migrants have often been associated with peasants and unskilled workers (Kyle and Koslowski 2001; Smith 1997). The irregular migration of Chinese traders to developing countries with large populations of ethnic minorities, such as in the Philippines, has received much less attention in academic studies, despite the fact that, the repercussions there of the many irregular Chinese migrants (an estimated 80,000–100,000 persons) are severe and unlike the consequences of irregular migration in industrialized countries. In this light, this chapter has been included although it is not primarily based on empirical research, but provides an account of the present situation of contemporary Chinese migrants in Philippine society as accounted for in newspapers and perceived by an ethnic Chinese political activist.

Teresita Ang See demonstrates in her study that Chinese traders opt for destination countries such as the Philippines, because of its weak bureaucratic and legal institutionalization, and widespread corruption. In contrast to developed countries with more strict control of irregular migrants, Philippine society offers irregular migrants the possibility of bribing corrupt government officials in the Philippine Bureau of Immigration, the Bureau of Customs and other government agencies to become regularized, import Chinese merchandise and obtain better stall locations on markets. Consequently, this favouring of Chinese migrants means that Filipino vendors lose the better stall locations to Chinese vendors, thereby creating intense racial hostility and resentment.

Moreover, to counteract the livelihood of the Chinese trading migrants, a Retail Trade Law banning foreigners from undertaking retail trade has been passed. Frequent police raids are conducted against undocumented migrants and foreign retail traders resulting, in many cases, in the violation of the human rights of those being arrested. Simultaneously, the Filipinos of Chinese descent have also become the victims of police raids and are now facing racial discrimination by the mainstream society, thus creating unrest and insecurity among all ethnic Chinese.

The two case studies of Chinese migrants conducting wholesale and retail businesses in Italy and the Philippines demonstrate the impact of global capitalism on both sending and receiving societies in relation to human mobility. China's integration into the global economy as the producer of inexpensive products (caused by low salary levels and restricted legal and institutional constraints on production) has created new opportunities for Chinese traders and entrepreneurs in the global market. Countries with weak links to the global economy and without severe restrictions on migration and/or the possibilities of circumvention by bribery or of applying for amnesties seem especially to attract Chinese migrants as both wholesalers and retailers of competitive products produced in China.

Ceccagno's and See's chapters show that in Italy and the Philippines legal measures to confine the activities particularly of Chinese migrants have been implemented to constrain their commercial activities. In late 2003, global competition from Chinese migrants was curbed in Italy by implementing strict national import and custom restrictions on goods directly imported from China. After a worldwide quota system expired on 1 January 2005, countries in Southern Europe have, moreover, pressured the European Commission to apply new import quotas on textiles from China. Such strong receiving state reactions designed to curb the import and sales of Chinese manufactured products reflect that production in these countries has not adjusted well to the spread of global capitalism and production in low income countries such as China, nor have they adjusted to the new type of commercial migrant taking advantage of their translocal linkages to, and information about, production in China.

The case studies in this volume and other ethnographic studies on Chinese trading migrants suggest that a new and different category of migrant, albeit numerically small compared to the overall number of Chinese migrants, has emerged as a result of globalization and China's economic position on the global market. Additional investigations are needed to demonstrate whether these traders adapt a distinctive form of economic activity based on regular translocal entrepreneurship that differs from other Chinese migrants and whether or not such economic activities also imply that these migrants are less likely to settle permanently outside China.[18]

CONTEMPORARY CHINESE MIGRATION: TRANSLOCAL RELATIONS OF PROFESSIONAL AND ECONOMIC MIGRANTS

Entrepreneurship is one issue among others related to the recent introduction of 'transnationalism' as an analytical tool in migration studies. 'Transnationalism' has, in anthropological, sociological and cultural studies, been conceived as an alternative focus within the field of migration studies to assimilation and adaptation of migrants to receiving societies. Instead of primarily directing attention to traditional concerns about migrants, in relation to destination societies, the transnational perspective focuses more on economic, political and cultural interactions and identity constructions between places of origin and destinations of migrants and the impact that such activities have across borders on communities at both ends of the migration stream (see e.g. Appadurai 1990, 1993; Basch et al. 1994; Guarnizo and Diaz 1999; Kyle 2000; Levitt 2001; Ong and Nonini 1997; Smith and Guarnizo 1998).

In this new analytical perspective, migrants are argued increasingly to live dual or fluid lives with unceasing attachments to both their localities of origin and destination, not at least due to technological conditions supporting a higher level of border crossing connections and activities than previous migrants (Levitt 2001). In a Chinese context, migrants of the past appear as sojourners with a clear notion about 'home' as a stable unified locality in China linked to their ancestors and to where they would return to be buried (Sinn 1989). Contemporary Chinese migrants, who in contrast to their predecessors are likely to enjoy less racial discrimination and exclusion where they choose to settle and have easier access to their localities of origin may identify 'home' as being in various localities. However, as Wang Gungwu, Wang Cangbai and Wong Siu-lun as well as Maggi Leung all argue in this volume 'home' as an analytical concept applied to contemporary conditions should be redefined and separated from traditional notions of home on a grounded and material territory. Instead, 'homemaking' needs to be studied as the product of diverse power relations and struggles in a translocal space. Such power relations still encompass the nation-state as we are reminded by Live Yu-Sion's ethnographic study of ethnic Chinese on Reunion Island whose recent identity shaping processes of cultural belonging are significantly affected by the novel presence of the PRC.

The chapters in this section all focus on issues of translocal identity, belonging and homemaking constructions as a novel feature of contemporary Chinese migrants and as a new development that is also contingent on China's rising attractiveness and the Chinese party-state's increasingly active presence among Chinese migrant populations. The section starts with Wang Gungwu's theoretical discussion about the new type of contemporary Chinese students-turned-migrants, who settle after graduation or completed study programmes, rather than returning to China. Wang Gungwu proposes the new concept of 'migranthood' to refer to this life situation of home and nationality located spacially in between nations, localities and cultures.

It has already been argued above that students need to be regarded as part of contemporary Chinese migration. Student migrants only constitute a fraction of all international migrants, but student migration has a long history in Asia, and, as argued by Ronald Skeldon in this volume, PRC students constitute a significant part of the number of new Chinese migrants. Despite intensive efforts by PRC authorities, including a change in propaganda slogan from 'return to serve the country' [guiguo fuwu] to 'to serve the country' [weiguo fuwu] and economic advantages by returning to China, a large although waning proportion of China's overseas students stay in their countries of study.

Wang Gungwu's discussion in Chapter 8 addresses the complex issue of a distinct form of students-turned-migrants' mobility. Wang argues that when students decide to settle after having completed their studies and acquire permanent residence, they also start sustaining a migrant-like existence, or they obtain 'migranthood'. Wih this new concept Wang suggests that these highly skilled persons are neither students, nor migrants, but in an intersticial position 'in-between'. It is argued that with the latest developments of international mobility and educational exchange the concepts of migrants and 'migranthood' would seem to interact and blend, but the case of Chinese students or graduates suggests that they do not easily become regular migrants. Globalization enables them to regard China as a possible place to serve from afar, but not necessarily to return to settle.

Wang's concept of 'migranthood' applied specifically to students-turned-migrants, who postpone their decision to go back to China and find ways to contribute both to their country of settlement and in this case to China, underlines contemporary migrants' propensity to simultaneously maintain close attachments beyond a single nation-state. Applying this analytical perspective 'home', conceived of as a national-territorial bounded entity related to migrants' countries of ancestry that is lost forever when moving beyond the borders of the nation-state, is contested.

In Chapter 9, Wang Cangbai and Wong Sui-lun also question the interpretation of 'home' as related to a national-territorial locality that only exists in migrants' country of origin. In relation to contemporary migrants, 'home' as a social science concept also needs to be reconceptualized as a social entity that can be reconstructed in an 'extra-territorial' space by borrowing shared social and cultural elements. On the basis of an ethnographic study of Indonesian Chinese migrants in Hong Kong, it is argued by Wang and Wong that these migrants effectively reconstruct a cohesive and symbolic home. In the case of the Indonesian Chinese, the reconstruction of a new home in Hong Kong has been undertaken by borrowing concepts from the traditional Chinese lineage system and transferring these into a new type of unique association – the alumni association – to create fictive blood ties and define a shared geographic locality of origin. This study of Indonesian-Chinese migrants demonstrates that although they identify themselves as being ethnically Chinese, China is merely a cultural symbol or ancestral home. Indonesia is their emotional home and Hong Kong is their functional home. Finding China an undesirable place to live and Indonesia unsafe, these migrants have opted to settle in Hong Kong where they, with great efforts and through struggles of power, reconstruct a new permanent home by employing traditional forms of symbolic attachment.

Maintaining a position 'in-between' also applies to contemporary migrants from China living in Germany. Maggi Leung in Chapter 10 discusses this perception of 'home' among first- and second-generation Chinese migrants with close family relations in China and specifically in Hong Kong. These migrants define home as existing in multiple places and as with the case of the Indonesian Chinese, their claims of belonging are closely linked to social, political and economic processes of exclusion and inclusion. Moreover, Maggi Leung argues that 'homemaking' is influenced by other aspects such as the commercialization of diaspora tourism. The ethnic tourist industry targeting migrants – private or state-run – commodifies the notion of 'home' and 'homing desire' to gain a profit from transnational migrants. Being of Chinese ethnicity, these travel agents apply their ethnic background and knowledge of China to appeal to Chinese migrants by commodifying 'home' as a locality in China and festival celebrations as required events for a Chinese person, thus asserting features of a genuine home for ethnic Chinese as located in China. In this contested space of global capitalism and nation-states, contemporary Chinese migrants, supported by new communication and transportation technologies, construct and re-construct, according to Leung, new notions of belonging to homes in multiple sites.

Fluid lives and multiple homes are defined by diverse factors related to contemporary migration, but the impact of the nation-state on contemporary migrants' notions of belonging is still fundamental for our understanding of the migrants of today. In particular, the case of China with its expanding economic and cultural presence across Asia and the Pacific offers a case worth studying in regard to migrants' responses to their country of origin. Even among third- and fourth-generation ethnic Chinese living in creolized societies, we see, as described and analysed by Live Yu-Sion in Chapter 11, that ethnic and cultural identity changes are prompted by China's changing global position. In contrast to earlier times, Chinese migrants of older generations no longer look at China with embarrassment or as a politically sensitive location of ethnic attachment, but as a potential alternative home.

Live Yu-Sion discusses these identity changes among ethnic Chinese born after the Second World War in Reunion Island's multicultural society. That part of the population in Reunion Island who still identify as being Chinese has, as a result of an encompassing creolization process, instigated by colonial French rule, lost its ability to speak Cantonese or Hakka in favour of a Creole language (a mixture of French with African, Asian and Malagasy languages) and elements of Chinese culture have gradually vanished. In the mid-1980s, French direct political control ended and political decentralization permitted the formation of ethnic associations proclaiming distinct ethnic identities and ancestries, rather than a colonial policy intending a 'frenchification' of the island. As China became more visible and reachable as a source of a long lost Chinese cultural heritage, ethnic Chinese associations started to arrange tours to southern China to let participants rediscover their roots, Chinese languages and cultural practices. Having been exposed to live versions of Chinese culture enacted in the villages of their ancestors, a quest for ancestry and authenticity materialized in Reunion Island as descendants of Chinese migrants returned from China and started enacting elements of their newly discovered Chinese heritage. As a result, a development to strengthen ethnic Chinese identities among the second, third and fourth generations of former Chinese migrants arose.

These attempts to recover a lost cultural heritage, Live Yu-Sion argues, was initially not very successful as the social context of Reunion is genuinely creolized, rather than consisting of disparate cultural minorities advancing separate ethnic identities. Instead, support to boost Chinese identification came in 2003 with an ever stronger presence of political, economic and cultural delegations dispatched from China to Reunion Island. The high profile visit of a Chinese vice-premier, the opening of a Chinese representative office, a sister-cities programme, financial support for Chinese language teaching at various levels and finally an elaborate celebration of a Chinese hero-warrior supported by local authorities in 2004 were all contributing elements to the recent local assertion of a Chinese ethnic identity. According to Live Yu-Sion, it is premature to assess the outcome of this new confident Chinese presence for the ethnic Chinese in Reunion, but the re-assertion of a Chinese ethnic identity by re-enacting linguistic and cultural heritage demonstrates the powerful influence of the transnational activities of states such as France and the PRC.

Recently, the continuing role of the nation-state in transnational processes has been given more attention than in the early years of transnational research. The role of the nation-state has, however, primarily been explored in relation to its attempts to liaise with first-generation migrants, who already have established direct connections with people and institutions in their places of origin (Glick Schiller 1999; Guarnizo and Diaz 1999; Smith and Guarnizo 1998). Live Yu-Sion's study demonstrates how the Chinese state, as primary initiator, is also empowering 'diasporic' identities among second- and third-generation migrants with limited transnational contact by directly supporting financial, cultural and educational projects in Reunion Island.[19] Hence, it is pertinent to recognize that transnationalism is not limited to actions and reactions of contemporary migrants. We need to be equally attentive to nation-states' – especially to nation-states on the rise – coping strategies in relation to migration and ethnic attachments.

The transnational approach mentioned above has contributed to our understanding of migration processes as more complex than simple mobility from sending to receiving states and integration of migrants in the latter. However, attempts to reconceptualize translocal linkages and translocal social fields may also fall prey to overstating or reifying translocal agents' homogeneous ethnicity as well as ignoring class and political differences. Also easily forgotten are the connections among migrants and minorities of diverse ethnicities in localities where migrants move and settle. The last chapter in this volume, on new cross-cultural alliances between the ethnic minorities of Chinese and Aborigines in Australia, is a reminder to move the field of migration studies beyond essentialized concepts of diaspora communities and reified transnational fields.

In Chapter 12, Peta Stephenson examines hybrid political, cultural and social alliances undertaken by Chinese migrants and indigenous Australians. Historically, alliances between Chinese and indigenous communities have been produced by the exclusion of both groups by mainstream Australian society. Stephenson explores how these cross-cultural alliances today are also invoked in artistic co-operation through the case studies of a Chinese painter and a Chinese photographer. The painter is contested by the majority society, because he, as an ethnic minority member, takes Aborigines as his motive and the photographer is likewise criticized by the majority society for his depictions of Aborigines. These types of cross-cultural and cross-ethnic activities of minority groups such as contemporary Chinese migrants and indigenous populations are informing alternative history writings and conceptions of belonging that we need to consider for a more varied understanding of migrants' lives.

CONCLUSION

Contemporary Chinese migrants are no longer confined to closed enclaves such as Chinatowns or secluded mines and plantations. They constitute a global phenomenon of young male and female migrants who, affected by global capitalism and local structural changes migrate into diverse geographical locations. Contemporary Chinese migration encompasses various socio-economic groups who, in contrast to previous migration flows, are directed primarily to developed countries and global cities, rather than destinations in South-east Asia. In these new destinations and in the more traditional locations of settlement as well, some Chinese migrants make use of new information technology and affordable transportation to act beyond the boundaries of nation-states in their economic, ethnic, political and cultural pursuits.

Similar types of political and economic migration among contemporary Chinese migrants have been documented as a characteristic feature of Chinese migration in the late nineteenth and early twentieth centuries, but, as it is made clear in the contributions in this volume, translocal economic activities among contemporary Chinese migrants differ markedly in range, flexibility and intensity compared to the earlier period. However, more empirical studies focusing on Chinese migrants engaged in translocal pursuits are necessary to determine whether or not contemporary Chinese migrants really exhibit a novel form of adaptation to receiving societies at variance from earlier migrants.

Although new technologies undoubtedly offer new possibilities for contemporary Chinese migrants to act beyond the boundaries of both sending and receiving nation-states in translocal fields of economic, social and ethnic relations, the chapters in this book also reflect the need to consider translocalism from above. In common with numerous other migrant sending states, the Chinese party-state, at central and local levels, vigorously ventures beyond the confines of national territory to address migrant movements by endorsing novel policies and activities to direct migration streams, and to liaise and to seek economic and political support among contemporary migrants. The PRC has a history of attracting migrant support dating back to the beginning of the twentieth century, but China's recent rise as an economic world power, and the determination of the Chinese party-state to use migration as a strategy in its modernization programme, are factors which seem to have changed the scope and strength of state actions affecting migration flows, migrants' economic decisions and migrants' ethnic identification with China.

After a period of more than 30 years since Chinese have been permitted to leave the country, contemporary Chinese migration is again becoming part of the larger global system of migration. As the following chapters show, China is no longer unique in being the largest exporter in Asia of coolie labour, but contemporary Chinese migration has become manifold and, as such, an important case to study in understanding world migration today.

Introduction

AUTHOR'S NOTE

The author is grateful to the anonymous reviewer and Arif Dirlik for their invaluable suggestions to earlier drafts of this introduction and wants to thank Peta Stephenson for her careful language revisions.

NOTES

[1] The number of regular Chinese migrants who have left China since the beginning of the early 1980s is unknown owing to lack of reliable data and unclear definitions of who qualifies as a migrant. In the PRC census for 2000, 760,000 Chinese were registered as having given up their permanent household registration (Guowuyuan renkou pucha bangongshi and Guojia tongjiju renkou he shehui keji tongjisi 2002: 11), but far from all Chinese migrants give up their household registration or are reported as officially living abroad. The difficulties of measuring the numbers of irregular migrants are discussed in Massey and Capoferro, 2004.

[2] Chinese working on work contacts abroad in e.g. the Middle Eastern countries are not included. By the end of 2003 they amounted to 525,000 according to official data. 'Chinese seeking jobs overseas,' *People's Daily Online*, 25 Nov. 2004, http://english.people.com.cn/200411/25/eng20041125_165183.html; 'More Chinese workers join overseas labor market,' *People's Daily Online*, 18 Nov. 2004, http://english.people.com.cn/200411/18/eng20041118_164327.html (accessed Aril 2006).

[3] See e.g. articles from the last ten years in the PRC journal *Huaqiao huaren lishi yanjiu* [Overseas Chinese history studies].

[4] See the analysis and discussion of this term in Wang Gungwu, 1994.

[5] This issue is also discussed in Cheng, 2005.

[6] 'Zhongguo guanyuan: Zhongguo yi shixing 'shuangchong guoji' xiyin haiwai youxiu' [A Chinese official: China plans to implement 'dual citizenship' to attract overseas talent]. 29 Dec. 2004, *Zhongguo xinwenwang* [*Chinanews*]. http://www.chinanews.com.cn/news/2004/2004-12-29/26/522242.shtml (accessed Aril 2006).

[7] See more discussions on this terminology change in Nyíri, 2001; Thunø, 2001; Wang Gungwu, 2004.

[8] In 1990 according to official data, migrants from Beijing and Shanghai made up 49 per cent of all migrants from the PRC. Migrants from the provinces of Fujian and Guangdong constituted 20 per cent (Guowuyuan renkou pucha bangongshi and Guojia tongjiju renkou tongjisi 1993: 7).

[9] 'More Chinese studying abroad return to make career,' *People's Daily Online*, 18 January 2006, http://english.people.com.cn/200601/06/eng20060106_233368.html (accessed Aril 2006).

[10] 'Record 20,100 Chinese students return home in 2003'. In *China Daily* (electronic version), 16 February, 2004. http://english.people.com.cn/200402/16/eng20040216_134955.shtml (accessed April 2006).

[11] 'China tops world in number of students studying abroad,' *People's Daily Online*, 18 November 2005, http://english.people.com.cn/200511/18/eng20051118_222349.html (accessed April 2006).

[12] See also Wang Gungwu's chapter in this volume on early Chinese overseas students.

[13] From the 1880s, Chinese and other Asians were virtually excluded from Australasia and the Americas for almost 80 years.

[14] It has been estimated that China in 2000 received US$7 billion in remittances, which was the same as received in the Philippines and in Mexico, but only half of the remittances received in India (Sorenson 2004: 8). In 2003, remittances received in China were estimated to make up US$10 billion (IOM 2005: 127).

[15] Chinese officials estimate that 60 per cent of all foreign direct investments originates from investors of Chinese descent (IOM 2005: 126).

[16] Studies on economic investments from the perspective of transnational relations of Chinese migrants to China include Bolt, 1996; Douw et al., 1999; Douw et al., 2001; Lever-Tracy et al., 1996.

[17] An analysis of recent PRC migration policies is available in Thunø, 2001.

[18] Transnational entrepreneurship is discussed in Portes et al., 2002 and in Zhou, 2004.

[19] Although cross-border activities carried out by the Chinese state may be defined as international for the sake of distinguishing transnational activities at the grass-root level from activities of nation-states (Portes 2003: 877), the implications for Chinese second and third migrants in Reunion is likely to be the empowerment of translocal identities and translocal activities.

REFERENCES

Aldrich, H. and R. Waldinger (1990) 'Ethnicity and entrepreneurship'. *Annual Review of Sociology*, vol. 16, pp. 111–135.

The Associated Press (2005) 'EU and China reach deal on textile imports'. *International Herald Tribune*, 5 September, URL: http://www.iht.com/bin/print_ipub.php?file=/articles/2005/09/05/asia/web.euchina.php (accessed 17 September 2005).

Bailey, Paul (1998a) 'Chinese students in Japan in the early 20th Century'. In Lynn Pan (ed.) *The Encyclopedia of the Chinese Overseas*. Singapore: Archipelago Press and Landmark Books, p. 335.

—— (1998b) 'The work study movement'. In Lynn Pan (ed.) *The Encyclopedia of the Chinese Overseas*. Singapore: Archipelago Press and Landmark Books. 318

Bieler, Stacey (2004) *'Patriots' or 'Traitors': A History of American-educated Chinese Students*. Armonk, N.Y.: M.E. Sharpe.

Introduction

Basch, Linda G., Nina Glick Schiller and Cristina Blanc-Szanton (1994) *Nations Unbound: Transnational Projects, Postcolonial Predicaments and Deterritorialised Nation-States*. Langhorne, PA: Gordon and Breach.

Bolt, Paul J. (1996) 'Looking to the Diaspora: The Overseas Chinese and China's Economic Development'. *Diaspora*, vol. 5, no. 3, pp. 467–496.

—— (2000) *China and Southeast Asia's Ethnic Chinese: State and Diaspora in Contemporary Asia*. Westport, CT: Praeger Publishing.

Castells, Manuel (1989) *The Informational City Information Technology, Economic Restructuring, and the Urban-Regional Process*. Oxford: Basil Blackwell.

Castles, Stephen and Mark J. Miller (1993) *The Age of Migration: International Population Movements in the Modern World*. New York: Guilford Press.

Chen Ta (1940) *Emigrant Communities in South China: A Study of Overseas Emigration and its Influence on Standards of Living and Social Change*. New York: AMS.

Cheng, Xi (2000) 'Rencai liushi yu xinyimin,' [Brain drain and new migrants]. *Huaqiao huaren lishi yanjiu* [Overseas Chinese history studies], no. 4, pp. 17–25.

—— (2003) *Dangdai Zhongguo liuxuesheng yanjiu* [A study of contemporary China's overseas students]. Hong Kong: Hong Kong Press for Social Sciences, Ltd.

—— (2005) *Qiaowu yu waijiao guanxi yanjiu – Zhongguo fangqi 'shuangchong guoji' de huigu yu fansi* [A study of Overseas Chinese affairs and foreign affairs – reviewing and rethinking China's abolishing of dual citizenship]. Beijing: Zhongguo huaqiao chubanshe.

Cohen, Robin (1997) *Global Diasporas: An Introduction*. London: UCL Press.

Douw, Leo, Cen Huang and Michael R. Godley (eds) (1999) *Qiaoxiang Ties: Interdisciplinary Approaches to 'Cultural Capitalism' in South China*. London: Kegan Paul International and International Institute for Asian Studies.

Douw, Leo, Cen, Huang and David Ip (eds) (2001) *Rethinking Chinese Transnational Enterprises: Cultural Affinity and Business Strategies*. Richmond, Curzon.

Gao, Weinong (2004) 'Qianlun huaqiao huaren xueke jianshe zhong de xueshu piping)' [On academic criticism in relation to the establishing of overseas Chinese studies as an academic field]. *Huaqiao huaren lishi yanjiu* [Overseas Chinese History Studies], no. 3, pp. 1–9.

Gao, Weinong and Shi Cangjin (2002) *Zhongguo de huaqiao huaren yanjiu (1979-2000): dui ruogan huaqiao huaren yanjiu qikan zaiwen de zhaiping* [Overseas Chinese studies in China (1979–2000): selected criticism of publications in all kinds of overseas and ethnic Chinese journals]. Beijing: Zhongguo huaqiao chubanshe.

Glick Schiller, Nina (1999) 'Transnational nation-states and their citizens: the Asian experience'. In K. Olds et al. (eds) *Globalisation and the Asia Pacific: Contested Territories*. London: Routledge, pp. 202–218.

Guarnizo, L. E. and L. M. Diaz (1999) 'Transnational migration: a view from Colombia'. *Ethnic and Racial Studies*, vol. 22, no. 2, pp. 397–421.

Guo, Liang (2003) 'Zhongguo de huaqiao huaren yanjiu yu xueke jianshe' [Overseas

Chinese studies and establishing an academic discipline]. *Huaqiao huaren lishi yanjiu* [Overseas Chinese history studies], no. 1, pp. 1–7.

Guowuyuan Qiaoban Qiaowu Ganbu Xuexiao (2005) [Cadre school on overseas Chinese matters under the Office for Overseas Chinese Matters of the State Council] (ed.) *Huaqiao huaren gaishu* [Outline of Overseas Chinese and ethnic Chinese]. Beijing: Jiuzhou chubanshe.

Guowuyuan renkou pucha bangongshi (1993) [Population Census Office under the State Council]and Guojia tongjiju renkou tongjisi [Dept. of Population Statistics, National Bureau of Statistics of China] *Zhongguo 1990 nian renkou pucha ziliao* [Tabulation of the 1990 population census of the People's Republic of China]. Beijing: Zhongguo tongji chubanshe.

Guowuyuan renkou pucha bangongshi [Population Census Office under the State Council] and Guojia tongjiju renkou he shehui keji tongjisi (2002) [Dept. of Population, Social, Science and Technology Statistics, National Bureau of Statistics of China] *Zhongguo 2000 nian renkou pucha ziliao* [Tabulation of the 2000 population census of the People's Republic of China]. Beijing: Zhongguo tongji chubanshe.

Haugen, Heidi Ø. and Jørgen Carling (2005) 'On the edge of the Chinese diaspora: the surge of *baihuo* business in an African city.' *Ethnic and Racial Studies*, vol. 28, no. 4, pp. 639–662.

International Organization for Migration (IOM) (2005) *World Migration 2005: Costs and Benefits of Migration*. Section 1. Geneva: International Organization for Migration.

Kyle, David (2000) *Transnational Peasants: Migrations, Networks, and Ethnicity in Andean Ecuador*. Baltimore, MD: Johns Hopkins University Press.

Kyle, David and R. Koslowski (2001) *Global Human Smuggling: Comparative Perspectives*. Baltimore and London: Johns Hopkins University Press.

Lever-Tracy, C., David Ip and Noel Tracy (1996) *The Chinese Diaspora and Mainland China: An Emerging Economic Synergy*. Houndmills: Macmillan.

Levitt, Peggy (2001) *The Transnational Villagers*. Berkeley: University of California Press.

Li, Anshan (1999) *Feizhou huaqiao huaren shi* [A history of Overseas Chinese and ethnic Chinese in Africa]. Beijing: Zhongguo huaqiao chubanshe.

—— (2002) 'Huaqiao huarenxue de xueke dingwei yu yanjiu duixiang' [Chinese overseas studies: academic orientation and subject matter]. *Huaqiao huaren lishi yanjiu* [Overseas Chinese history studies], no. 1, pp. 1–15.

Li, Minghuan et al. (1999) '"To get rich quickly in Europe!" – reflections on migration motivation in Wenzhou'. In Frank Pieke and Hein Mallee (eds), *Internal and International Migration: Chinese Perspectives*. Surrey: Curzon Press.

—— (2003) 'Yige lü Ou xin qiaoxiang de xingcheng, yingxiang, wenti yu duice' [The emergence of a new *qiaoxiang*: Its developments, impact, problems and political counter measures]. *Huaqiao huaren lishi yanjiu* [Overseas Chinese history studies], no. 4, pp. 8-15.

Liang, Zhiming (2002) 'Shiji zhi jiao Zhongguo dalu xueshujie guanyu huaqiao huaren de yanjiu' [Overseas Chinese studies in Mainland China at the turn of the century]. *Huaqiao huaren lishi yanjiu* [Overseas Chinese history studies], no. 1, pp. 1–8.

—— (2003) 'Luntao huaqiao huaren xueke de xingcheng yu dingwei' [Discussing the form and position of overseas Chinese studies as an academic field]. *Huaqiao huaren lishi yanjiu* [Overseas Chinese history studies], no. 4, pp. 1–7.

Light, Ivan (1984) 'Immigrant and ethnic enterprise in North America'. *Ethnic and Racial Studies*, vol. 7, pp. 195–216.

Liu, Hong (2005) 'Overseas Chinese nationalism'. *Journal of Contemporary China*, vol. 14, no. 43, pp. 291–316.

Ma, Laurence J. C., 'Space, place, and transnationalism in the Chinese diaspora'. In Laurence J. C Ma and Carolyn Cartier (eds), *The Chinese Diaspora: Space, Place, Mobility, and Identity*. Oxford: Rowman & Littlefield, pp. 1–49.

Massey, Douglas S. and Chiara Capoferro (2004) 'Measuring undocumented migration'. *The International Migration Review*, vol. 38, no. 3, pp. 1075–1102.

Massey, Douglas S. et al. (1993) 'Theories of international migration: a review and appraisal'. *Population and Development Review*, vol. 19, no. 3, pp. 431–466.

Massey, D. S. et al. (1998) *Worlds in Motion: Understanding International Migration at the End of the Millennium*. Oxford, Clarendon Press.

Nieto, Gladys (2003) 'The Chinese in Spain'. *International Migration*, vol. 41, pp. 215–237.

Nyíri, Pàl (2001) 'Expatriating is patriotic? The discourse on "new migrants" in the People's Republic of China and identity construction among recent migrants from the PRC'. *Journal of Ethnic and Migration Studies*, vol. 27, no. 4, pp. 635–653;

—— (2003). 'Chinese migration to Eastern Europe'. *International Migration*, vol. 41, pp. 239–265.

Ong, Aihwa and Nonini, Donald (1997) *Ungrounded Empires: The Cultural Politics of Modern Chinese Transnationalism*. New York and London: Routledge.

Østergaard-Nielsen, Eva (2003) *International Migration and Sending Countries: Perceptions, Policies and Transnational Relations*. Houndmills and New York: Palgrave Macmillan.

Pieke, Frank, Pàl Nyíri, Mette Thunø and Antonella Ceccagno (2004) *Transnational Chinese: Fujianese Migrants in Europe*. Stanford: Stanford University Press.

Piore, Mihael J. (1979) *Birds of Passage: Migrant Labor in Industrial Societies*. New York: Cambridge University Press.

Portes, Alejandro (2003) 'Conclusion: theoretical convergencies and empirical evidence in the study of immigrant transnationalism'. *The International Migration Review*, vol. 37, no. 3, pp. 874–892.

Portes, Alejandro, W. Haller and L. E. Guanizo (2002) 'Transnational entrepreneurs: an alternative form of immigrant adaptation'. *American Sociological Review*, no. 67, pp. 278–298.

Portes, Alejandro and R. D. Manning (1986) 'The immigrant enclave: theory and empirical examples'. In Suzanne Olzak and Joane Nagel (eds), *Competitive Ethnic Relations*. Orlando: Academic Press, pp. 47–68.

Russell, Sharon S. (1986) 'Remittances from international migration: a review in perspective'. *World Development*, vol. 14, no. 6, pp. 677–696.

—— (1992) 'Migrant Remittances and Development'. *International Migration*, vol. 30, no.3/4, pp. 267–287.

Saich, Tony (2004) *Governance and Politics of China*. 2nd edition. New York: Palgrave Macmillan.

Sassen, Saskia (1988) *The Mobility of Labor and Capital: a Study in International Investment and Labor Flow*. Cambridge: Cambridge University Press.

—— (1991) *The Global City: New York, London, Tokyo*. Princeton, N.J.; Princeton University Press.

—— (1998) *Globalization and Its Discontents*. New York: New Press.

Sinn, Elisabeth (1989) *Power and Charity: the Early History of the Tung Wah Hospital*. Hong Kong: Oxford University Press.

Sinn, Elisabeth (1995) 'Emigration from Hong Kong before 1941: general trends'. In Ronald Skeldon (ed.) *Emigration from Hong Kong: Tendencies and Impact*. Hong Kong: The Chinese University Press, pp. 11–34.

Skeldon, Ronald (1997) *Migration and Development: A Global Perspective*. London: Longman.

—— (2000) *Myths and Realities of Chinese Irregular Migration*. IOM Migration Research Series, no. 1. Geneva: IOM.

Smith, M. P. and L. E. Guarnizo, (eds) (1998) *Transnationalism from Below* (Special Issue of Comparative Urban and Community Research, 6). New Brunswick, NJ: Transaction Publishers.

Smith, Paul J. (1997) 'Introduction'. In Paul J. Smith (ed.) *Human Smuggling: Chinese Migrant Trafficking and the Challenge to America's Immigration Tradition*. Washington, DC: Center for Strategic and International Studies, pp. viii–xv.

Smith, Robert C. (2003) 'Migrant membership as an instituted process: transnationalization, the state and the extra-territorial conduct of Mexican politics'. *International Migration Review*, vol. 37, no. 2, pp. 297–344.

Sorensen, Ninna Nyberg (2004) *The Development Dimension of Migrant Remittances*. Migration, Policy, Research - Woking Paper Series, no. 1. Geneva: International Organisation for Migration. URL: http://www.old.iom.int//DOCUMENTS/PUBLICATION/EN/mpr1.pdf (accessed April 2006).

Thunø, Mette (2001) 'Reaching out and incorporating Chinese overseas: the trans-territorial scope of the PRC by the end of the 20th century'. *The China Quarterly*, no. 168, pp. 910–929.

Thunø, Mette and Frank N. Pieke (2005) 'Institutionalizing recent rural emigration from China to Europe: new transnatioal villages in Fujian'. *International Migration Review*, vol. 39, no. 2, pp. 485–514.

Wang, Gungwu (1994) [1991]*China and the Chinese Overseas*. Singapore: Times Academic Press.

—— (2004) 'New migrants: how new? why new?'. In Gregor Benton and Hong Liu (eds), *Diasporic Chinese Ventures: The Life and Work of Wang Gungwu*. London: RoutledgeCurzon, pp. 227–238.

Wong, Bernard P. (1988) *Patronage, Brokerage, Entrepreneurship and the Chinese Community of New York*. New York: AMS Press.

Ye, Weili (2001) *Seeking Modernity in China's Name: Chinese Students in the United States, 1900-1927*. Stanford: Stanford University Press.

Yuan, Zujun (2005) 'Weiyuan jianyi chengren shuangchong guoji, yu yimin canyu guonei zhengzhi' [Committee members propose to acknowledge dual citizenship and to permit emigrants to participate in domestic politics], *Xinhua News*, web edition, http://news.xinhuanet.com/newscenter/2005-03/13/content_2690019.htm (accessed April 2006).

Zai, Liang and Hideki Morooka (2004) 'Recent trends of emigration from China: 1982–2000'. *International Migration*, vol. 42, no. 3, pp. 145–164.

Zhang, Guochu (2003) 'Migration of highly skilled Chinese to Europe: trends and perspective'. *International Migration*, vol. 41, no. 3, pp. 73–97.

Zhao, Hongying (2000) 'Jin yiershi nianlai Zhongguo dalu xin yimin ruogan wenti de sikao' [Reflection on all kinds of questions relating to the new Chinese migrants of the last two decades]. *Huaqiao huaren lishi yanjiu* [Overseas Chinese history studies], vol. 4, pp. 7–16.

Zhou, Min (2004) 'Revisiting ethnic entrepreneurship: convergencies, controversies, and conceptual advancements'. *The International Migration Review*, vol. 38, iss. 3, pp. 1040–1074.

Zhou, Nanjing (ed.) (2001) *Huaqiao Huaren Baikequanshu – Zhuzuo xueshujuan* (vol. 9) [Encyclopedia of Chinese Overseas, Volume of Academic Work (9)]. Beijing: Zhongguo huaqiao chubanshe.

Zhuang, Guotu (2001) *Huaqiao huaren yu Zhongguo de guanxi* [On relations between Overseas Chinese and China]. Guangzhou: Guangdong Gaodeng jiaoyu chubanshe.

Zweig, David and Chen Changgui (1995) *China's Brain Drain to the United States* (China Research Monograph 47). Berkeley: Institute of East Asian Studies.

Zweig, David, Chen Changgui and Stanley Rosen (2004) 'Globalization and transnational human capital: overseas and returnee scholars to China'. *The China Quarterly*, no. 179, pp. 735–755.

PART I

Contemporary Chinese Migration: Ordinary and Distinct

Chapter 2

The Chinese Overseas: The End of Exceptionalism?

Ronald Skeldon

The issue of exceptionalism and migration in China was raised in an earlier publication (Skeldon and Hugo 1999), but in an introductory chapter to a book on recent research on old and new migrations from China, the idea is worth pursuing as it retains its influence in the field. It needs to be emphasized, however, that the 'end of exceptionalism' remains a question rather than a statement as, from certain, mainly theoretical, points of view, exceptionalism may be over, but from other very practical points of view it can still be applied. Of course, with some justification, it can always be argued that simply because of its vast demographic size, at 1,324 million in mid-2006, China will always be 'exceptional': it is a world all to itself. Nevertheless, size alone does not necessarily dictate exceptionalism, and common patterns consequent upon the incorporation of China into a global economy appear to be emerging.

Every individual, every group, every society can be seen to be exceptional in one way or another. However, as social scientists, we have to simplify to make sense of what we see so we have clearly generalized to create categories such as 'the Chinese' or the 'Chinese Overseas'. Nevertheless, we can legitimately ask the question whether the Chinese form a very particular migrant group that is quite distinct from other migrant groups in both its patterns of movement and its types and forms of behaviour. A substantial literature argues clearly that, yes, indeed, the Chinese did and do form a distinct migrant group. The case is perhaps strongest for the historical patterns of migration from China. The vast majority of those who migrated were men, mostly unskilled, and they migrated with the intention of returning to China: the sojourner. There was relatively little variation within the flows, dominated as they were by uneducated men who fell within certain age groups.

There is much of substance in the above argument, although we must be careful not to over-emphasize the exceptionalism of the Chinese migration in the nineteenth century. As students of migration from Britain at the same time discovered, much of the migration from Europe to North America during the so-called 'Great Migration' was of sojourners. Dudley Baines has gone so far as to suggest that it was possible that most emigrants expected ultimately to return (Baines 1991: 40). He estimated that perhaps one quarter of all emigrants from Europe to the Americas returned during the period 1815–1930. Between 1861 and 1913, just under 40 per cent of English and Welsh returned. Many were young men going overseas to seek their fortunes in ways reminiscent of most of the Chinese who migrated at the same time. Nevertheless, the movement of families, and in the later period the movement of young independent women, that were seen in European flows, were not seen in the Chinese flows.

Here, another of the themes of Chinese migration is worth highlighting. We talk of Chinese migration and migration from China, but, as we all know, it was nothing of the sort: it was migration from very particular and limited parts of that vast country. The migration was essentially from the three coastal provinces of Guangdong, Fujian and Zhejiang, and from particular districts and even towns within these provinces. These areas were marginal to the Chinese state, marginal, too, in terms of resource base but, most importantly, those areas were the earliest and those most intensively affected by the seaborne expansion of European colonial powers. They were thus those areas that were early linked to a wider global system. Origin and destination flows were quite exceptional in terms of their sub-ethnicity and often occupation.

When we look at the migration from Europe to North America it, too, was characterized by very particular origin and destination flows. The characteristic of migration from Europe across the Atlantic was its diversity. A magisterial study of early British migration to the United States shows how the impact of four specific migration streams from Britain during the seventeenth and into the eighteenth centuries is reflected in American life today: from the eastern counties of England to New England and primarily Massachusetts; from the southern counties of England to Virginia; from the northern Midlands of England to Delaware; and from highland Britain towards the backcountry of the Americas (Fischer 1989). These migrations gave rise to four separate culture regions in the United States that are reflected in attitudes, mannerisms and dialects today.

Much more could be made of the various Chinese culture regions. However, perhaps the critical difference between European and Chinese migrations at that time was that Europeans were moving into areas that they controlled or came to dominate ethnically and politically; the Chinese were marginal geographically and politically in the Americas, so marginal that they could be 'excluded' altogether. So, although there are parallels between Chinese and European migrations in the nineteenth century, the differences between them were perhaps enough to sustain the idea that the migration of the Chinese was indeed exceptional at that time.

Chinese migrations between 1949, the year of the foundation of the People's Republic of China, and 1978 were also quite exceptional. These were very few, and the migrations that did take place were tightly controlled, reflecting in part the tight control of internal migration during much of this period. The great campaigns to move people to and from cities domestically represented some of the greatest examples of planned population movements ever seen. Migrations overseas were essentially temporary and were limited to other parts of the socialist world of which China saw itself a part: primarily to the former USSR, but also to outposts in Africa such as Tanzania.

However, it is to the migrations after1978 that we must turn to see if the incorporation of China into the global community has seen the end of exceptionalism as far as its form and types of migration are concerned. The end of 1978 and the beginning of the economic reforms that have transformed China form a convenient dividing line between the 'old' and the 'new' migrations. The old migrations were much less varied in their composition than the new that are associated with China's increasing economic wealth and are an integral part of the increasing prosperity of large segments of its population. Just as the rapid economic growth of Europe in the nineteenth century became associated with a period of emigration across the Atlantic, so, too, is China's current development associated with its 'new' migration. While Chinese migration to North America, Australasia and even Europe is certainly not 'new', what is new is its increasing volume after many decades of little international movement. Also, unlike the nineteenth-century migrations that came from a politically and economically moribund state, today the movement is associated with a country that has the potential to rival, or even surpass, the economically developed parts of the world. At the risk of oversimplifying, the principal reasons for the increasing migration from China today are associated with that state's growing participation in the global economy. The migration is essentially a function of globalization and it has come to be viewed with some concern by destination countries. In the following discussion, both immigration and emigration will be considered.

By 2000, China had become one of the world's leading trading nations in terms of imports and exports of both manufacturing goods and services (see Tables 2.1 and 2.2). Yet, in terms of its immigration, it was still clearly different from the leading North American or European states.

Table 2.1. Manufacturing trade and the relative importance of immigration, 2000

	Export		Import		Migrant stock (% of total population
	%	rank	%	rank	
United States	12.3	1	18.9	1	12.4
Germany	8.7	2	7.5	2	9.0
Japan	7.7	3	5.7	3	1.3
France	4.7	4	4.6	5	10.6
United Kingdom	4.5	5	5.1	4	6.8
Canada	4.3	6	3.7	6	18.9
China	3.9	7	3.4	8	0.0
Italy	3.7	8	3.5	7	2.8
Netherlands	3.3	9	3.0	10	9.9
Hong Kong SAR	3.2	10	3.4	9	39.4
Belgium	2.9	11	2.7	12	8.6
Republic of Korea	2.7	12	2.4	13	1.3
Mexico	2.6	13	2.7	11	0.5
Taiwan Province of China	2.3	14	2.1	15	--
Singapore	2.2	15	--	--	33.6

Sources: Dicken (2003): 40; United Nations (2002): wall chart.

China could not be seen as a country of immigration and its pattern is much closer to those of Japan and South Korea in this respect. It is worth noting that the rapidly growing economies of Singapore and Hong Kong did exhibit high levels of immigration, although the figure for migrant stock for Hong Kong has to be treated with some care as the majority of those migrants are China-born.

Table 2.2. Relative importance of trade in services, 2000

	Export		Import	
	%	rank	%	rank
United States	12.3	1	13.8	1
United Kingdom	7.0	2	5.7	4
France	5.7	3	4.3	5
Germany	5.6	4	9.2	2
Japan	4.8	5	8.1	3
Italy	4.0	6	3.9	6
Spain	3.7	7	2.1	12
Netherlands	3.6	8	3.6	7
Hong Kong SAR	2.9	9	1.8	15
Belgium and Luxembourg	2.9	10	2.7	9
Canada	2.6	11	2.9	8
China	2.1	12	2.5	10
Austria	2.1	13	2.0	13
Republic of Korea	2.0	14	2.3	11
Singapore	1.9	15	--	--

Source: Dicken (2003): 44.

The focus of this chapter, however, will be on the migrations from, rather than to, China. After three decades of very little outmigration (excluding sporadic waves of movement to Hong Kong), China again became a major player in global patterns of migration after 1978. This migration consists not just of workers going overseas on short-term contracts but also of settlers and students. Looking first at workers, which in some way is a continuity with earlier circular migrations of male contract labourers from China, Chinese sources estimate that, since opening the economy from 1979, more than 2.45 million workers have been employed overseas. The vast majority of these were employed either on engineering and construction projects or on government-to-government projects of international labour co-operation. In November 2003, some 520,000 Chinese workers were estimated to be overseas, up from 485,000 a year previously. During the first 11 months of 2003, 180,000 workers had been sent overseas (Ma 2004). The volume of remittances returned to China from the Chinese Overseas was perhaps around US$1 billion per annum throughout the 1990s, which was small compared with other countries such as India. This amount was tiny compared with the around US$40 billion per annum that flowed into China as foreign direct investment, about half of which came from the Chinese Overseas (figures cited in Newland 2004). Such figures do need to be taken with some degree of caution as significant proportions would have been from groups not normally associated with the Chinese Overseas such as those in Hong Kong or Taiwan. Also, difficulties arise with capital exiting China to cities such as Hong Kong and re-entering China as foreign direct investment.

China is not quite in the same league as the Philippines, which had 868,000 workers sent overseas during 2003, from a population of 81.4 million and an annual remittance income of US$7.6 billion. Nevertheless, China by the twenty-first century was emerging as a major supplier of labour. Like the Philippines, substantial numbers of Chinese workers are entering the merchant marine of several countries where currently some 20,000 are employed. Chinese labour contracts extend to 180 countries and territories around the world.

Table 2.3. Fertility decline, China and selected other areas, 1965–2000

	1965–70	1970–75	1975–80	1980–85	1985–90	1990–95	1995–2000
China	6.06	4.86	3.32	2.55	2.46	1.92	1.80
Hong Kong	4.02	2.89	2.32	1.80	1.31	1.22	1.10
Singapore	3.46	2.62	1.87	1.69	1.71	1.76	1.57
Japan	2.0	2.07	1.81	1.76	1.66	1.49	1.39
Korea	4.71	4.28	2.92	2.23	1.60	1.70	1.51
United States	2.55	2.02	1.79	1.83	1.92	2.05	2.05
Australia	2.87	2.54	2.09	1.93	1.87	1.87	1.77
Canada	2.51	1.97	1.74	1.63	1.62	1.70	1.56
Denmark	2.25	1.97	1.68	1.43	1.54	1.75	1.75
United Kingdom	2.52	2.07	1.72	1.80	1.81	1.78	1.70

Source: United Nations (2003).

Will this labour migration continue to increase? Over the short term it is likely to increase, but it need not necessarily increase indefinitely and dominate global labour markets. The experience of a near neighbour, South Korea, is instructive, with its sharp rise from 1974 to 1982 and then sharp decline to the mid-1990s. However, China need not necessarily follow the experience of South Korea, although common and significant regional and global demographic trends underlie the patterns of migration (see Table 2.3).

The sharp declines in childbearing across the region are notable with, in the case of China, a decline from over six children per woman in the second half of the 1960s to less than two by the end of the 1990s. China today has a level of fertility reached by women in Japan from the mid-1970s. Certainly, Japan's fertility decline was much longer and more gradual than that of China, but there may be lessons to be drawn as far as migration is concerned and it is worth briefly considering the Japanese case.

Japan is presently facing a rapidly ageing society. Its labour force is projected to decline continuously from 87.2 million in 1995 to 57.1 million in 2050 (United Nations 2001: 53), and pressures for immigration have increased. This discussion should not imply that immigration can in any way replace the cohorts 'lost' to fertility decline; the numbers of immigrants required would be just too large to be socially or politically possible, but migrants can fill critical shortages in particular sectors of the economy. In Brazil and Peru, Japan has turned to the *nikkeijin*, people of Japanese descent – effectively, the Japanese overseas – as a source of immigrant labour. The experience of the *nikkeijin* has been an interesting one for the Japanese. In 1999, some 224,299 Japanese of Brazilian descent were living in Japan, with increasing signs that many of them did not intend to return to Brazil (de Carvalho 2003). They look Japanese, but culturally they are Brazilian. Important differences also exist between Peruvian and Brazilian Japanese. Their presence is causing the Japanese to question what is 'Japaneseness' and even their own identity, just as the *nikkeijin*, too, question their own identity as overseas ethnic Japanese.

While there is no law of economic development to say that China will follow the same path as that of Japan, the trend in fertility in China will generate not too dissimilar age pyramids from Japan over the next decades (see Figure 2.1).

If China is to continue its double-digit economic growth into the near future and emerge as the world's second largest economy, as some predict, what will be the impact for regional and global labour markets? It is interesting to speculate whether the current concern with emigration from China will be but a temporary issue and the long-term issue will be one of immigration. The massive rural-to-urban migration in China and the rapid capital accumulation that we see in the present economy of China may give rise to a phase of much lower capital accumulation as more and more domestic workers enter higher-wage, higher-productivity sectors.

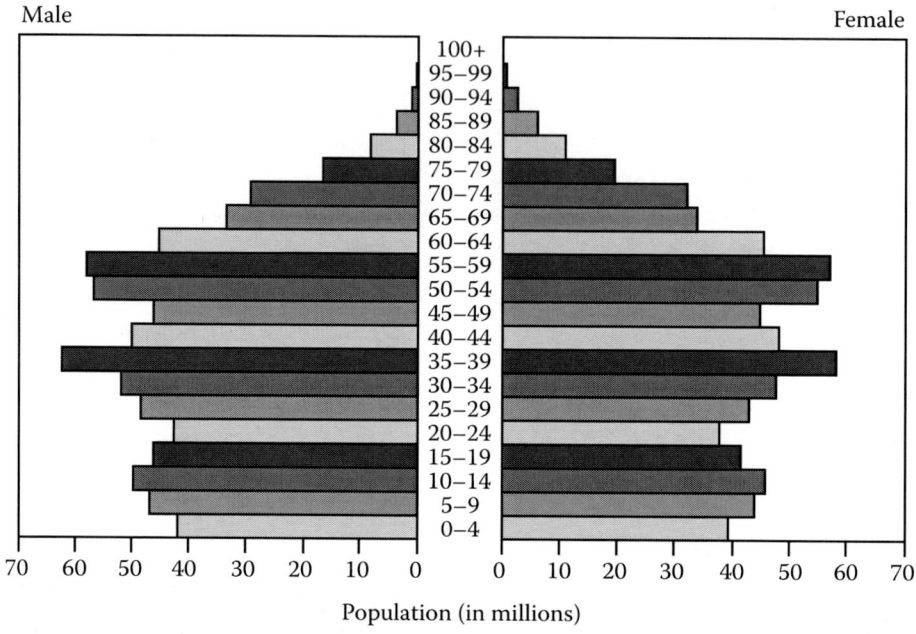

Figure 2.1. Population Pyramid Summary for China, 2025
Source: U..S. Census Bureau, International Data Base

Of course, there is no means of knowing whether China in the future will follow such a path but it may be that we should think the unthinkable and foresee a time when China will need to import labour. Even now, China is importing labour in certain high-skill sectors from overseas. At present, perhaps some 250,000 'foreign experts', most in managerial positions, are in China, but how many of these are ethnic Chinese is not known. However, already up to two million job vacancies were reported in the south-east coastal region in 2004 (*Economist*, 9–15 October 2004) and labour shortages spread north into the Yangtze River and the north coastal region in 2005 (Wang and Gao 2005). Although these shortages must reflect bottlenecks in the domestic labour market for certain types of less-skilled labour, recent evidence does suggest that these shortages may be structural rather than cyclical. As prosperity has spread inland, migrants who might have travelled to the coast go only as far as local or regional towns to look for work. The era of cheap labour in China may be drawing to a close (*International Herald Tribune*, 3 March 2006). To which sources of supply will China turn for labour? Will China recruit workers mainly from among the Chinese communities overseas? However, if ethnic Chinese are recruited for work in China, like the Japanese experience with the ethnic Japanese, they will not be Chinese in the sense of Chinese from China – they will be ethnic Chinese but Americans, Canadians, Australians or other nationalities and cultures.

It is also necessary to look at other types of migrants from China, and particularly settlers and students. The numbers of China-born in the United States, Canada and Australia have increased dramatically since the 1970s. Between 1980 and 2000, the 1China-born (not the number of ethnic Chinese as US-born Chinese are excluded) increased from 286,120 to 1,518,652 and the rate of increase accelerated from one decade to the other (see Table 2.4).

Table 2.4. Increase in China-born in selected destinations, various years

	Foreign-born (total)	China-born	Taiwan-born	Hong Kong-born
United States				
2000	31,107,889	1,518,652	326,215	203,580
1990	19,767,316	529,837	244,102	147,131
1980	14,079,906	286,120	75,353	80,380
1970	9,619,302	172,132		
Canada				
2001	5,647,125	345,520	70,615	240,045
1996	5,137,785	238,485	52,480	249,175
1991	4,566,300	168,355	19,725	163,400
Australia				
2001	4,105,688	142,781	22,418	67,124
1996	3,908,173	111,009	19,547	68,430
1991	3,754,841	78,835	13,025	58,955

Sources: US Census Bureau, Washington DC; Statistics Canada, Ottawa; Australian Bureau of Statistics, Canberra.

The China-born in the United States between 1990 and 2000 increased by 186.6 per cent compared with an overall increase among the foreign-born of 57.4 per cent and just 13.2 per cent for the population as a whole. These are stock figures. Data on the flows of recent migrants into the main settler countries reveal that China has emerged as a major source area for permanent immigrants. In fact, China is the major source of immigrants to Canada and is the third most important source of immigrants to the United States, a long way after Mexico and quite a bit behind India. China is also the third most important source of immigrants to Australia, after New Zealand and the United Kingdom. Chinese, too, have been moving to Europe in increasing numbers.

The reasons for the increasing flows of Chinese to the countries of the developed world lie mainly in the global shifts in the international migration system. The declining fertility of the traditional source areas of migration to North America in Europe that caused the latter areas themselves to shift from net-emigration to net-immigration; the continuing demand for migrants in North America; the increasing development of East Asia that gave greater numbers of Asians the prosperity and education to allow them to migrate; and the dismantling of discriminatory immigration policies in the main settler societies as more liberal regimes came to the fore after 1945, have all contributed to the transformation of the global migration system in which the Chinese have played, and are playing, a major role.

These flows of settlers are entering the developed countries as potential citizens. Today, unlike the old Chinese migrants of the nineteenth century, they are not excluded as marginal groups but are part of multicultural societies. To look at them as Chinese Overseas in a way seems strange as the various European migrant groups to these countries today are not considered as British overseas, or Danes overseas. These latter may be expatriates but they are all immigrants to Canada, Australia or the United States. Some will return, as they always did, but others will stay and integrate in one way or another. Some will marry someone they met overseas; others will have children at school and not wish to take them out and it is surely the children who will be of critical importance in any future decision to return or to integrate. The children grow up speaking English, without a strong command of the Chinese written language, playing baseball, cricket or ice hockey. Are they Chinese, or are they Americans, Australians or Canadians, to say nothing of the various European countries to which increasing numbers of Chinese are migrating? The simple answer is that they are both but, critically, increasing numbers will chose to remain in their adoptive societies. They are not sojourners.

Estimates of the number of Chinese in Europe around the year 2000 vary enormously, owing to the importance of irregular migration, from a low of 200,000 to 1 million or more, but all appear to agree on the recency and the rapidity of the migration. For example, numbers of Chinese residents more than doubled in Italy and increased more than sixfold in Spain over the last decade of the twentieth century. At the end of 2002, the 62,314 Chinese in Italy represented the fifth most important foreign national group in that country (ISMU 2004: 212). This migration appears to be less skilled than the movements to Australasia and North America, with large numbers going into low-order services and trading and manufacturing. Large numbers of Chinese are also moving into Japan, the Russian Far East and in smaller numbers to other destinations as widely dispersed as the islands of the Pacific and countries in Latin America, but all influenced by the global distribution of the Chinese as established by previous migrations.

Settlers are only one part of the legal flow to settler societies; there are also skilled migrants: to take just one example, those who gain access to the United States through the H1-B visa category for skilled migrants. Most of these go into the IT sector. In 2001, for example, some 384,191 were admitted into the United States under this category, 17,192 from China, or some 5 per cent of the total, but this figure is small compared with the number from India, which accounted for fully 27 per cent. In 2001–2002, there were some 63,211 Chinese students in American degree-granting institutions. Increasingly, Australia, Canada and the United States are using non-settler or non-immigrant channels as pathways towards later immigration as students, and other categories of skilled migrants, are offered the opportunity for permanent settlement after being trained or having obtained experience in destination economies.

The point is that the Chinese Overseas conceived of as a diaspora is deceptive (see also Skeldon 2003). It is a highly heterogeneous phenomenon and essentializing it into a transnational community of Chinese Overseas is not doing justice to the real situation. Rather than conceptualizing the migration from China as a unique diaspora, it can be understood more clearly with reference to other migrant groups. This statement certainly does not mean to imply that all migrant groups are the same – far from it – but that differences within the Chinese flows can be as great as any between Chinese and non-Chinese migrant groups. The cultural 'Chineseness' has perhaps been overemphasized at the expense of migrant situation.

One of the Chinese characteristics of the migration out of Hong Kong and Taiwan that has been identified is the trans-Pacific circulation of heads of family, sometimes including spouse as well, that created the 'astronaut' and 'parachute kids' syndromes (Skeldon 1994). This circulation saw the emergence of bi-local, transnational families with women and children in North America and Australasia and the male breadwinner back in Asia. However, by the early twenty first century, the Hong Kong-born populations of both Canada and Australia appeared to have declined between 1996 and 2001 (see Table 2.4, p. 43). Many of those who left Hong Kong for those countries before the 1997 handover may have returned. The case for a transnational community based upon continuous systems of human circulation was perhaps overstated. A more measured interpretation suggests that, after an initial period of flux, with intense circulation between origins and destinations, the system stabilizes, with some migrants returning but others making a longer-term commitment to destination societies. More integration and assimilation have been going on than was perhaps first assumed.

The critical point of this discussion is the heterogeneity of the flows of migration from China: a heterogeneity in type and in geographical origin within China. There are unskilled workers, skilled workers, settlers, circulators and students. The migrants to the mid-1990s came from the three traditional coastal provinces of origin, but also from the largest urban areas of Beijing and Shanghai and other large cities in the north, as well as from southern coastal cities. Recent data suggest, however, that migration from Beijing and Shanghai may have slowed in the last five years of the twentieth century (Liang and Morooka 2004). This shift is due perhaps to the booming urban economies, suggesting a 'migration turnaround' from these provinces in a telescoped variant of what has been seen at the national levels for South Korea and other boom economies in East and South-east Asia (Abella 1994). However, the difficulty of finding adequate data on the origins of migrants from China must be emphasized. Most countries simply classify migrants as 'from China' irrespective of their origins in that vast country. Apart from these differences in types and origins of migrants from China there are of course the irregular flows, still primarily from Fujian, but also from Zhejiang, the provinces of the North East, and other parts of China and increasingly using the land route to Europe as well as various air routes. This heterogeneity is typical of migrant flows in general, not just of the Chinese.

China is presently going through one of the most dramatic phases of economic development in its history and one that is associated with a rapid transition to low fertility. A vibrant economy now exists to which migrants and students can return. The diaspora is playing a significant role in this development, with millions of dollars being invested through Overseas

Chinese business networks every year. Some 190,000 of the estimated 440,000 'foreign experts' in China in 2001 were from Hong Kong, Macau or Taiwan, and many of the others are likely to have come from Singapore, and North American and Australasian Chinese communities. Nevertheless, the idea of a homogeneous Chinese diaspora oriented to the homeland is too much of a simplification. The Chinese diaspora is a highly segmented entity whose various members are as likely to do business with non-Chinese as they are to be linked with China. In terms of migration, however, we can expect increasing numbers of Chinese to return to China or to circulate within transnational networks of the highly skilled and of business in a variant of past sojourner strategies. It may be significant that the migration from Hong Kong has reversed and that from Taiwan stabilized. China, too, or at least parts of that vast country, may progress through a migration transition from emigration to immigration. As China develops economically and its population ages, perhaps the greatest consequence for migration and the West will be its contribution to increasing competition for labour within the global system as it, too, needs to seek out workers for its economy. Whatever the outcome, China is now clearly a major participant in the global migration system and has moved away from its exceptional and marginal phase of international migration. Its patterns of migration are perfectly understandable within a global framework and with reference to other regional and global flows. While some aspects of the migrations in, from and to China will obviously remain unique to that vast country, they are now only to be understood with reference to the wider context. The driving forces, the resultant patterns and the consequences of the migrations are today primarily a function of broader and global processes. China's phase of exceptionalism in its patterns of migration, assuming that it ever existed, is over.

REFERENCES

Abella, Manolo I. (1994) 'Turning points in labor migration', *Asian and Pacific Migration Journal*, vol. 3, no. 1, special issue, pp. 1–6.

Baines, Dudley (1991) *Emigration from Europe 1815–1930*. London: Macmillan.

De Carvalho, Daniela (2003) 'Nikkei communities in Japan'. In R. Goodman, C. Peach, A. Takenaka and P. White (eds), *Global Japan: The Experiences of Japan's New Immigrant and Overseas Communities*. London: Routledge, pp. 195–208.

The Economist (2004) 9 October, vol. 373, no. 8396, p. 69.

Dicken, Peter (2003) *Global Shift: Reshaping the Global Economic Map in the 21ˢᵗ Century*. London: Sage Publications (fourth edition).

Fischer, David H. (1989) *Albion's Seed: Four British Folkways in America*. New York: Oxford University Press.

International Herald Tribune (2006), 3 March, pp. 1; 13.

ISMU (Initiatives and Studies on Multi-ethnicity) (2004) *The Ninth Italian Report on Migrations 2003*. Milan: ISMU Foundation.

Liang, Zai and Hideki Morooka (2004) 'Recent trends of emigration from China: 1982–2000'. *International Migration*, vol. 42, no. 3, pp. 145–164.

Ma, Yongtang (2004) 'Country Report: People's Republic of China', paper presented at the Workshop on International Migration and Labour Market in Asia, The Japan Institute for Labour Policy and training and OECD, Tokyo, 5–6 February.

Newland, Kathleen (2004) 'Beyond remittances: the role of diaspora in poverty reduction in their countries of origin. A scoping study for the Department of International Development'. Washington DC: Migration Policy Institute.

Skeldon, Ronald (ed) (1994) *Reluctant Exiles? Migration from Hong Kong and the New Overseas Chinese*. New York: M. E. Sharpe.

—— (2003) 'The Chinese diaspora or the migration of the Chinese peoples?'. In L. J. C. Ma and C. Cartier (eds), *The Chinese Diaspora: Space, Place, Mobility, and Identity*. Lanham, MA: Rowman and Littlefield, pp. 51–66.

—— and Graeme Hugo (1999) 'Conclusion: of exceptionalisms and generalities'. In Frank N. Pieke and Hein Mallee (eds), *Internal and International Migration: Chinese Perspectives*. Richmond: Curzon, pp. 333–345.

United Nations (2001) *Replacement Migration: Is It a Solution to Declining and Ageing Populations?* New York: Population Division, Department of Economic and Social Affairs.

—— (2002) *International Migration 2002*. New York: Population Division, Department of Economic and Social Affairs, wall chart.

—— (2003) *World Population Prospects: The 2002 Revision*. New York: United Nations Population Division, Department of Economic and Social Affairs.

Wang, Dewan, Cai Fang and Gao Weshu (2005) 'Globalization and internal labor mobility in China: new trend and policy implications'. Beijing: Chinese Academy of Social Sciences, mimeo.

Chapter 3

The 'Distinctiveness' of the Overseas Chinese as Perceived in the People's Republic of China*

Cheng Xi

INTRODUCTION

This chapter points out that since China's reforms and open-door policies commenced in 1978, increasing attention has been attached to the study of Overseas Chinese in both the People's Republic of China (PRC) and in other countries. It is argued that this vivid research focus among scholars of different positions and viewpoints has come into existence because of an increasing number of contemporary Chinese migrants, contemporary Chinese migration adapting to modern migration practices, but the distinct relationship of the Overseas Chinese to China. This chapter discusses Chinese migration and the relationship of the Overseas Chinese to China from the perspective of international politics in order to enhance the understanding of the character of some distinctive features of the Overseas Chinese as migrants. This approach is adapted to initiate reflections on both the general and more exceptional traits of contemporary Chinese migrants as well as contributing to decreasing political sensitivities regarding Overseas Chinese studies and, ultimately, to enable more and better migration studies on recent migrants from the PRC.

---

* Translated from Chinese by Mette Guldberg.

RESEARCHING OVERSEAS CHINESE: THE SIGNIFICANCE OF NUMBERS

An important reason for the perception of Chinese migration as a politically sensitive and complicated issue, especially in South-east Asia, is the scope of historical migration from China to these countries. Still, contemporary Chinese migration is limited and needs to be perceived as much less threatening in terms of numbers and as comparable to migration flows from other Asian countries. As a starting point, some scholars argue that some 60 million migrants originate from China by including descendants of Chinese migrants (approximately 30 million in South-east Asia, approximately five million in North America, Europe, Oceania and in other parts of the world, as well as 28 million in Hong Kong, Macau and Taiwan). However, the populations of Hong Kong, Macau and Taiwan should not be regarded as Chinese migrants. According to Chinese authorities it is more correct to reckon with a total sum of Overseas Chinese at presently around 30 million people (Fang and Xie 1993: 4–17).

Statistical data compiled by the Overseas Chinese Affairs Commission (Taiwan) state there were approximately 37.5 million Overseas Chinese in 2003 (Overseas Chinese Affairs Commission, ROC 2005). PRC scholars generally estimate the total sum of Overseas Chinese who emigrated after the Second World War to be around four to five million (including migrants from Hong Kong, Macau and Taiwan, as well as Chinese ethnic remigrants from countries in South-east Asia constituting approximately 1–1.5 million people) (Zhu 2002; Zhuang 2001: 352–356). Seen in a larger international migration perspective China, with the world's largest population (1.3 billion), is by no means the largest sending nation of migrants.

According to estimates from international migration organizations, world migration from the middle of the nineteenth century to the middle of the twentieth century amounted to more than 100 million people, of which Chinese migrants constituted approximately 10 per cent (Qiu 2000: 2–3). Numbers provided by the United Nations Population Division show that the total number of migrants (population residing outside their country of birth) in the world increased from 75 million in 1965 to 120 million people in 1990, making the total number of international migrants in the 1990s at 135–140 million people (Castle 2001). Other data also provided by the United Nations Population Division show that the total number of international migrants was approximately 154 million in 1990, increasing to approximately 175 million in 2002 (United Nations Population Division 2002: 1).

According to the above-mentioned calculations, Chinese migrants only accounted for approximately 10 per cent of the total number of global migrants prior to 1940; after 1945, PRC migration was reduced to a percentage almost not worth mentioning in the global perspective. In relation to China's total population, the proportion of Chinese migrants is even less significant. Consequently, regardless of applying data on Chinese migrants in absolute numbers or in relative numbers, they do not constitute any exceptionally large group in the total number of migrants. Nor is China the largest sending country of migrants in Asia.[1]

At present, popular and scholarly concern with the scope of contemporary Chinese migrants appears to be somewhat exaggerated. Nevertheless, since China has a huge latent transient population resource, a long migration tradition combined with China's rising economic position in the world may serve as additional explanations for this concern.

RESEARCHING OVERSEAS CHINESE: THE SIGNIFICANCE OF CULTURAL DISTINCTION

The anxiety outside of the PRC towards the development of Chinese migration can also be partly explained by the burgeoning research focus on the 'distinctiveness' of Overseas Chinese among PRC scholars within the field of Chinese migration studies or 'Overseas Chinese studies' [*huaqiao huaren yanjiu*]. In the PRC prior to the economic reforms, studies on Overseas Chinese issues were also politically sensitive, due to the political status of Overseas Chinese as harmful and treacherous social elements. Since the economic reforms and open-door policies started in 1978 and the political redefinition of Overseas Chinese as pertinent for China's economic reforms, studies of Overseas Chinese inside the PRC have unceasingly gained speed and expanded in both quantity and quality, albeit initially being a politically difficult topic of study (Li, Anshan 2002). This new development has even assumed the strength so that discussions of establishing a regular academic discipline for Overseas Chinese studies have emerged among academics in the PRC.[2]

In this process, an important issue for research among PRC scholars has been the need to determine the 'distinctiveness' or 'significance' of the Overseas Chinese's relationship to China.

From outside the PRC, this development within Chinese scholarship has occasionally been regarded as giving too much prominence to the cultural affinity of the Overseas Chinese to China (Cai 2002). For example, some Chinese scholars argue that the Overseas Chinese are inextricably bound to China by national sentiment, cultural identity, mentality and similar determinants. Within this perspective, the Overseas Chinese are regarded as a substantial dynamic force for China's present and future economic development. Research topics such as Overseas Chinese hometowns (*qiaoxiang*), the uniqueness of Chinese business management and analytical concepts such as 'Greater China's economic sphere' (*da Zhonghua jingji quan*) or 'ethnic Chinese economy' (*huaren jingji*) (Guo 2002) all reflect the standpoint of culturally determined economic activities working to the advantage of China's economic development (Cheng 2002).

However, Chinese scholars differ in their views when analysing Overseas Chinese and their relationship to China. A second group of scholars views the issue of Overseas Chinese from the perspective of the receiving countries, being basically in opposition to the above-mentioned standpoint. Scholars working within this framework contest considering the Overseas Chinese and China as an 'integrated whole', or regarding the Overseas Chinese as an extension of China. Instead, research is focused on 'indigenization' and it is maintained that research on Overseas Chinese should include the political, economic and social development of the receiving countries in order to understand the local cultural and social context into which the Overseas Chinese settle. Attention should be paid to the relationship, interaction and assimilation of the Overseas Chinese with local ethnic groups (Cheng 2002).

Finally, a third group of Chinese migration scholars may be situated between the two above-mentioned groups (Cheng 2002). This group of scholars considers the Overseas Chinese more as a 'network of resources' and believes that the confrontations and conflicts between the Overseas Chinese and the PRC during the 1950s and the 1960s have been replaced by positive interactions after the PRC implemented the economic reforms and open-door policies to the benefit of both parties. In this perspective, some scholars have started to analyse the 'two worlds' of the Overseas Chinese (Li, Minghuan 1999) by refraining from considering the Overseas Chinese as cultural or ethnic communities in opposition to their host countries.

With the economic market reforms in the PRC, scholarship within the field of Overseas Chinese has developed and become more diverse. Today, anxieties about contemporary Chinese scholarship being generally one-sidedly focusing on cultural uniqueness and rejecting the possibilities of integration of Overseas Chinese in destination countries may be regarded as unwarranted.

OVERSEAS CHINESE STUDIES: 'DISTINCTIVENESS' AS A RESEARCH TOPIC

It is understandable that a focus on the primordial and cultural ties of Overseas Chinese to China provokes great anxieties, especially in countries 'hosting' large groups of overseas and ethnic Chinese. The relationship between the PRC and the Overseas Chinese, however, is 'distinct' by being primarily embedded in political structures, rather than in cultural attachments and affinities. In our studies of the Overseas Chinese, it is necessary not only to examine the Overseas Chinese from the micro-level, but also to consider macro-level determinants such as: the position of the Overseas Chinese within the political system of the PRC; the significant financial contributions of the Overseas Chinese to China's economic development; and the significance of the Overseas Chinese as being citizens of a nation aspiring to become a super power.

The Special Position of the Overseas Chinese in the Political System of the PRC

For more than a century, the PRC has had special government institutions for dealing with Overseas Chinese work within the state administration.3 In the twentieth and twenty-first centuries, Chinese leaders have through these political organs attended to the interests of the Overseas Chinese as well as attracting resources from the Overseas Chinese to serve the modernization process. At present, a large and extensive network of political organs and institutions from the centre in Beijing down to the county level work to liaise with ethnic Chinese and Overseas Chinese as well as returned Chinese migrants. This network of government institutions may be considered the largest and most comprehensive of any country in the world.

The Chinese system of Overseas Chinese government organs and institutions stretches across legislative and administrative organs and across political parties and mass organizations. In fact, five different organs and institutions or the so-called Five Overseas work to maintain contacts with the Chinese living outside mainland China:

(a) Overseas Chinese Affairs Office of the State Council [Guowuyuan qiaowu bangongshi]

(b) Committee for Overseas Chinese under the National People's Congress [Quanguo renda huaqiao weiyuanhui]

(c) All-China Federation of Returned Overseas Chinese as a Mass Organisation [Qiaolian]

(d) Committee for National Overseas Chinese in Hong Kong, Macau and Taiwan under the Chinese People's Political Consultative Conference [Quanguo zhengxie GangAoTai qiaoweiyuanhui]

(e) Organs under China's Zhigong Party

These five organs and institutions exist from the central to the local levels of Chinese society in most provinces. By the end of 2000, the PRC had in 30 provinces, autonomous regions and government municipalities (except in Tibet and Taiwan) established more than 8,000 local committees of All-China Returned Overseas Chinese, constituting a network covering most of the country from top to bottom. Similarly by the end of 2000, 94 small groups in charge of Overseas Chinese affairs had been established at various departments and bureaus under the State Council (Cheng 2005: 10).

The Overseas Chinese Affairs Office under the State Council has several domestic institutions under its jurisdiction including among others: the Overseas Chinese Investment Company, the China Travel Agency, the China Overseas Chinese Travel Agency, the China News Agency, overseas farms and forests for returned Overseas Chinese, Chinese Schools for Overseas Chinese and Overseas Chinese Universities. Internationally, the work of the Overseas Chinese Affairs Office has developed through what is known in Chinese as the 'three treasures' of the Overseas Chinese communities' – being the Overseas Chinese associations, Overseas Chinese newspapers and journals/magazines and Overseas Chinese schools.

The targets of the work for these institutions and government organs mentioned above encompass both ethnic Chinese, Overseas Chinese, returned Chinese migrants (to China) as well as relatives of Chinese migrants still living in China. The target groups for Overseas Chinese work are thus described well by the Chinese idiom: 'the previous three generations and the coming next three generations'. Moreover, legislation emphasizes special rights for and protection of returned Overseas Chinese and their relatives in China.4 The promotion and implementation of this law has been the object of many of the above mentioned government organs and institutions.

In addition, one should remember that the same kind of work regarding the Overseas Chinese is also undertaken in Taiwan in strong competition with the institutions in mainland China.[5]

The Special Position of the Overseas Chinese in the Market Economy Reforms of the PRC

The reason why the extensive government system on Overseas Chinese affairs holds such an exceptional position in China's current political system is due to its historical origin. At the beginning of the twentieth century, the Qing government attempted for the sake of national interests to rely on Overseas Chinese resources to facilitate the modernization of the empire. It changed its policies of 'no communication whatsoever' with the Overseas Chinese to setting up overseas offices of protection for them and issued the 'Qing dynasty Nationality Regulation', based on the principle of blood relationship. The Overseas Chinese's economic significance to China began with this undertaking.

The stipulations in the 'Qing dynasty Nationality Regulation' and the subsequent revisions in the Nationality Laws of 1912 and 1929 under the Republic of China all confirmed the national belonging to China of the Overseas Chinese on the basis of blood relations. These nationality laws became the bond by which the Overseas Chinese became linked to China and 'which within a certain time produced specific positive effects on the protection of the rights and interests of the Overseas Chinese, and which influenced all previous Chinese government policies regarding the Overseas Chinese' (Gao and Shi 2002: 137). The laws on the blood relationship doctrine strengthened the Overseas Chinese's national consciousness and their sense of belonging to China, as well as promoting unity among Overseas Chinese communities. Former President of the Republic of China Sun Yat-sen called the Overseas Chinese 'the revolution's mother'. Even though he did not have much knowledge or understanding of the history of the Overseas Chinese, this statement reflects the significance of the Overseas Chinese for modern China.

After the establishment of the People's Republic of China in 1949, the political conditions under the Cold War made it difficult to allow original relations come into play. Under these circumstances, the Department for

Overseas Chinese Affairs was one of the few government departments to be in touch with the outside world and it became an essential and effective supplement within diplomacy and foreign trade. For example under the First Five Year Plan (1953–1957), the trade deficit was extensive, but remittances from Overseas Chinese amounted to 1.17 billion US dollars, which almost made up for the foreign-trade deficit (Lin 1992).

From the 1950s and the following four decades, the focus of the government's work in Overseas Chinese affairs mainly targeted relatives and dependants of the Overseas Chinese in the PRC, but in consideration of the relationship of the Overseas Chinese to the PRC. In 1956, it was officially expressed in this way: 'Every small issue and step domestically can affect the Overseas Chinese abroad, as they can also affect the perceptions towards our country of the people residing where Overseas Chinese have settled,' so we must 'handle the issues of the returned Overseas Chinese and their relatives well and expand the influence of our country'.[6] Officially it was only in the beginning of the 1990s that the Overseas Chinese Affairs Office proposed to officially focus its work on the Overseas Chinese living outside China, but as the speech above and other sources reflect, the perspective has always been to consider and nurture good relationships with the Overseas Chinese.[7]

Today, some of the most important slogans concerning work with the Overseas Chinese, such as 'collaborating with domestic enterprises while introducing advanced technology and capital from abroad' or 'using the Overseas Chinese as a bridge' also reflect this focus. During the past two decades, official changes in policies have attracted a large amount of foreign direct investments in the reconstruction of China's market economy. Of foreign direct investments in mainland China 70–80 per cent are believed to originate from ethnic Chinese primarily living in South-east Asia, Taiwan and Hong Kong. Guangdong province, where most hometowns of Overseas Chinese are located, is the leading province in China in terms of attracting foreign direct investments. Fujian province, the second largest province of Overseas Chinese hometowns, occupies the second position nationwide in attracting foreign direct investments. Thus, the importance of the Overseas Chinese for China's modernization is evident.

Some scholars also believe that in a comparison of the reform progress of China with that of the former Soviet Union and Eastern European countries, China has made great achievements economically, due to the benefits of the links with the Overseas Chinese. The Overseas Chinese have, as shown above, brought capital and technology to China, but even more important are the regulations of the market economy and the shortcuts for entering the global commercial markets and networks that they have provided.

> As an overseas community resource, the Overseas Chinese and their fellow compatriots from Hong Kong and Macau have not only through donations, remittances, purchases and direct investments participated on a grand scale in and greatly promoted the economic reform process of their hometowns' economy, they have also through their close relationships with local governments and ordinary people, provided them the opportunity to learn how to set up enterprises, improve management and expand into domestic and international markets. They have also widened their field of vision, liberated their thoughts and have eliminated many obstructions, benefiting the continued reform developments and open-door policies ... Their exemplary role has to a great extent reduced the slow reform processes of other areas, and has lowered the reform costs of successive areas. (Long 2003: 224–225)

Seen also from this perspective, the Overseas Chinese are 'distinct' due to their significant contributions to the modernization and, most recently, the economic reforms in China.

The Special Position of the Overseas Chinese in the PRC's Pursuit for Great Nation Status

The anxiety about China as a rising economic world power is another fundamental reason why the Overseas Chinese should be regarded as distinctive in relation to other migrant groups. In Deng Xiaoping's economic market reform strategy and opening up to the outside world, he placed the Overseas Chinese in an important position:

> To say that the 'overseas relations' are complex and not to be trusted is reactionary. At present, we do not have too many overseas relations, but too few. Overseas relations are a good thing, and may open various kinds of relations. (Guowuyuan qiaowu bangongshi and Zhong-Gong zhongyang wenxian yanjiushi 2001: 6)

> We also have several millions of patriotic fellow countrymen overseas who hope to see China flourish and develop, and this [situation] is unparalleled in the world ... As for China, there are actually not many possibilities to develop on a grand scale. China is different from all countries in the world with its own unique opportunities. For instance, we have several tens of millions of patriotic fellow countrymen overseas, and they have made many

contributions to their ancestral land. (Guowuyuan qiaowu bangongshi and Zhong-Gong zhongyang wenxian yanjiushi 2001: 12)

Deng Xiaoping's famous statements, also called the 'Unique Opportunity Theory' [Dute jiyulun], on China's future relations with the Overseas Chinese gave new vitality to the political organs and institutions committed to Overseas Chinese affairs, as well as making people reflect on the significance of the role of the Overseas Chinese in relation to China's development. Some non-Chinese scholars and media tend to combine the forces of the Overseas Chinese with the economic development of China to make conclusions about the economic and political strengths of this alleged unity. By adding the populations of Taiwan, Hong Kong and Macau to the 30 million Overseas Chinese to make the total sum of 'Overseas Chinese' amount to 60 million people, they point to a possible capital force of 200 to 300 billion US dollars in the hands of 'the Chinese'.[8] As a result, some Western scholars believe that China has the potential to use the Overseas Chinese to form a new cultural and economic community that could strengthen its position on the international stage enormously (Brzezniski 1997).

Claiming Overseas Chinese significance on this circumstantial basis is mistaken. The PRC has not given up its pursuit of being regarded as one of the great nation-states, but it is not a status to be achieved via the Overseas Chinese. Deng Xiaoping said: 'In a multipolar [world], China is one of the poles. China does not want to belittle itself, it is one pole no matter what' (Deng 1993: 353). The late Qing government only implemented the nationality law based on blood relation in order to rely on the Overseas Chinese to rescue the empire from complete decline. In 1955, China renounced the principle of holding dual nationality to demonstrate its intentions of peaceful co-existence with countries especially in South-east Asia. By doing this, China re-established its position as a great nation in the world system and as a reliable partner and player in the new post-war order of international relations.

There are good reasons to believe the Chinese government's sincere intentions in 1955 not to interfere in other countries affairs by renouncing the principle of 'dual nationality' (Chen 1998: 231–239; Wang 1987: 266). However, China did not completely turn away from the resources of the Overseas Chinese. Overseas Chinese who had become naturalized in their countries of settlement were quickly described as 'daughters or children who were given away', but still had relations to China. One may interpret this position of regarding ethnic Chinese of foreign nationalities as married-out daughters as also meaning that they are different in their relations to China from those still retaining their Chinese nationality. Ethnic Chinese are still considered part of the Chinese family and thus treated differently from other foreign citizens.[9] In doing this, the Chinese government was anticipating that the Overseas Chinese would still function as contacts or intermediaries between China and their countries of settlement to establish good relations between China and these countries. Since China renounced the policy of 'dual nationality', however, China's policy of maintaining contacts with naturalized Chinese has not gone one step beyond this line.

In short, the Overseas Chinese are 'distinct' from other migrants, because of the great importance they have played in the past in the modernization of China, and today for their enormous economic contributions to the development of China. The Chinese government is fully aware of the role and pertinence of the Overseas Chinese and has established clear policies and a major bureaucratic apparatus to maintain links and close relationships with Chinese migrants all over the world. The Overseas Chinese have become an active part of China's development strategy and its pursuit of great nation status. As a consequence, in our investigations of the Overseas Chinese, this distinct position and relation to the PRC needs to be taken into account.

CONCLUSION

Voluntary and forced migration has been part of Chinese history for centuries and produced large numbers of ethnic Chinese communities around the world. Compared with migrants from other countries, the relations between the Overseas Chinese and their countries of destination are also in many cases particularly sensitive. In a historical perspective, it is noticeable that when China did not care much about the Overseas Chinese, the receiving countries did not allow or encourage the Overseas Chinese to become naturalized, but once China started to attach more importance to them, the relevant countries also tried hard to woo them into becoming citizens.[10]

From the perspective of the nation-state, the present concern with the Overseas Chinese can roughly be divided into two geographical regions:

Asian countries situated in China's periphery and industrialized countries. The first region has historically been the main receiver of Chinese migrants and even now perceptions of the Overseas Chinese are still influenced by former ideological contradictions. The second region has been the main 'host country' for Overseas Chinese emigrants and remigrants since the end of the Second World War. The perception of Overseas Chinese in these countries, especially as regards 'new Chinese migrants' arriving within the last 20 years, is basically informed by increasing labour force demands, challenges to social welfare systems, potential ethnic contradictions and the potential for high numbers of future emigrants from China.

Increasing academic attention outside China with regard to the Overseas Chinese has by some researchers been evoked by the potential number of Chinese migrants, especially illegal Chinese migration, but contemporary Chinese migration is relatively limited compared to migrants from other countries. Some scholars and popular media have expressed their concern that the Overseas Chinese might be a potential liability given the PRC's rapid economic development. Such fears and anxieties are not based on available migration data, nor on historical facts such as the PRC's maintained policies of single-nationality, but they reflect economic globalization and how migration has become as a key element in national production and in national security. As a result, industrialized and post-industrialized countries vigorously try to attract skilled migrants, but simultaneously they struggle to exclude or return non-skilled labour migrants or illegal migrants, pointing to accelerating ethnic conflicts and social problems. Developing countries, on the other hand, while hoping to profit by sending out migrants also experience 'brain drain' if parts of the highly-skilled population do not return. It is probably unavoidable that there are inherent contradictions and conflicts between migrants and the geopolitical strategies of nation-states.

Overseas Chinese may be regarded as are other migrants as both beneficial and a liability to 'host societies'. In order to analyse, understand and theorize about contemporary Chinese migrants, it is important to consider that Chinese migrants have become part of modern migration systems, but in migration studies we also need to take into account the distinct characteristics of Overseas Chinese. The historical contributions and political role of the Overseas Chinese since the early twentieth century have contributed to today's official perception of the Overseas Chinese as paramount for China's development. Since the reopening of the PRC to the outside world in the early 1980s, the Overseas Chinese have been identified as a main key for economic reforms, and their heavy financial investments have sustained and perpetuated the Chinese government's policies and practices with regard to its migrant population.

NOTES

1. For related studies, see Zhou 2002.

2. See discussions in various issues of *Huaqiao huaren lishi yanjiu* [Overseas Chinese history studies] published since 2002.

3. The development of China's policies towards the Overseas Chinese affairs is analysed in 'Qiaowu weiyuanhui zuzhi yanbian jingguo gaikuang' 1991: 1 and in Li, Yinghui 1997: 17, 44–62.

4. 'Law for the Protection of the Rights and Interests of the People's Republic of China's Returned Overseas Chinese and their Relatives' in Guowuyuan qiaoban zhengyansi 1999: 517–630.

5. A recent sign of this competition is the establishment by mainland China of the Promotion Association for a Peaceful Unification for Overseas Chinese to encourage activities to 'oppose independence and promote unification' and the parallel establishment by Taiwan of All Alien Residents' Alliance for Democracy and Peace all over the world to 'collaborate to secure Taiwan's position, stability and prosperity'.

6. Speech entitled "Promoting Overseas Chinese Affairs by Implementing Further Relevant Policies " by He Xiangning at the Third Meeting of the First Session of the National People's Congress in 1956 (He 1985: 759).

7. On 5 May 2002, the General Office of the Central Committee of the Chinese Communist Party and the State Council stated that the 'principal part of the work on Overseas Chinese affairs is abroad' ('Guowuyuan Qiaoban, Waijiaobu guanyu jinyibu jiaqiang guowai qiaowu gongzuo de yijian' 2002).

8. For a critique of this see Liang 2002: 147.

9. In the 1983 directive issued by the Central Committee of the Chinese Communist Party 'Issues regarding the strengthening of work on Overseas Chinese and Chinese of foreign nationalities' [Guanyu jiaqiang huaqiao, waiji huaren gongzuo wenti de zhishi], and more explicitly in the 'Basic guiding principles for the work on Chinese foreign nationals' [Guanyu waiji huaren gongzuo de jiben fangzhen] circulated in 1989, it was emphasized to paying more attention to a differentiation between Chinese migrants of Chinese citizenship and ethnic Chinese who were naturalized in their countries of settlement, but on the other hand not to treat the ethnic Chinese as non-Chinese in the hope of catering for their national sentiments and to strengthen their attachments to China.

   On 5 May, 2002, the General Office of the Central Committee of the Chinese Communist Party and the State Council issued the 'Suggestions from the State

Council's Overseas Chinese Affairs Office and the Ministry of Foreign Affairs on how to strengthen the work regarding the Overseas Chinese' [Guowuyuan Qiaoban, Waijiaobu guanyu jinyibu jiaqiang guowai qiaowu gongzuo de yijian] in which these requests were reaffirmed. Since the majority of Overseas Chinese have become naturalized in their countries of settlement, the number of 30 million 'overseas compatriots' primarily include ethnic Chinese and as such they are also the main target of Overseas Chinese policies. In attracting foreign capital, ethnic Chinese (including persons from Hong Kong, Macau and Taiwan) enjoy the same treatment as the Overseas Chinese, although legislation only speaks about Overseas Chinese.

[10] Cai Renlong has studied the historical development of Overseas Chinese naturalization in Indonesia during the 380 years of Dutch colonial rule and discovered that Indonesian-Chinese kept vacillating between 'not wanting to' and 'wanting to' become naturalized (Cai 2000: 204). Similar experiences were also observed and examined in my studies on the nationality issue of Indonesian Chinese (Cheng 2005).

REFERENCES

Brzezniski, Zibgniew (1997) *The Grand Chessboard: American Primary and Its Geostrategic Imperatives*. New York: Basic Books.

Cai, Renlong (2000) Yinni huaqiao yu huaren gailun [A general discussion of Indonesian Overseas Chinese and the Chinese people]. Hong Kong: Nandao chubanshe.

Cai, Zhenxiang (2002) 'Shilun Zhongguo haiwai yimin de gongtongxing yu teshuxing wenti' [A discussion of the commonalities and particularities of China's emigrants]. *Huaqiao huaren lishi yanjiu* [Overseas Chinese history studies], no. 2, pp. 35–40.

Castle, Stephen (2001) 'Ershiyi shiji chu de guoji yimin: quanqiuxing de qushi he wenti' [International migration at the beginning of the twenty-first century: global trends and issues]. Guoji yimin 2000 [International migration 2000], vol. 18, no. 3, pp. 26–27.

Chen, Dunde (1998) *Zhou Enlai fei wang Wanlong* [Zhou Enlai flies to Bandung]. Beijing: Zhongguo qingnian chubanshe.

Cheng, Xi (2002) 'Guanyu muqian huaqiao huaren yanjiu ruogan wenti de guancha yu sikao' [Observations and reflections on present issues related to Overseas Chinese studies]. *Huaqiao huaren lishi yanjiu* [Overseas Chinese history studies], no. 4, pp. 1–6.

—— (2005) *Qiaowu yu waijiao guanxi yanjiu: Zhongguo fangqi shuangchong guoji de huigu yu fansi* [Overseas Chinese affairs and national diplomacy: review and thoughts on China's abandonment of dual nationality]. Beijing: Zhongguo huaqiao chubanshe.

Deng, Xiaoping (1993) *Deng Xiaoping wenxuan* [Selected works of Deng Xiaoping], vol. 3. Beijing: Renmin chubanshe, 1993.

Fang, Xiongpu and Xie Chengjia (1993) *Huaqiao huaren gaikuang* [A general survey on Overseas Chinese]. Beijing: Zhongguo huaqiao chubanshe.

Gao, Weinong and Shi Cangjin (2002) *Zhongguo de huaqiao huaren yanjiu (1979–2000) – dui ruogan huaqiao huaren yanjiu qikanzaiwen de zhaiping* [Overseas Chinese studies in China (1979–2000) – discussions of selected research publications on Overseas Chinese]. Beijing: Zhongguo huaqiao chubanshe.

'Guanyu jiaqiang huaqiao, waiji huaren gongzuo wenti de zhishi' [Issues regarding the strengthening of work on Overseas Chinese and Chinese of foreign nationalities] (1983). Not published.

'Guanyu waiji huaren gongzuo de jiben fangzhen' [Basic guiding principles for the work on Chinese foreign nationals] (1989). Not published.

Guo, Liang (2002) 'Huaren jingji yanjiu ruogan wenti pingxi' [Analysis and discussions of studies on ethnic Chinese economy]. In Hao, Shiyuan (ed.), *Haiwai huaren yanjiu lunji* [Collection of discussions of Overseas Chinese studies]. Beijing: Zhongguo shehui kexue chubanshe, pp. 159–173.

'Guowuyuan qiaoban, Waijiaobu guanyu jinyibu jiaqiang guowai qiaowu gongzuo de yijian' [Suggestions from the State Council's Overseas Chinese Affairs Office and the Ministry of Foreign Affairs on how to strengthen work on the Overseas Chinese]. Document no. 11 (2002). Not published.

Guowuyuan qiaoban zhengyansi (ed.) [The Overseas Chinese Affairs Office of the State Council's Office for Political Studies] (1999) *Qiaowu fagui wenjian huibian (1955–1999)* [Collection of documents on the laws and regulations on Overseas Chinese affairs (1955–1999)]. Beijing: Internal publication.

Guowuyuan qiaowu bangongshi and Zhong-Gong zhongyang wenxian yanjiushi (eds) [The Overseas Chinese Affairs Office of the State Council and the Document Research Department of the Central Committee of the Chinese Communist Party] (2001) *Deng Xiaoping lun qiaowu* [Deng Xiaoping discusses Overseas Chinese affairs]. Beijing: Zhongyang wenxian chubanshe.

He, Xiangning (1985) 'Jinyibu guanche zhixing qiaowu zhengce, kaizhan qiaowu gongzuo' [A step further in implementing the Overseas Chinese affairs policy and in developing the work on Overseas Chinese affairs]. In Shang Mingxuan and Yu Yanguang (eds), *Shuangqing Wenji* [Two complete collected works], vol. 2 Beijing: Renmin chubanshe, pp.752–760.

Li, Anshan (2002) 'Ming Qing shiqi youguan huaqiao huaren de dianji biji he yanjiu gaishu' [Ancient writings and research overviews regarding Overseas Chinese during the Ming and Qing dynasties]. *Huaqiao huaren lishi yanjiu* [Overseas Chinese History Studies], no. 2, pp. 41–47.

Li, Minghuan (1999) *We Need Two Worlds: Chinese Immigrant Associations in a Western Society*. Amsterdam: Amsterdam University Press.

—— (2002) *Ouzhou huaqiao huaren shi* [History of the Overseas Chinese in Europe]. Beijing: Zhongguo huaqiao chubanshe.

Li, Yinghui (1997) *Huaqiao zhengce yu haiwai minzu zhuyi (1912–1949)* [Overseas Chinese policies and overseas nationalism (1912–1949)]. Taibei: Guoshiguan yinhang.

Liang, Yingming (2002) 'Haiwai huaren jingji huodong yanjiu ruogan wenti' [Some questions regarding the studies of Overseas Chinese economic activities]. In Zhou Nanjing (ed.), Huaqiao huaren baikequanshu – zonglun juan [Encyclopedia of Chinese Overseas, general studies volume]. Beijing: Zhongguo huaqiao chubanshe, pp. 139–159.

Lin, Jinzhi (1992) 'Qiaohui dui Zhongguo jingji fazhan yu qiaoxiang jianshe de zuoyong' [The effects of Overseas Chinese remittances on China's economic development and on the construction work in the hometowns of Overseas Chinese]. *Nanyang wenti yanjiu* [The journal of Nanyang studies], no. 2, pp. 21–34.

Long, Denggao (2003) *Haiwai huashang jingying guanli tanwei* [A short inquiry into the operations and management of Overseas Chinese merchants]. Hong Kong: Xianggang shehui kexue chubanshe youxian gongsi.

Qiu, Liben (2000) *Cong shijie kan huaren* [The Overseas Chinese seen from a world perspective]. Hong Kong: Nandao chubanshe.

Overseas Chinese Affairs Commission, ROC (2005). URL: www.ocac.gov.tw/english/public/public.asp?selno=1166&no=1166&level=C (accessed July 2005).

'Qiaowu weiyuanhui zuzhi yanbian jingguo gaikuang' [Survey of the organizational developments of the Overseas Chinese Affairs Commission] (1991). In Guangdongsheng danganguan [Archives of Guangdong Province] (ed.), *Huaqiao yu qiaowu shiliao xuanbian (2)* [Selected historical documents on Overseas Chinese and Overseas Chinese affairs (2)]. Guangdong: Guangdong renmin chubanshe.

United Nations Population Division (2002) *International Migration Report 2002*. New York. www.un.org/esa/population/publications/ittmig2002/2002ITTMIGTEXT22-11.pdf from URL: www.un.org/esa/population/publications/publications.htm (accessed April 2006).

Wang, Gungwu (1987) *Dongnanya yu huaren – Wang Gengwu jiaoshou lunwen xuanji* [South-east Asia and the Chinese people – selected works of Professor Wang Gungwu's research papers]. Beijing: Zhongguo youyi chuban gongsi.

Zhonghua renmin gongheguo waijiaobu, zhong-gong zhongyang wenxian yanjiushi bian [The Foreign Ministry of the People's Republic of China and the Research Department of the Central Committee of the Chinese Communist Party] (eds), (1990) *Zhou Enlai waijiao wenxuan* [Selected diplomatic works of Zhou Enlai]. Beijing: Zhongyang wenxian chubanshe.

Zhou, Nanjing (2002) 'Huaqiao huaren wenti gailun' [Outline of questions related to the Overseas and ethnic Chinese]. In Zhou Nanjing (ed.), *Huaqiao huaren baikequanshu – zonglun juan* [Encyclopedia of Chinese Overseas, general studies volume]. Beijing: Zhongguo huaqiao chubanshe, pp. 8–26.

Zhu, Huiling (2002) '21 shiji shangbanye fada guojia huaqiao huaren shehui de fazhan taishi' [The development situation of Overseas Chinese communities in developed countries in the first half of the twenty-first century]. *Huaqiao huaren lishi yanjiu* [Overseas Chinese history studies], no. 2, pp. 28–34

Zhuang, Guotu (2001) *Huaqiao huaren yu Zhongguo de guanxi* [The relations between the Overseas Chinese and China]. Guangzhou: Guangdong gaodeng jiaoyu chubanshe.

PART II

Contemporary Chinese Migration: Changing Economic Impact and Host-Country Responses?

Chapter 4

Remittances, Donations and Investments in Qingtian County since 1978*

Zhang Xiuming

Qingtian County is famous in Zhejiang province and all over China as a migrant sending community.¹ At present there are 210,000 people from Qingtian scattered over more than 120 countries and regions. As a community with distinct regional and cultural characteristics, the Qingtian Overseas Chinese have attracted much attention in Chinese academic circles and government departments. The Overseas Chinese Research Center of Zhejiang Teachers' University established in 1990s is one of the key centers in the People's Republic of China (PRC) for research on Zhejiang's Overseas Chinese and it publishes the journal *Huaqiao huaren yanjiu luncong* [Collection of research essays on Overseas Chinese].² Chief Editor Chen Murong recorded the history and present situation of the Qingtian Overseas Chinese in *Qingtian Xianzhi* [Qingtian County gazetteer] (1990) and Director of Zhejiang Teachers' University's Overseas Chinese Research Center Zhou Wangsen has compiled the *Qingtian Xian Huaqiao Zhi* [Qingtian County gazetteer on Overseas Chinese]. In 2002, the Qingtian County Overseas Chinese Research Institute was established by Qingtian County government and Zhejiang Teachers' University in order to promote research on the Qingtian Overseas Chinese.

Chinese migration to Europe is closely linked to the Qingtian Chinese who were among the first major groups of Chinese migrating to Europe. Even today, more than 80 per cent of Qingtian migrants are still

---

* Translated from Chinese by Mette Guldberg.

concentrated in Europe. Consequently, research on the Qingtian Chinese has also increasingly been carried out by European-based researchers (Benton and Pieke 1998; Christiansen 2003; Li Minghuan 2002; Pieke and Mallee 1999). These studies draw out the general migration history and the present situation of the Qingtian migrants.

This chapter will contribute to the empirical studies on Qingtian migrants, but primarily from the perspective of the migrants' influence on their hometown. This perspective has so far not been thoroughly investigated, despite the important contributions made by the Overseas Chinese towards Qingtian. This research interest was triggered when the author in May 1997 went to Qingtian as part of the New Chinese Migrant Investigation and Research Group under the All-China Federation of Returned Overseas Chinese. On this occasion, I obtained some initial knowledge and understanding of the local Qingtianese opinions and sentiments towards the Overseas Chinese. In October of the same year, I once again followed a delegation from the All-China Federation of Returned Overseas Chinese and visited France and Spain, with relatively high concentrations of Qingtian Chinese. During my travels, I became acquainted with many Qingtian overseas communities and community leaders and became inspired to write an initial article on the history and present situation of the Qingtian migrants (Zhang Xiuming 1998) based on data and source materials held by the Qingtian Overseas Chinese Historical Museum (established by Qingtian County's Federation of Returned Overseas Chinese).

The data in this article mainly derives from local Qingtian publications and news reports addressed to Qingtian migrants, such as the official newspaper *Qingtian Qiaoxiang Bao* [Qingtian hometown newspaper] published until 2004 by the local Qingtian County Committee of the Chinese Communist Party (CCP)[3] and the *Qiaolian Jianxun* [Brief news of the China Federation of Returned Overseas Chinese] published by the Qingtian Federation of Returned Overseas Chinese.

GEOGRAPHICAL FEATURES OF QINGTIAN COUNTY, ITS POPULATION AND CONTEMPORARY EMIGRATION

Qingtian County is situated in south-eastern Zhejiang province, in the middle and lower reaches of the Oujiang River. To the east, it is located by the Oujiang River close to Wenzhou municipality, but administratively it is subordinated to Lishui city. The total area is 2,493 square kilometers and the total population by the end of 2002 was 473,100. In 2002, the entire county brought in about 2,417 billion RMB in gross domestic products, an increase of 14.2 per cent over 2001; the gross domestic product per capita was 508.4 billion RMB, an increase of 22 per cent over 2001 (*Zhejiang Nianjian 2003*: 465–466).

Qingtian is situated in the mountains with limited arable land and is commonly referred to as the place with 'numerous mountains, little water and little land to cultivate'. Qingtian is economically developing, but it was not until 1998 that it managed to achieve an average income above the poverty level. Qingtian is known as the 'town of the carved stones', 'town of the Overseas Chinese' and as the 'town of famous people'. Overseas Chinese and stone carvings have become the major characteristics of Qingtian. There is a close relationship between Qingtian's stone carvings and the Qingtian Chinese going abroad. Nowadays, it seems that the Qingtian Chinese have generally adopted the view that 'the Qingtian Chinese was already selling Qingtian carved stones in Europe in the seventeenth – eighteenth centuries'; accordingly, the Qingtian Chinese already have a 300-year history of going abroad.[4]

There exist, however, different opinions on when the earliest Qingtian Chinese started to emigrate. The 300-year history of Qingtian migration seems to originate from a statement in the English edition of *The China Yearbook* of 1935 in which it is stated that 'As far back as during the seventeenth and eighteenth centuries there was a small number of our fellow countrymen who followed the land route through Siberia in order to get to Europe, and in the initial stages the majority of them were Qingtian Chinese, who sold carved stones from Qingtian'. Only no historical sources in China or Europe have been found to underpin this assertion (Zhou Wangsen 1997: 83–84). Oral and written sources in both Qingtian and Europe reveal that migration to Europe and America has taken place from at least the late nineteenth century (Thunø 1999: 162–164).

I think we can trace the earliest emigration movements of the Qingtian Chinese back to 1798, when a Qingtian stone trader went to Japan, and following him, during the nineteenth century traders went all over the world. According to local statistics some 2,000 Qingtian migrants ventured abroad prior to 1900 (Zhang Xiuming 1998: 49–50). Qingtian emigration history may thus be divided into four stages: the first stage runs from 1798 to the end of the nineteenth century; the second stage runs from 1900 to

1948; the third stage from 1949 to 1977; and the fourth stage from 1978 up to now (Zhang 1998: 48–51).

Numbers of people

Before the People's Republic of China (PRC) was established, there were 16,710 Chinese Qingtian living abroad (Chen 1990: 643). After the PRC was founded in 1949 but before the reform and open–door policies of 1978, the number of Qingtian people going abroad increased slowly due to the strict procedures for leaving the country. After the Great Proletarian Cultural Revolution (1966–76), China implemented open-door policies and relaxed the regulations for leaving or entering the country. Subsequently, the number of people from Qingtian emigrants sharply increased (Table 4.1).

Table 4.1. Qingtian people migrating abroad

Year	Number of people
1950–1959	152
1960–1965	124
1966–1976	91
1979–1986	10,948

Source: Chen 1990: 643.

After 1985 and China's sanctioning of emigration, the Qingtian Chinese's enthusiasm for going abroad continued to rise and has kept on rising ever since. Not only has the number of people going abroad kept on rising continuously, but the number of destination countries has also increased. However, the conventional distribution pattern has not yet been altered significantly, since Europe is still the main receiving continent, followed by America and Asia (Table 4.2).

Table 4.2. Distribution of Qingtian migrants

Year		1987	1995	1996
Number of people		20,030	62,336	84,700
Distribution	Europe	17,750 (87%)	55,825 (90%)	75,987 (90%)
	America	1,876 (9%)	5,022 (8%)	6,003 (7%)
	Asia	350	1,241	1,412
	Africa	47	231	1,231
	Australia	7	17	67
	Sub-total	46 countries and regions	59 countries and regions	62 countries and regions

Source: Data from 1987, Chen 1990: 646; data from 1995 and 1996, Zhang 1998: 54–56.

In 1997, 16,245 Qingtian Chinese applied for permission to leave the country and 11,948 people were approved. In 2000, the number of Qingtian Overseas Chinese reached 150,000 people in 70 countries and regions. One year later, 180,000 migrants from Qingtian were found in 120 countries and regions (Zhang 1998). At present, there are 210,000 Qingtian Overseas Chinese, distributed over 120 countries and regions.[5]

Occupations

Initially, when the Qingtian Chinese went abroad and had to find a way of living, the majority continued to trade in stone carvings. After stone carvings had become unmarketable, they gradually changed their occupations to trading in other sundries. Besides these peddlers, there were also a small number of people who started up companies and stores. After the Second World War, following the recovery and development of the Western European economy, the Chinese food industry in every European country developed rapidly. Besides this, an Overseas Chinese leather industry also developed in France, Italy and Spain. Against this background, the peddler-like economy of the Qingtian Overseas Chinese in Europe gradually transformed and diversified into different service industries, business and manufacturing, but the restaurant business still is the economic pillar of a majority of Qingtian migrants (Chen 1990: 647). According to data provided by the Museum for Qingtian Overseas Chinese History, a sample survey made in 1992 showed that of 30,000 Qingtian migrants in 1992, 70 per cent were still engaged in the catering industry (12 per cent worked in business and trading; 4 per cent were engaged in the leather industry, 3 per cent in the garment industry and only 1 per cent were made up of students) (Zhang 1998: 56).

Since the late 1990s, an increasing number of Qingtian migrants have become involved in business and trading, as a result of China's economic rise and importance on the global markets. In the 1990s, the business opportunities on the Chinese market combined with the Central and Eastern European market gave Qingtian migrants new economic opportunities. Qingtian migrants and Chinese migrants from other parts of China with funds rushed into Central and Eastern European markets and expanded their activities into international trade. In shipping containers or via air transport they imported inexpensive daily sundries and garments to trade on the Central Eastern European markets. As trade flourished, an increasing number of

Qingtian migrants became engaged in importing goods from China and selling them in Europe.

In 1998, 30,000 Qingtian Chinese had settled in Central and Eastern European countries and were engaged in international trade worth three billion US dollars. By the beginning of 2004, half of the 2,000 Chinese merchants in Bulgaria originated from Qingtian.[6] These Qingtian migrants working as traders and merchants in Central and Eastern Europe became major clients in markets for sundries and specialized products from towns and cities in the vicinity of Qingtian (Yiwu, Wenzhou, Luqiao and Wenling). Starting to become more prosperous, some Qingtian migrants based in Europe also began to travel back to their home villages to establish manufacturing enterprises and trading companies. As a result, international trade and industrial zones started to emerge in Hecheng, Wenxi and Chuanliao.[7]

Associations and organizations

Initially, Qingtian migrants did not found their own associations, but in regions of Europe where Qingtian migrants congregate, they entered the local Overseas Chinese associations and in some they now hold leadership positions. As their numbers increased during the 1990s, Qingtian migrants started to organize their own independent associations to maintain contacts with their native villages, exchanging information and mutually helping each other (see Table 4.3).

In Central and Eastern Europe, Qingtian associations have also been established as the numbers of Qingtian migrants increased in the early 2000s, such as the Romania–Qingtian Association and the Bulgaria–Qingtian Association. Qingtian umbrella associations linking regional Qingtian associations across Europe have also emerged. On 22 October 2002, the fourth session of the Europe–Qingtian Association of Fellow Provincials was held in Madrid. The topic of the meeting was 'Love your country and your hometown, oppose estrangement and promote unity; we unite as one and together we grow'. Leaders of the local Qingtian associations in France, Italy, The Netherlands, Austria, Spain, Belgium and Germany attended this meeting.[8] Qingtian migrants also participate as members and leaders in federations of regional or European Overseas Chinese associations, such as Federation of Overseas Chinese in Europe and the Promotion Association for Peace and Unity between Europe and China.

Table 4.3. Qingtian associations in Europe

Name of organization	Year of establishing
Zhejiang Qingtian Association of Fellow Provincials in Holland	1986
Qingtian Association of Fellow Provincials in Belgium and Luxembourg	1988
Luxemburg–Qingtian Association	2003
The France–Qingtian Association of Fellow Provincials	1994
Northern Italy–Qingtian Association of Fellow Provincials	1995
Europe–Qingtian Association of Fellow Provincials	March 1996
Spain–Qingtian Association of Fellow Provincials	August 1996
Germany–Qingtian Association of Fellow Provincials	May 1998
Austria–Qingtian Association of Fellow Provincials	February 1999
Italy–Qingtian Association of Fellow Provincials	July 1999

Source: Li 2002: 679–680; 'Lusenbao Qingtian tongxianghui chengli' [The founding of the Luxemburg–Qingtian Association] Qingtian zai xian, Haiwai xinwen [The Qingtian on-line – overseas news] URL: www.521m.com (accessed 20 February 2004).

THE RELATIONS BETWEEN QINGTIAN MIGRANTS AND QINGTIAN COUNTY

The majority of Qingtian migrants are now first-generation migrants, having gone abroad since the early 1980s; as such they still carry profound sentiments towards their native country and hometowns. They are concerned about and dedicate mental and physical efforts to the development of their hometowns. Every year many Qingtian Chinese return to their hometowns for visits, travels, to make sacrifices to their ancestors, to make investments etc. The Qingtian Overseas Chinese have become an important link in the contacts between Qingtian County and the rest of the world, and have caused Qingtian County to have natural links with the global economy and civilization. The influence of the Qingtian Overseas Chinese on Qingtian County is multifaceted, and they have had a positive influence on the economic development of Qingtian County, on social progress, in making culture prosper, on diplomatic and foreign relations, etc.

Remittances

Remittances sent back home by Chinese migrants constitute the most direct and basic contribution to their villages and towns of origin, and the Qingtian migrants are not an exception. Following the founding of the PRC and before the start of the economic reform, remittances to Qingtian started to increase. After 1979, remittances grew substantially. Remittances received in Qingtian County amounted to 19,000 RMB in 1950, 186,000 RMB in 1955, 339,000 RMB in 1960, 1.16 million RMB in 1965, 1.26 million RMB in 1970, 1.86 million RMB in 1975, 4.28 million RMB in 1980 and 9.89 million RMB in 1986 (Chen 1990: 655).

According to data from the *Qingtian Qiaoxun* [Qingtian overseas news report] and from the *Qiaolian Jianxun* [China federation of returned Overseas Chinese news], the remittances sent back home to Qingtian have in recent years reached 300 million US dollars. Until the end of May 2001, Qingtian County's foreign currency savings deposits reached 309 million US dollars, for the first time ever passing 300 million US dollars. Compared with the corresponding period in 2000, they had increased by 83 million US dollars, a growth rate of 13 per cent.[9]

In 2002 the remittances sent to Qingtian amounted to 302 million US dollars, the export trade amounted to 8.72 million US dollars, 26 per cent of the total sum of the exports and imports of the entire county that amounted to 33 million US dollars.[10]

According to statistics from the Qingtian branch of the People's Bank of China, the Qingtian branch in all received 50,976 monetary donations in 2003, which in all amounted to 366.45 million US dollars, a substantial increase over former years.[11]

Donations

In the period from 1949 to 1978, donations contributed by Qingtian migrants to their hometowns were primarily placed in education, sanitation, communication and other public welfare projects. From 1960 to 1966, these donations amounted to 58,000 RMB, from 1967 to 1976 to 331,700 RMB. After the beginning of the reform period, Overseas Chinese donations increased substantially. From 1977 to 1987, donations increased to 2.185 million RMB and were mainly contributed to public welfare projects such as Taihe Park, the Overseas Chinese Hotel and Qingtian middle school (Chen 1990: 653–654).

From the beginning of the 1990s and following the strengthening of the economic situation of many Overseas Chinese, donations became more substantial and frequent. In the period from 1978 to 2001, donations from Qingtian migrants (including migrants in Hong Kong and Macau) reached 150 million RMB.[12] In 2003, Qingtian County's improvements within the fields of communication, sanitation and education all involved Overseas Chinese donations of around 11 million RMB.[13]

Since the 1990s, the Overseas Chinese have mainly contributed to the following community projects:

- Museum for Qingtian Overseas Chinese History (the entire project of 2.86 million RMB was financed by donations from Overseas Chinese)
- Xiakang Gymnasium (the entire project of one million RMB was donated by one Overseas Chinese living in Belgium)
- Oujiang Bridge located in Qingtian (three million RMB were donated by Overseas Chinese)
- Taihe Bridge located in Qingtian (two million RMB were donated by Overseas Chinese)[14]
- Fuqing Highway (five million RMB were donated by Overseas Chinese)[15]

Apart from these infrastructural and cultural projects, Qingtian migrants have also substantially contributed to raising the educational level by implementing scholarship programs. In 1988, a married couple, Sun Mingquan and Chen Yuhua, who were living in Italy, established the Sun Mingquan and Chen Yuhua Scholarship for Educating the Talented. As a foundation with a capital of 60,000 US dollars (later increasing to 100,000 US dollars), 20 students with the best results at the annual university entrance examinations are awarded a scholarship every year. From 1988 to 1996, 180 students with outstanding entrance examination results have obtained this award (Qing, Bao et al. 1997: 172–182). As the first type of scholarship for students in all of Qingtian County, this award program has had an important influence on the motivation of students to perform better at the university entrance examination. It has contributed to improving a rather poor-performing educational system in Qingtian County.

Similarly, in October 1989 two Qingtian migrants living in Austria, established the Lu Jiaxian and Gao Wenying Scholarship for Progresses in Science and Technology with a donation of 10,000 US dollars to reward scientific research projects contributing to the development Qingtian County. By August 2002, four reward sessions had been held.[16]

In townships with high concentrations of Overseas Chinese, the donations of the migrants are even more prominent. In Fangshan township, migrants have made major contributions to the development of various kinds of enterprises in their home villages. According to incomplete statistics, by the end of 1998 donations from Overseas Chinese compatriots in Hong Kong, Macau and Taiwan reached 6,89 million RMB, which was spent on improving the infrastructure, education, sanitation and similar communal projects in the entire township.[17] In 1998, Fangshan also became the first township in Zhejiang province where all 20 villages had international telephone connections.[18]

Investments

Apart from extending donations, an increasing number of Qingtian migrants also invest in their hometowns. While donations are a relatively simple virtuous act, investments may involve various difficulties in relation to local financial circumstances and or investment policies and regulations. As a result, many Overseas Chinese 'squander money' when donating to their hometowns, but when asked to make financial investments they hesitate to come forward. Qingtian migrants seem to be no exception.

In the 1980s, Qingtian migrants established or helped to establish such enterprises as a dairy factory and 26 other enterprises with a total of 2.5 million RMB in direct investments (Chen 1990: 654–655). It was only by the end of the 1990s that a major upsurge in financial investments by Qingtian migrants in their hometowns took place. By 1997, 67 private, foreign and joint venture enterprises had been established in the county with foreign investments of 140 million RMB.[19] In 2001, Qingtian County attracted 2.37 million US dollars in Overseas Chinese and foreign capital to establish seven private, foreign and joint venture enterprises (*Zhejiang Nianjian, 2003*: 519). In 2002, the total amount of investments originating from Qingtian migrants reached 600 million RMB.[20]

This upsurge in direct financial investments made by Qingtian migrants in their hometowns was closely linked to the successful economic reforms in China and to Qingtian County goverment's strategy of promoting a local export-oriented economy based on Overseas Chinese capital investments. Since 2001, this 'Project of Overseas Chinese as the key element to return flows' (*Huaqiao yaosu huiliu gongcheng*) has been enthusiastically implemented, and a kind of 'Overseas Chinese economy' has developed into a positive force, boosting Qingtian's development.

Qingtian County's local Communist Party committee and local government emphasize policies of 'double priorities', in other words paying attention to both Overseas Chinese affairs and optimizing conditions for financial investments. These policies were also clearly stated when Qingtian County government on 1 July 2002 held the Forum on WTO and the Overseas Chinese Economy. The focus of the forum was the three topics of 'Overseas Chinese capital', 'the backbone of the Overseas Chinese economy' and 'how to establish an Overseas Chinese economy'. At the conference, it was assumed that the Overseas Chinese economy had already permeated into local politics, economy, culture and other fields. It was also found necessary to venture one step further in promoting 'close relations with the Overseas Chinese', 'protecting the Overseas Chinese' and 'encouraging the Overseas Chinese', as well as expanding the realm of the Overseas Chinese investments and in all ways strengthening overseas relations.[21]

As a result of the implementation of the 'double priorities' policies, Overseas Chinese investments have surged. In recent years, major Overseas Chinese investments in Qingtian encompass:

- Qingtian Huanen Power Station Company Limited, in charge of building and running the Huanen Power Station in Shankou that officially started to generate electricity in 1997. The investment amounted to eight million RMB.[22] The company won the year 2000–2002 title as Outstanding Overseas Chinese Enterprise in Zhejiang province.
- Qingtian New Century Building, a modern multi-commercial building was built in 2001 in Lishui city. The investment amounted to 100 million RMB.[23]
- Jiangnan and Huaguang mansions were built in 2001 in Hecheng city. The investment amounted to 80 million RMB. Foreign real estate management was adopted in running the mansions, and the main customers were the Overseas Chinese living in Europe.[24]
- Zhejiang Province Changxing Shenghua Market Development Company Limited was established in 2001 as a Chinese–foreign joint-venture enterprise engaged in wholesaling of agricultural by-products. The Overseas Chinese investment amounted to 70 million RMB.[25]
- A three-star hotel and a business centre located in Qingtian city. Overseas Chinese investment amounted to 110 million RMB (Guo and Zhou 2003: 291).
- The Ba Yuan Power Station went into operation on 31 January 2004. Investments constituted 76 million RMB. The electricity generated by the power station every year amounts to 15.85 million kilowatt-hours. Besides generating electricity, the station also controls irrigation for the lower levels of the river.[26]

Since the late 1990s, foreign investments made by Qingtian migrants have reached over 600 million RMB, which constitutes more than half of all foreign direct investments made in Qingtian County. Migrant investments have profoundly improved the economic development of migrant hometowns and transformed the county centre of Hecheng city into a more modern city able to attract tourists and it is believed that more than 1 million locals have been offered jobs, as a result of Overseas Chinese investments.[27]

In general, Qingtian migrants' investments have been a success and many have profited from them, due to preferential treatment policies and improvement of the investment environment. However, a small number of unsuccessful enterprises established by Qingtian migrants have also been encountered.[28] In October 2004, Qingtian migrant investors established the Association for Returned Qingtian Overseas Chinese Investors reflecting the number of migrant investors and the popularity of such actions.

CONCLUSION

Data on remittances, donations and investments indicate that during the last couple of decades Qingtian migrants have contributed to the development of their hometowns. It is, however, difficult to assess the direct economic impact of migrants, because foreign direct investments are not marked specifically as originating from persons or companies of Chinese ancestry. By comparing Qingtian's development with neighbouring counties, it only becomes evident that the effect of Overseas Chinese economic activities has been paramount in Qingtian.

Among the eight county and cities administered by Lishui city, the economy of Qingtian County has in recent years been among the best. In 2002, the number of industrial enterprises with an annual income of more than five million RMB was the second highest in Qingtian County, which also had the highest number of foreign-invested enterprises (Qingtian had ten foreign-invested companies, while the other counties and cities only had one each or none). In Qingtian County, the share of the foreign-invested companies in relation to the total value of industrial production was 15 per cent, while foreign-invested companies in Songyang County only made up 6 per cent of the total value of production. The foreign-invested enterprises in other counties and cities had an even smaller share (Lishui Shi Tongjiju 2003:

62). The positive effect of the Qingtian Overseas Chinese on the development of Qingtian's industry is evident.

In 2002, Qingtian County assumed a vanguard position among all counties administered under Lishui city, with investments in real estate and house construction amounting to 480 million RMB, fixed assets reaching 190 million RMB and an area of building construction (including housing) covering 500,000 square meters (Lishui Shi Tongjiju 2003: 115). It is not surprising that investments in real estate and house construction is high in Qingtian County compared to neighbouring counties, since Overseas Chinese typically return to their hometowns as soon as they have enough savings to buy real estate to build lavish houses. In recent years, following the development of Qingtian's economy, many Overseas Chinese have one after another purchased real estate spurring the development of Qingtian County's real estate industry.

International tourists and the income generated from international tourism are also among the highest in all of Lishui city's counties. In 2002, some 423,000 travellers made it to Qingtian County. Of these, 14,000 came from outside China and constituted 62 per cent of all international travellers who came to counties under the jurisdiction of Lishui city. The income from international tourism in Qingtian County amounted to 29 million US dollars, constituting 68 per cent of Lishui city's annual international tourism income (Lishui Shi Tongjiju 2003: 135). Since there are no particular tourist sites in Qingtian, we may safely assume that the high number of international travellers to Qingtian County is caused by Overseas Chinese visitors, who return to visit family and friends, make investments and per form similar activities.

The dominant position of the Overseas Chinese for the local development of Qingtian County's economy has been shown above, but in comparison to other counties in Zhejiang province Qingtian's economic development is still lacking behind. In 2002, Qingtian County ranked 42nd out of 58 counties and cities in Zhejiang province *(Zhejiang nianjian, 2003*: 477–478*)*. As observed in many other migrant-sending communities (Russell 1992), migrants' economic resources are primarily made as family remittances, which are used for consumption and/or placed in real estate. Productive investments from migrants have been more difficult to attract to Qingtian and as a result the local government in Qingtian has recently formulated a development strategy in which local industry is to be the main economic force, tertiary industry is to provide economic dynamics and the Overseas

Chinese economy will be the driving force. With the implementation of this strategy, it seems that local authorities have recognized that the Overseas Chinese are only an exterior driving force and that domestic industry needs to develop first, but that the unique situation of being an emigrant county can make the Overseas Chinese into a driving force that can assist in triggering the economic takeoff of Qingtian County.

NOTES

1. The author is particularly grateful for the large amount of material provided by former Chairman of the Qingtian County Federation of Returned Overseas Chinese Chen Yaodong.

2. *Huaqiao huaren luncong* is compiled in collaboration with the Federation for Returned Overseas Chinese of Zhejiang Province.

3. In 2004, this journal changed title to *Qingtian qiaoxun* [Qingtian overseas news reports] and is now published by the local Qingtian Federation of Returned Overseas Chinese.

4. This time frame seems to have become consensus among the Qingtian Chinese themselves. See e.g. the Zhejiang Xinhua internet site where Qingtian is presented: 'As a native place of Overseas Chinese, Qingtian has an Overseas Chinese history of more than 300 years'. Xinhua wang Zhejiang zhengfu wangqun, Qingtian xian [Xinhua Newsweb, Zhejiang government website]. URL: www.zj.xinhua.org/df/qingtian/history/history.htm (accessed 25 February 2004).

5. Xinhua wang Zhejiang zhengfu wangqun, Qingtian xian [Xinhua Newsweb, Zhejiang government website]. URL: www.zj.xinhua.org/df/qingtian/history/history_09.htm (accessed 20 February 2004).

6. 'Fengeng Ouzhou: Zhongguo shangren chuangfu Ouzhou de gushi' [Fengeng Europe: a story about the Chinese businessmen enriching Europe], *Qingtian zai xian, Haiwai xinwen* [The Qingtian on-line – overseas news] . URL: www.521m.com (accessed 18 February 2004).

7. *Qingtian qiaoxiang bao* [Qingtian hometown newspaper], 14 October 1999.

8. Bihua xinwenwang [Belgian Chinese newsweb]. URL: www.bihua.org/messages/107.html (accessed 20 February 2004).

9. *Qiaolian jianxun* [Brief News of China Federation of Returned Overseas Chinese], no. 7. 20 June 2001.

10. *Qiaolian jianxun* [Brief News of China Federation of Returned Overseas Chinese], no. 6. 30 June 2003.

11. *Qingtian qiaoxun* [Qingtian overseas news report], no. 3. 13 January 2004.

12 Xinhua wang Zhejiang zhengfu wangqun, Qingtian xian [Xinhua Newsweb, Zhejiang government website]. URL: www.zj.xinhua.org/df/qingtian/history/history_09.htm (accessed 20 February 2004).

13 *Qiaolian jianxun* [Brief News of China Federation of Returned Overseas Chinese], no. 1. 3 March 2004.

14 Xinhua wang Zhejiang zhengfu wangqun, Qingtian xian [Xinhua Newsweb, Zhejiang government website]. URL: www.zj.xinhua.org/df/qingtian/history/history_09.htm (accessed 20 February 2004).

15 *Qiaolian jianxun* [Brief News of China Federation of Returned Overseas Chinese], no. 4. 30 April 2003.

16 *Qiaolian jianxun* [Brief News of China Federation of Returned Overseas Chinese], no. 8. 20 September 2002.

17 *Qingtian qiaoxiang bao* [Qingtian hometown newspaper], 26 November 1998.

18 *Qingtian qiaoxiang bao* [Qingtian hometown newspaper], 17 December 1998.

19 Xinhua wang Zhejiang zhengfu wangqun, Qingtian xian [Xinhua Newsweb, Zhejiang government website]. URL: www.zj.xinhua.org/df/qingtian/history/history_09.htm (accessed 20 February 2004).

20 *Qiaolian jianxun* [Brief News of China Federation of Returned Overseas Chinese], no. 2. 27 February 2003.

21 *Qiaolian jianxun* [Brief News of China Federation of Returned Overseas Chinese], no. 6. 11 July 2002.

22 *Qingtian qiaoxiang bao* [Qingtian hometown newspaper], 17 June 1999.

23 *Qiaolian jianxun* [Brief News of China Federation of Returned Overseas Chinese], no. 10. 5 September 2001.

24 *Qiaolian jianxun* [Brief News of China Federation of Returned Overseas Chinese], no. 6. 30 May 2001.

25 Ibid.

26 *Qingtian qiaoxun* [Qingtian overseas news report], no. 7. 3 February 2004, first edition.

27 Bihua xinwenwang [Belgian–Chinese newsweb]. URL: www.bihua.org/messages/107.html (accessed 25 February 2004).

28 Private information from former official.

REFERENCES

Benton, Gregor and Frank N. Pieke (eds) (1998) *The Chinese in Europe*. Houndmills, Basingstoke, Hants: Macmillan; New York: St. Martin's Press.

Chen, Murong (ed.) (1990) *Qingtian Xianzhi* [Gazetteer of Qingtian County]. Hangzhou: Zhejiang renmin chubanshe.

Christiansen, Flemming (2003) *Chinatown, Europe: An Exploration of Overseas Chinese Identity in the 1990s*. London: RoutledgeCurzon.

Guo, Yuhuan and Zhou Wangsen (2003) 'Haiwai yangfan, chizi qinghuai' [Hoisting sail overseas and genuine sentiments]. In Zhou Wangsen (ed.), *Huaqiao Huaren Yanjiu Luncong* [Collection of research essays on Overseas Chinese], no. 6. Beijing: Zhongguo huaqiao chubanshe, pp. 280–292.

Li, Minghuan (2002) *Ouzhou Huaqiao Huaren Shi* [History of the Overseas Chinese in Europe]. Beijing: Zhongguo huaqiao chubanshe.

Lishui Shi Tongjiju [Lishui City Statistics Department] (ed.) (2003) *Lishui Tongji Nianjian, 2003* [Lishui statistical yearbook, 2003]. Beijing: Zhongguo tongji chubanshe.

Pan, Jiawei and Sun Jianguo (eds) (2003) *Zhejiang Nianjian, 2003* [Zhejiang Yearbook, 2003]. Hangzhou: Zhejiang nianjian she.

Pieke, Frank N. and Hein Mallee (eds) (1999) *Internal and International Migration: Chinese Perspectives*. Richmond, Surrey: Curzon Press.

Qing, Bao et al. (eds) (1997) *Qingxi Changcheng – Sun Mingquan, Chen Yuhua Kangli Shengping Shilu* [Concerns about the Great Wall – authentic record of the lives of the married couple Sun Mingquan and Chen Yuhua]. Hongkong: Xianggang haiyang guoji chubanshe.

Russell, Sharon S. (1992) 'Migrant Remittances and Development'. *International Migration*, vol. 30, no. 3/4, pp. 267–287.

Thunø, Mette (1999) 'Moving Stones from China to Europe: The Dynamics of Emigration from Zhejiang to Europe'. In Frank N. Pieke and Hein Mallee (eds), *Internal and International Migration: Chinese Perspectives*. Richmond, Surrey: Curzon Press.

Zhang, Xiuming (1998) 'Qingtianren chuguo de lishi yu xianzhuang chutan' [An initial exploration of the history of Qingtian Chinese going abroad and of their present situation]. *Huaqiao huaren lishi yanjiu* [Overseas Chinese History Studies], no. 3, pp. 48–58, 47.

Zhou, Wangsen (1997) 'Qingtian shidiao yu Qingtian huaqiao – lun Qingtian huaqiao de qiyuan wenti' [Qingtian stone carvings and Qingtian Overseas Chinese – a discussion of the origin of the Qingtian Overseas Chinese]. In Zhou Wangsen (ed.), *Huaqiao Huaren Yanjiu Luncong* [Collection of research essays on Overseas Chinese], no. 2. Beijing: Zhongguo huaqiao chubanshe, pp. 83–88.

—— (ed.) (forthcoming) *Qingtian Xian Huaqiao Shi* [History of Overseas Chinese in Qingtian County].

Chapter 5

Detraditionalized and Renewed *Qiaoxiang* Areas:
Case Studies of Panyu and Wenzhou in the Reform Period since 1978

Yow Cheun Hoe

INTRODUCTION

Not all the *qiaoxiang* (sojourner homeland) areas that experienced massive emigration before 1949 took on the same development pathway in the reform period that commenced in China in 1978. In the context of China's rise as a great manufacturing base and a huge investment destination, some of these old *qiaoxiang* areas shed their traditional features, while some resumed emigration with new elements. This study is based on Panyu and Wenzhou, the former located in Guangdong and the latter in Zhejiang. It demonstrates how these two localities in the reform period have been different from their landscapes in the pre-1949 period. In a more detailed examination, it discusses what they have in common and how they differ in their relations with Chinese emigrants and their descendants.

In view of the disparate scenarios demonstrated in the reform period, there is an obvious need to challenge and re-examine the concept of *qiaoxiang* areas as well as other related issues, such as *huaqiao* (Overseas Chinese) and new migrants. In fact, it has always been a set of complex political, social, and economic factors inside and outside China that have defined and redefined the old *qiaoxiang* areas in the age of globalization. Migration trajectories, migrants' inspiration and state policies have interacted with each other amid expanding global capitalism and have generated different degrees of impact on *qiaoxiang* areas. This chapter shows that various groups of ethnic Chinese responded in different ways to their ancestral homelands in China and thus the impacts varied across different *qiaoxiang* areas

After China embarked on its open-door policy and economic reform in 1978, both central and local governments made efforts to re-establish relations with the ethnic Chinese living all over the world and engage them in the social and economic agendas being carried out in their ancestral homelands, or the so-called *qiaoxiang* (literally sojourner district) areas. Apart from extending large economic benefits, the promotion of primordial sentiment and kinship ties are among the strategies used to attract the Chinese overseas. More than two decades after China's opening to the world, however, *qiaoxiang* areas have witnessed very different socioeconomic changes and relations with Chinese overseas. The first part of this chapter attempts to explain, on the basis of existing literature, what a *qiaoxiang* area is. Then, it outlines three periods of *qiaoxiang* evolution that took place in Guangdong province in South China. Subsequently, a comparative study is made of two well-known *qiaoxiang* areas, Panyu and Wenzhou, the former located in Guangdong, the latter in Zhejiang province, examining how the two localities, in terms of demography, have changed from a shared traditional landscape of pre-1949 and then differed from each other after 1978, moving on to discuss the deep involvement of Hong Kong people in Panyu's economic transformation and the limited ethnic Chinese influence on Wenzhou's vigorous economy. It also explores the changes in the local mentality amid the economic developments and emigration trajectories. In conclusion, it attempts to pin down different types of *qiaoxiang*, arguing that Panyu has been detraditionlized, while Wenzhou is expanding with new elements.

WHAT IS A *QIAOXIANG*?

A combination of *qiao* (sojourner) and *xiang* (district), the term *qiaoxiang* implies a locality from where a high percentage of people originally left but with the ultimate intention to return one day. It is related to the term *huaqiao* (Overseas Chinese) used to designate Chinese migrants, but literally meaning 'Chinese sojourners' and implying a political loyalty to China and a primordial sentiment towards their country of origin.[1] Different Chinese governments at different points of time did not clearly define the characteristics of a *qiaoxiang*, but such emigrant villages or districts seem to earn their name when they attain certain numbers of *huaqiao, guiqiao* [returned Overseas Chinese], and *qiaojuan* (family members of Overseas Chinese in China) (Pan 1998: 27–30).

Qiaoxiang, as a term, was seldom used in the literature written in both China and Overseas Chinese communities during the late Qing and Republican periods, a time when massive overseas migration occurred in South China, and the majority of Chinese migrants had not yet been naturalized or assimilated into other parts of the world. The term gained unprecedented currency after economic reform was initiated in 1978 and has since been widely employed indiscriminately by local government organs, particularly by the Qiaoban (Overseas Chinese Affairs Office) and by the so-called mass organization Qiaolian (Returned Overseas Chinese Association) to pinpoint certain localities and their relations to the ethnic Chinese in South-east Asia, North America, Hong Kong, Europe and elsewhere around the world.[2] Meanwhile, some scholarly writings also employed the term and the concept without much heed to its definition and its diversity of meanings (Douw et al. 1999; Wang Benzun, 2000; Zhuang Guotu, 2000).

First of all the application of the term causes confusion among ethnic Chinese, particularly those living in South-east Asian countries. It is politically dubious, if not unacceptable, to make use of the concept of *qiaoxiang* to relate a locality in China to certain Chinese overseas, because the majority of these ethnic Chinese are no longer *huaqiao* but citizens of their respective countries.[3] Local Chinese designations of these particular areas as *qiaoxiang*, thus, appear to be in contrast to the foreign policy of the PRC clearly demarcating Overseas Chinese [*huaqiao*] and compatriots [*tongbao*] in Hong Kong, Macau, and Taiwan. The local definition of *qiaoxiang* ignores, whether deliberately or not, the fact that Hong Kong, Macau, and Taiwan compatriots are not *huaqiao* and that in other parts of the world there are more ethnic Chinese who are foreign nationals.[4] Secondly, applying the term *qiaoxiang* to many emigrant communities in South China seems to imply a shared developmental path based on central and local policies and similar ethnic Chinese involvement, but as I will show below this is not the case.

THREE PERIODS OF *QIAOXIANG* EVOLUTION: GUANGDONG EXPERIENCE

What has happened in Guangdong province tells us that the formation and transformation of the so-called *qiaoxiang* areas have been essentially contingent on the strength and content of their relations at different periods of time with the Chinese emigrants originating from these areas. More specifically, it is a set of complex political, economic and social factors, involving China as well as the countries of residence, that have conditioned the different ways various Chinese emigrants and descendants have responded to and defined the landscapes of many towns and villages across Guangdong (as well as other places). Generally speaking, the *qiaoxiang* evolution can be divided into three periods. The first is the formation and developmental period, which started in the mid-nineteenth century and lasted until 1949 when the People's Republic of China was founded. During this period, deteriorating economic conditions, serious political chaos and social insecurity led many Chinese to leave their native villages and towns (Wakeman 1966). On the other hand, the thriving economies outside China, particularly in South-east Asia (Purcell 1980) and North America (Chan Sucheng 1986; Wickberg 1982), needed cheap labour, thus inducing the setting up of many Western and Chinese agents who facilitated labour trafficking from South China (McKeown 1999). More importantly, what made possible the construction of *qiaoxiang* areas was that the Qing court in the late nineteenth century abandoned its policy of regarding Chinese emigrants as traitors and instead made many efforts to enlist financial support from them (Douw 1999: 31–36; Fang Xiongpu 2000). This change encouraged Overseas Chinese to have relations with their homelands in China and the inflow of monies. Subsequently, the Republican government also endeavoured to engage Chinese emigrants in China's development.

In this period, the *qiaoxiang* areas can best be described as emigrant communities, featuring high percentages of young males who worked overseas and supported their old people, wives, and children who stayed put. These areas received immeasurable remittances for family expenditure and donations for social welfare,[5] but lacked significant industrial investments as such actions did not appear as promising in the then chaotic environment.[6] Among the local people, the returned migrants [*guiqiao*] and the dependants of emigrants [*qiaojuan*] became financially privileged and had extravagant lifestyles. In Guangdong, many of these emigrant communities had formed before the Second World War, particularly in the Sanyi and Siyi areas in the Pearl River Delta, Shantou areas, Meixian and Xinyi in the mountainous inland areas, and Wenchang and Qionghai in Hainan Island (see Map 5.1).[7]

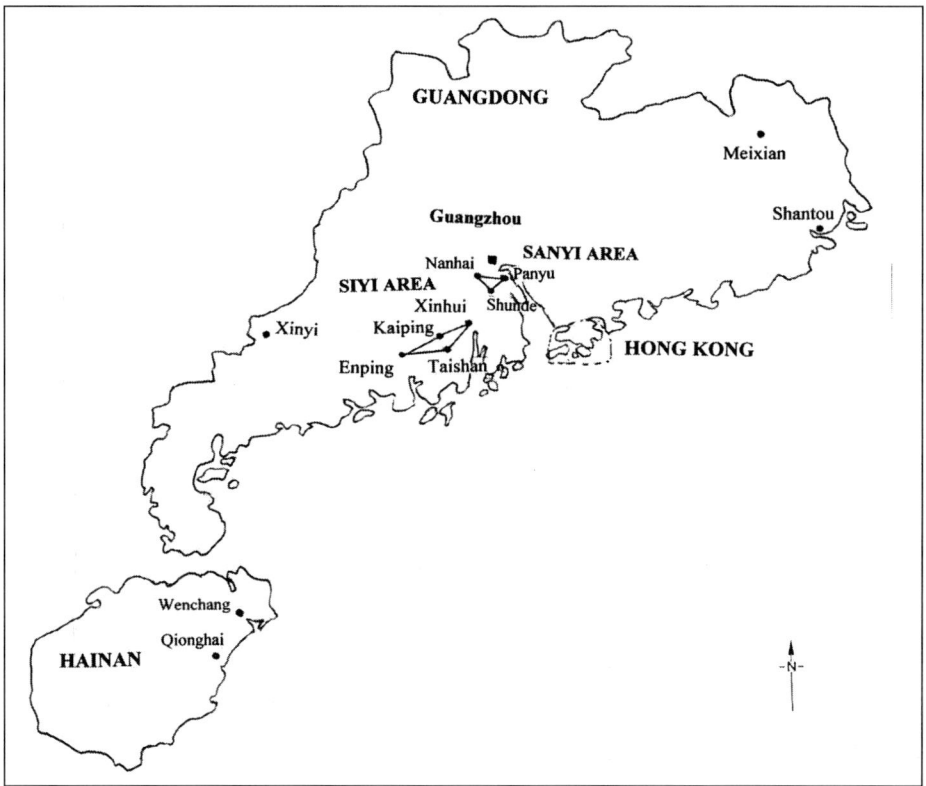

Map 5.1. Major *qiaoxiang* areas in Guangdong

The second period, spanning 1949 to 1978, is the isolation period. The first few years after 1949 witnessed the return of many emigrants from their living and working places abroad, whether voluntarily or not, to the new China. However, before long, these returnees, as well as dependants of emigrants, were cut off from their overseas kinsfolk following China's isolation from the international political stage. During the Land Reform Campaign (1951–1953) and the Cultural Revolution (1966–1976), contacts with overseas family members were cut off and many were severely criticized for their overseas connections, which the Communist government regarded as treacherous, and their properties were confiscated (Zhuang

1998; Fitzgerald 1972: 162–184). As a direct result, there was an economic setback in the *qiaoxiang* areas. On the other hand, despite the severed *qiaoxiang* links, the Chinese overseas communities, particularly in South-east Asia and North America, thrived with descendants born locally. Hong Kong continued to receive immigrants from mainland China and somehow maintained some business and social connections with Guangdong (Chan Ming K. 1995; Lui Ping-Keung 2000). These demographic changes have largely determined the different ways the Overseas Chinese and the Hong Kong compatriots responded to the *qiaoxiang* areas in the third period.

The third period, commencing from 1978, is the transformation period. Since 1978, for the purpose of family reunion, a considerable number of kinsfolk left these *qiaoxiang* areas to join their counterparts in Hong Kong and smaller numbers went to North America. Few went to South-east Asia, where countries, except Singapore, did not welcome Chinese immigrants. Large-scale emigration from these old *qiaoxiang* areas in Guangdong never resumed, while new or renewed sources for sending workers, students, and talents emerged in other parts of China, including Wenzhou.[8] During this period, the old *qiaoxiang* areas in Guangdong and Fujian were institutionalized with the rehabilitation or new establishment of many Qiaoban and Qiaolian at local levels of township and village. Nevertheless, different *qiaoxiang* areas have, since 1978, gone along different development pathways.

While all the *qiaoxiang* areas generally demonstrated the same features in the first and second periods, they presented diverse pictures in the third period, involving three patterns. The first pattern is observable in such economically prosperous places as Panyu and Dongguan, which are located adjacent to the international financial hub of Hong Kong. They have registered high economic growth, rapid industrialization and successful urbanization as a result of an unprecedented huge inflow of business and productive investments, coupled with immeasurable donations to public welfare, primarily from and through Hong Kong.[9] In contrast to the economically fast-growing first pattern, the second pattern is associated with such mountainous and remote areas as Xinyi (Yow 2004). Receiving the fewest donations and investments, they have modernized least and floundered in economic problems. The third pattern is evident in such localities as Taishan and Kaiping (Johnson and Woon 1997; Woon 1990), located outside the fast-developing areas spanning Guangdong's administrative centre Guangzhou southwards to Hong Kong, but not having the geographical diversity of the province's inland part. They absorbed less investment than did the first-pattern localities. However, with closer links to North American Chinese, they received more donations than the second-pattern localities did.

DIFFERENT DEMOGRAPHIC CHANGES

Having discussed the Guangdong experience in general, the examination now turns to two prominent *qiaoxiang* areas, Panyu and Wenzhou municipality (see Maps 5.1 and 5.2).

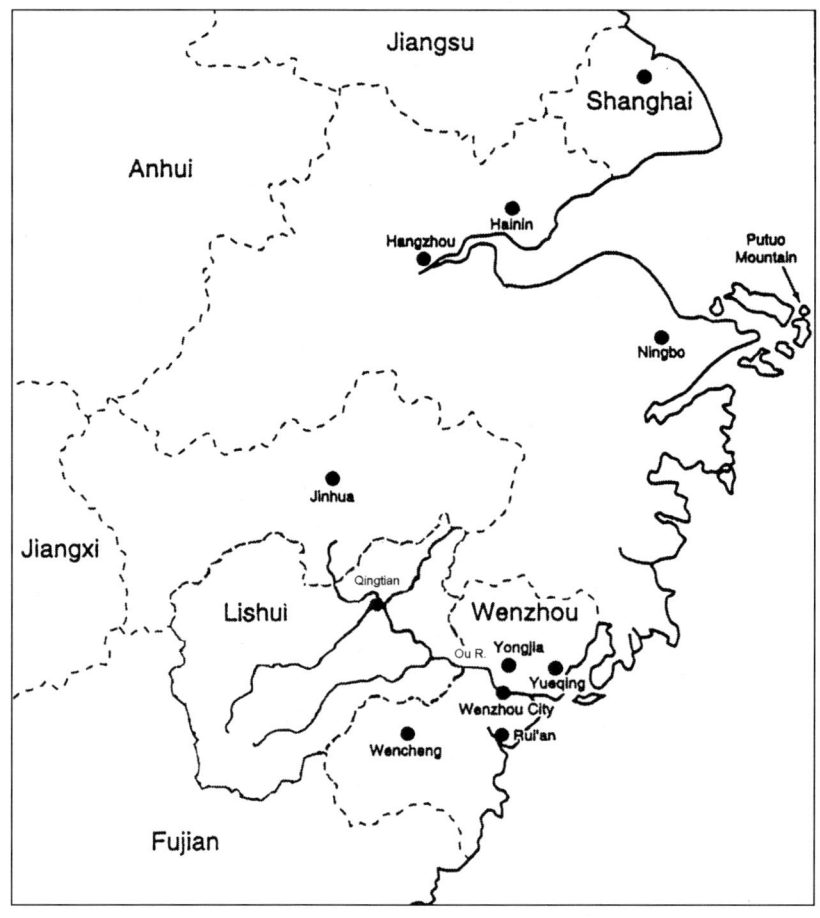

Map 5.2. Wenzhou in Zhejiang Province

Like many other old *qiaoxiang* areas across Guangdong, both Panyu and Wenzhou experienced significant emigrations before 1949. Commencing from the mid-nineteenth century, particularly after the Opium War, tens of thousands of Panyu natives went overseas as labourers to South-east Asia and North America (Luo 1995: 923–924; Panyu qiaowu bangongshi: 1–17). After Wenzhou became a treaty port in 1816, it also witnessed its merchants sail to South-east Asia and Africa's east coast to trade in handicrafts and other goods, but more Wenzhou people went abroad as coolies, the largest destination for whom being Western Europe (Zhang 1991: 1–12; 1987: 13). While the Wenzhou emigration came to a halt in 1937 with the outbreak of Sino-Japanese War (Zhang 1987: 4), Panyu migrants stopped flocking overseas and went instead to Hong Kong and Macau throughout the period from 1949 to 1978 (Panyu qiaowu bangongshi: 85–86).

In the reform era since 1978, demographic changes have taken place in both Panyu and Wenzhou and altered their traditional features as *qiaoxiang* that were a result of a high percentage of natives living overseas. These changes can be seen in how four groups of people have defined the demographic contours of both localities: (1) residents in the localities themselves; (2) emigrants and their descendants living overseas and in Hong Kong and Macau; (3) the people who ventured out from the both localities but migrated internally inside China and (4) migrant workers coming into both localities.

Table 5.1. Demographic profiles of Panyu (1997) and Wenzhou municipality (2001)[10]

	Panyu	Ratio of residents in Panyu	Wenzhou	Ratio of residents in Wenzhou
Residents	880,103	1	7.4 million	1
Emigrants and their descendants	494,182	0.56	400,000	0.05
Internal migrants	insignificant	–	1.6 million	0.21
Migrant workers	347,063	0.39	1.53 million	0.20

Note: 1997 and 2001 were chosen because data for all the four groups were available for these years.
Sources: Luo Jingxiang 1998: 3; Cai and Zhu 2002: 23; Cai Xiaozhen 2002: 11; WN 2002: 396.

As shown in Table 5.1, in 1997 Panyu had 880,103 residents and 494,184 people from there resided overseas, in Hong Kong and in Macau. It attracted 347,073 migrant workers into its growing job market, while the numbers of its people moving out as internal migrants in China were minuscule. Proportionally, for each 100 residents in Panyu, there were 56 living overseas and 39 migrant workers.

While residents in Wenzhou outnumber those in Panyu, Wenzhou emigrants and their descendants are fewer as compared to Panyu. In 2001, Wenzhou residents reached 7.4 million, while people from there living outside mainland China only totalled 400,000. The internal migrants from Wenzhou and migrant workers received by Wenzhou, numbering 1.6 million and 1.53 million respectively, were far larger than those in Panyu. For each 100 residents in Wenzhou, there were 21 internal migrants inside China, 20 migrant workers in the city itself and only 5 emigrants and their descendants.

The demographic statistics above show that, after two decades of successful economic transformation since 1978, Panyu has changed from being a destablized locality sending substantive labour overseas in the pre-1949 period to a prosperous one receiving migrant workers from elsewhere in China in 1997. The bulk of the migrant workers came from less-developed counties in western Guangdong and interior provinces such as Hunan, Jiangxi, and Sichuan.[11] They were employed primarily as manual labour in factories, construction sites, shops and restaurants, with a few of them in seasonal agricultural activities (Luo 1998: 3). The inflow of migrant workers was a result of numerous job opportunities created in businesses and factories invested in primarily by Chinese emigrants living in Hong Kong. In this sense, emigrants and their descendants have detraditionalized Panyu as a *qiaoxiang* which had in the past large numbers of natives because of the local poverty. In fact, this phenomenon appeared after 1978 in other *qiaoxiang* localities in Guangdong and Fujian that had benefited from foreign investments, a significant portion of which came from Chinese overseas and Hong Kong and Macau residents.[12]

While the foreign-investment-driven economy in Panyu attracted migrant workers, the booming local private enterprises in Wenzhou also turned the city into a favoured destination for migrant workers, mainly from impoverished provinces such as Hunan, Hubei, Jiangxi, Anhui, Henan, Sichuan, and Guizhou (WN 2002: 396). However, unlike Panyu, Wenzhou continued as a *qiaoxiang* by resuming overseas migration as well as internal migration into other parts of China.

The configuration of the Panyu and Wenzhou people outside mainland China needs closer examination as these diverse experiences define and determine the development of the two *qiaoxiang* areas quite differently.

Out of the 494,182 Panyu emigrants and their descendants in 1997, 74 per cent resided in Hong Kong and Macau, while 26 per cent had settled in foreign countries (see Appendices 1 and 2).[13]

The numerous Panyu migrants in Hong Kong and Macau was a result of out-migration that continued even after 1949, whereas in South-east Asia, the number of Overseas Chinese increased out of natural growth after the Second World War. The overseas Panyu people, mainly in South-east Asia and North America, evolved over a few generations and basically received no kinsfolk after the Second World War; they are now much rooted in the local societies where they live and their kinship ties with Panyu are weakening. On the other hand, Panyu people in Hong Kong have stronger links to Panyu, where they still have close family members and relatives.

While Panyu has never resumed the massive emigration it had before 1949, Wenzhou has since 1978 witnessed a new wave of emigration on a scale that is much bigger than the one before it (Li 1999b: 85). The major destinations for Wenzhou emigrants in the economic reform period were countries in Western Europe. This is partly because migratory chains were easier to reforge with the Wenzhou communities already established in Western Europe before 1937. At the same time, in the first half of the 1980s, immigrant policies based on family reunion schemes were more lenient in Western Europe, as opposed to those in South-east Asia (Li 1999a: 188–189). When European countries tightened their immigration policies in the late 1980s, many Wenzhou migrants arrived illegally, with the help of professional human traffickers, by land, air and sea routes via Hong Kong, Bangkok, Singapore, Moscow, and Prague (Giese 1999: 203–207).

It was estimated that in Europe by 1990, 70 per cent of the Chinese immigrants from Wencheng, one of the counties in Wenzhou, were new migrants who left their home villages after 1978 (Wencheng xianzhi 1996: 226). Two-thirds of the Wenzhou people outside China are residing in Western Europe, where the telling enclaves are located in France, the Netherlands and Spain (Cai and Zhu 2002). In 1990s' Paris, for instance, there were 130,000 Wenzhou people and the majority of them had arrived after 1978 (Wang Chunguang 2000: 15, 17). In the Florence–Prato area in Italy, also in the 1990s, about 90 per cent of the 10,000 Chinese there came from Wenzhou and its neighbor Qingtian (Tomba 1999: 283).[14] The bulk of the Wenzhou people in Europe found employment in Chinese restaurants while some run family enterprises manufacturing and selling garments and leather products (Tomba 1999:287). Thus, the concentration of Wenzhou people in Western Europe distinguishes them from the people of Guangdong origin residing in large numbers in South-east Asia and North America (GSH 1996: 59–60).

In general, Wenzhou emigrants were those lacking opportunities in the midst of the economic transformation in China. Neither the privileged top earners nor the underprivileged poor were the first to leave. Most emigrants hailed from a middle group who were aware of their own limits in China, but with certain financial possibilities that enabled then to afford the expenses of international migration. They did not necessarily come from a single class but might include both the son of a peasant and the daughter of an official (Giese 1999: 201–202).[15] Most of them worked abroad with the hope of improving their relative social position in the home community in Wenzhou (Li 1999a: 187). These new emigrants are supposed to have close linkages with Wenzhou at many levels. However, the magnitude of impact that ethnic Chinese can generate on their ancestral homelands is subject to their economic strength. Comparatively speaking, outside mainland China tycoons of Panyu origin are greater in numbers and wealth than business magnates of Wenzhou origin. As will be discussed subsequently, Panyu's economic development has benefited tremendously from its affluent emigrants and descendants mainly in Hong Kong, while Wenzhou has prospered without much of the involvement of its kinsfolk outside China.

DEEP INVOLVEMENT OF HONG KONG COMPATRIOTS IN PANYU

Over the past two decades, journalists and scholars have been paying increasing attention to Chinese business networks, discussing how ethnic Chinese have co-operated with each other outside China as well as how they have built connections with mainland China, including the many ancestral homelands of ethnic Chinese or the so-called *qiaoxiang* areas (Lever-Tracy et al. 1996; Tracy and Lever-Tracy 2000). Many of these writers view Chinese networks and linkages as a natural outcome of ethnic sameness and cultural affinity, and perceive economic activities conducted by ethnic Chinese as driven by primordial sentiment and kinship ties (Limlingan 1986; Redding 1990; Kotkin 1993; Hamilton 1996; Weidenbaum and Hughes 1996). Some scholars have posited their scepticism as to whether Chinese business practices truly involve some features particularly distinctive from those of other ethnic groups.[16] What is lacking is an evaluation of the different roles played by different groups of Chinese emigrants and their descendants and a comparison of the impact they have generated with those of other forces in that particular locality. Indeed, the formation and transformation of a *qiaoxiang* area are very much context – and location – specific (Yow 2002). Not all the *qiaoxiang* areas are the same, each is subject to the content and magnitude of the impacts engendered by various groups of ethnic Chinese at different periods of time.

During the reform period, Chinese emigrants and their descendants significantly helped Panyu succeed in industrialization and modernization. In the first decade after 1978, they donated immeasurably to lay down sound public infrastructure, including bridges, roads and schools for future economic development. In the 1990s, with improved infrastructure in Panyu, they, along with other Western companies, invested more in manufacturing and service sectors.

Historically, Overseas Chinese in the pre-1949 period donated largely to schools and hospitals in Guangdong as a whole and also in Panyu. Post-1978, Panyu witnessed the emergence of the production sector as a new object for donations. This shows that the Panyu people who were mainly residents of Hong Kong responded well to the economic reforms by donating machinery, material, and money to processing lines. Appendix 4 shows that from 1978 to 1996 the largest to receive donations was the production sector, with a total of HK$1,932 million.[17] Two traditional areas for donation, transportation and education, assumed the second and third positions with HK$1,533 million and HK$1,010 million respectively. Health centres and facilities also received a large donation of HK$ 635 million.

Where foreign investment is concerned, there were a number of companies from mainland China, registered in Hong Kong, which invested back to Panyu.[18] From 1980 to 1999, with the exception of these mainland Chinese companies, Hong Kong was the most important investor, with a total of around US$7,493 million. This amount vastly surpassed that of Scandinavia (US$182 million) and Taiwan (US$121 million), and even outstripped those by other countries. Where North America is concerned, Canada (US$7.6 million) and the United States (US$6.5 million) were far less significant in comparison to Hong Kong. From South-east Asia, the largest amount of investment was from Singapore with US$73.8 million, followed by Indonesia (US$13.6 million) and Malaysia (US$1.2 million) (Panyu Foreign Economic Relations and Trade Bureau 2000).

More specifically, it is the Hong Kong compatriots who outshone Chinese overseas in making donations and investments to generate economic transformation in Panyu. The emigration to Hong Kong that continued even after 1949 means that Hong Kong compatriots have a closer kinship and friendship with Panyu and thus are willing to do something good for the locality by making donations to the local social welfare. Geographical proximity is one of the obvious reasons for Hong Kong compatriots to invest in Panyu, which in fact is part of the great flow of relocation of factories and capital from Hong Kong to mainland China in search of cheaper labour and land. On the other hand, weakening kinship ties, long distances, limited wealth, and ample economic opportunities in their countries of residence have hindered many Chinese overseas from having as much financial commitment and economic involvement in Panyu as their Hong Kong compatriots.

The heavy involvement of Hong Kong compatriots can be seen more clearly by collating the data associated with the five groups of Panyu Honorary Citizens, conferred by the local government irregularly in 1993, 1994, 1996, 1998, and 2000. The honorary citizens were those who donated generously or invested significantly or did both in Panyu. Although no specific criterion was stated regarding the eligibility for the honour, the sums contributed individually by each honorary citizen appeared to be in large amounts, from a few ten thousands up to a few million *Renminbi*.

Appendix 3 gives the places of residence for all the 130 honorary citizens. Throughout, Hong Kong residents, amounting to 109, were definitely predominant. Those based in Macau (5), United States (4), and Taiwan (3), though assuming the next positions, were much less important. Among the countries in South-east Asia, where the bulk of Chinese overseas live, only Singapore had one of its nationals made an honorary citizen of Panyu.

One noteworthy feature is that Panyu was not a *qiaoxiang* for many of the honorary citizens. As shown in Appendix 4, out of 130 there were 74 honorary citizens who had their origin in Panyu, certainly not an overwhelming proportion. As for the others, some originated from other Cantonese-speaking localities (such as Nanhai and Shunde), Teochew-speaking areas (Shantou and Chaoyang), Fujian, Shanghai, Suzhou, Anhui, and some were non-Chinese foreigners hailing from Japan, Korea, the United States, the United Kingdom, Spain, and Australia. The existence of these non-kinfolk is not surprising, particularly in the context of the 1990s when Panyu, with its strategic location adjacent to Hong Kong and Guangzhou, became more attractive, in terms of infrastructure and economic environment, for investors from elsewhere, irrespective of their ancestral roots. On the other hand, this also implies that some honorary citizens of Panyu origin, who were involved actively in the local economic activities in the 1990s, might have been motivated by profit seeking – ancestral homeland sentiment was not pivotal for them.

LIMITED INFLUENCE OF EMIGRANTS ON WENZHOU ECONOMY

At the early stage of the economic reform, Wenzhou, like other places in China, was in need of capital to trigger economic growth and change. The local households were quick in generating capital for themselves and fostered private enterprises. On the other hand, the first batch of capital inflow from overseas Wenzhou people arrived in the form of enterprises established by dependants of Overseas Chinese (*qiaojuan*). The burgeoning of this type of enterprise was also common in the *qiaoxiang* areas in Guangdong in the early years after 1978 (Wang Benzun 2000: 49–61).

Table 5.2. *Qiaoshu* enterprises in Wenzhou municipality, 1985–1998

(1)	(2)	(3)	(4)	(5)	(6)
Year	No. of enterprises (as per cent of the total in Wenzhou)	No. of employees	Total investment in RMB million	Output in RMB million (as per cent of the total in Wenzhou)	Foreign exchange earnings in US$ million
1985	53 (0.08)	1200	2.3	12 (0.30)	–
1986	73 (0.13)	1716	3.2	20 (0.42)	4.6
1988	139 (0.28)	3300	13.9	74 (0.92)	5.9
1991	130 (0.38)	2824	13.8	105 (0.85)	5.5
1994	123 (0.08)	903	98.6	86 (0.16)	10.1
1996	205 (0.16)	–	–	780 (0.78)	14.4
1998	–	–	–	2635 (1.90)	64.9

Sources: The statistics from 1985 to 1994 were derived from WS 1998 and those of 1996 were from *Wenzhou huaqiao shi* 1997, with these of 1998 from WN 1998. The calculation of the percentages in (2) and (5) is based on the statistics provided in Cai Xiaozhen 2002: 195–196.

As shown in Table 5.2, the number of these *qiaoshu* enterprises in Wenzhou increased from 53 in 1985 to 205 in 1996. The total investment in *qiaoshu* enterprises increased from RMB2.3 million in 1985 to RMB98.6 million in

1994. By 1998, the Wenzhou's *qiaoshu* enterprises registered RMB2635 million in output and helped earn foreign exchange of US$64.9 million. These enterprises initially manufactured everyday goods like clothing and leather shoes as well as hardware. Subsequently, the products diversified into electrical appliances, machinery and chemical products (Cai and Zhu 2002: 23).

While *qiaoshu* enterprises were a major phenomenon in the early stage, *sanzi* enterprises later emerged as an important form of overseas participation when the economic environment became more conducive following the designation in 1984 of Wenzhou as one of the 14 coastal cities for foreign trade and investment. *Sanzi* (literally three financial capitals) enterprises refer to three forms of 'foreign-invested firm': wholly owned foreign firms, Sino-foreign equity joint ventures and Sino-foreign contractual joint ventures. The *sanzi* enterprises imply more direct economic participation by the Chinese overseas in comparison to the *qiaoshu* enterprises. As a matter of fact, these enterprises also thrived in Guangdong from the mid-1980s as a result of the increased inflow of foreign capital, primarily from Hong Kong (Cheng et al. 1998).

Table 5.3. *Sanzi* enterprises in Wenzhou municipality, 1984–1999 (US$ million)

Year	No. of approved enterprises	Total investment	Actual utilized foreign investment
1984	1	0.06	–
1985	3	0.64	0.03
1986	3	3.07	0.32
1987	3	1.70	1.04
1988	14	16.43	1.04
1989	28	16.09	5.74
1990	41	21.91	2.48
1991	57	34.36	7.66
1992	152	311.97	21.88
1993	377	650.24	57.44
1994	201	237.14	61.18
1995	159	236.35	73.52
1996	106	381.92	78.96
1997	87	204.23	60.50
1998	95	630.29	37.02
1999	70	132.32	56.15

Source: Cai and Zhu 2002: 24.

As shown in Table 5.3, the first *sanzi* enterprise in Wenzhou was founded in 1984 and the number of the enterprises increased to 377 in 1993, after which it declined to 70 in 1999. Although the enterprises received investment of only US$60,000 in 1984, in 1999 they attracted a total investment of US$132 million with an actual utilized foreign investment of US$56 million.

Although not every *sanzi* enterprise was invested in by overseas Wenzhou people, records show that the proportion of investment made by Chinese overseas, Hong Kong and Macau residents was remarkably large.[19] In 1989, there were altogether 52 foreign-invested enterprises with US$3.8 million, nine of which were invested in by Chinese overseas, accounting for 75 per cent of the total investment (*Wenzhou huaqiao shi* 1997: 265). In 1994, out of a total of 880 *sanzi* enterprises, there were 359 Chinese overseas-invested enterprises that contributed around half of the yearly output of RMB110 million (WS 1998: 415, 1802). By 1996, the number of Chinese overseas-invested enterprises was 787 (83 per cent of the total number of the *sanzi* enterprises), involving US$1,220 million (85 per cent of the total) in investment (*Wenzhou huaqiao shi*, 1997: 276). In 1998, the Chinese overseas-invested enterprises increased numerically to 1,090, with investments constituting around 80 per cent of the foreign capital received in Wenzhou (WN 1998: 498).

Until the early 1990s, Hong Kong and Taiwan were the major foreign investors in Wenzhou. Overtime, however, the sources of foreign capital have broadened to include countries in Western Europe and North America. In 1990, the 93 foreign-invested enterprises received capital from 15 countries and territories, of which the major ones were Hong Kong (39), Taiwan (23), France (6), the United States (6), Japan (5), Brazil (4) and Italy (2) (Cai and Zhu 2002: 25). By 1996, some countries appeared to have made a more pronounced investment and these included: France (117), the United States (95), Italy (72), the Netherlands (45), Japan (30), Singapore (25), Spain (24) and Austria (20) (*Wenzhou huaqiao shi* 1997: 272) . In 1998, 24 enterprises had investments from Europe and 22 from the United States, both of which combined to constitute 48 per cent of the foreign-invested enterprises in Wenzhou (WN 1998: 200).

A large number of foreign investors showed an interest in the manufacturing sector in Wenzhou. In 1999, 63 out of the total 70 contracts were in the manufacturing sector, involving US$29.3 million in foreign capital. Real estate was another large recipient sector with US$115 million contractual foreign capital and US$182 million utilized foreign capital.

In manufacturing, the major components were the production of leather shoes and clothing, but also included hardware, electrical appliances and chemical machinery. Finance, aquaculture and catering services also drew foreign investment (Cai and Zhu 2002: 25).

Nevertheless, it would be an exaggeration to conclude that foreign investment heavily shaped Wenzhou's economic landscape. In Wenzhou, from 1988 to 2001, the actual utilized foreign investment amounted to US$593 million, which only accounted for 9.2 per cent of total exports of US$6,441 million (Cai Xiaozhen 2002: 386, 388). In 2002, out of the total of Wenzhou's industrial output of RMB220 billion, 90 per cent was derived from private enterprises with local capital (Jiang and Yang). In other words, local entrepreneurs were more prominent than Chinese overseas in Wenzhou.

In fact, the major driving force in the development of the Wenzhou model has been the household and private enterprises making use of local people's capital. In Wenzhou, the local private sector has been booming, while foreign investors rarely come into the city (Dolven 2003). This is very different from the Zhujiang (Pearl River Delta) model, of which Panyu is a part.[20] While the Wenzhou model is defined by forces initiated from below that led to a thriving private economy, the Zhujiang model was influenced primarily by a combination of private forces, government regulations and foreign capital (Hu and Wu 2002: 330–332).

Apart from foreign investment, import and export trade has been another form of economic interaction between Chinese overseas and Wenzhou. Chinese overseas have thus played a significant role as a bridge between Wenzhou and many other countries, thus putting Wenzhou on track for globalization. They have helped introduce Wenzhou's products to the international market and hence gain foreign exchange. Equally, as in the case of foreign investment discussed before, the diaspora have brought in technologies that eventually lifted the productivity and quality of Wenzhou's products.

Since 1988, the Chinese central government has been adopting various policies and measures to reform foreign trade and decentralize power to local governments with regard to export matters. This facilitated, in the 1990s, the founding of many import and export companies by Wenzhou people in countries outside China. In the capital of Romania alone, for instance, more than 300 such companies were established by Wenzhou people. Major Wenzhou products exported included clothing, leather shoes, cigarette lighters, hardware and handicrafts. Meanwhile, the Chinese overseas also began to import machinery, textiles and leather goods (*Wenzhou huaqiao shi* 1997: 265–272).

Recent years also witnessed a surge in overseas investments by China's state-owned enterprises and private companies (Wong and Chan 2003a, 2003b). The capital surplus generated by the Wenzhou model is making forays onto the world market. While the success of outward investment is dependent on a wide array of factors, the Wenzhou people who settled abroad have had their own part to play in facilitating economic expansion.

DIFFERENT LINKAGES WITH AND VIEWS OF THE OUTSIDE WORLD

Since the 1980s, 'transnationalism' has emerged as a novel research field and has increasingly gained popularity among scholars studying sustained and regular networks between sending and receiving countries of migrants as a result of the globalization of capitalism, technological revolution in transportation and communication and the expansion of social networks (Guarnizo and Smith 1998; Portes et al. 1999). Initially, research on transnationalism focused on the transborder social and economic activities conducted by those migrants who went out from the poverty-stricken Central and South American countries and came to the United States as labour migrants after the Second World War (Smith and Guarnizo 1998; *Ethnic and Racial Studies* 1999). Later on, the concept became so popular that some scholars started adopting it to study Chinese emigrants and their descendants and their connections with China (Smart and Smart 1998; Sinn 1999). However, they seem to be forgetting that Chinese migration has a longer history and has experienced more complex changes over generations and politically. The magnitude and sustainability of the networks that towns and villages have with their diverse groups of natives and descendants in the reform period since 1978 may not be as strong and sustained as the proponents of transnationalism have thought.

In 2000, fieldwork conducted in Panyu revealed that many local residents had regular transterritorial contacts with Hong Kong people, but few sustained their transnational ties with the Chinese in South-east Asia and North America. The returnees (*guiqiao*) and dependants (*qiaojuan*) were losing their social and economic distinctions in Panyu. Most received no remittances from their kinsfolk living outside, because of weakening family bonds, but also because they benefited, along with other residents, from the local economic development that offered them job opportunities. As Panyu became a comfortably livable and job-promising place, all the local residents were reluctant to leave Panyu in search of another mode of life.

On the other hand, transnational linkages have been re-established and thus *qiaoxiang* mentality has been rekindled in Wenzhou, where a large number of people are attracted by migration to Western and Eastern Europe, the biggest destination for their predecessors before 1949. They are, as Li Minghuan (1999b: 83–93) observed, the people lacking the resources to participate in the booming economy in Wenzhou, and Europe still serve as the dreamland for them. The transnational networks have been effective in conveying information about the outside world, in transporting them to Western Europe, and later in connecting them to the families and friends in Wenzhou. The monies they made overseas were remitted to build magnificent houses and shrines, outstanding landmarks in the pre-1949 *qiaoxiang* areas. The extravagant expenditure by their dependants and by themselves when they went back has reinforced the *qiaoxiang* mentality, consolidating a 'trail of collective memory about another place and time' and creating 'a map of desire and attachment' (Appadurai and Breckenridge 1989: i). With such a view of the outside world, many people with overseas connections were not engaging actively in local economic activities (Wu 1995).

CONCLUDING REMARKS

The foregoing effort to compare and contrast different areas shows that diversities and divergences occurred where relations with Chinese emigrants and their descendants are concerned. All three types of *qiaoxiang* area mentioned in the discussion on Guangdong experience turn old in the reform period as they never sent fresh emigrants in the numbers they did before 1949 and as the ties with their emigrants and descendants weakened due to generation changes. In terms of economic development, they can be classified into three types (1) foreign-investment-driven, (2) capital-lacking, and (3) donation-supported.

The capital-lacking *qiaoxiang*, as evident in Xinyi, failed to lure substantial donations because of the generation change in their kinsfolk living outside. Nor did they succeed in attracting significant investment due to geographical adversity and remoteness. Still with close linkages with the ethnic Chinese in North America, the donation-supported *qiaoxiang*, as shown in Taishan and Kaiping, secured overseas funds for local public welfare and are finding economically tempting ways to attract more industrial investments.

The foreign-investment driven *qiaoxiang*, as the discussion on Panyu has shown, benefited from early opening up of Guangdong by the central government and also from the proximity to Hong Kong, where they have close kinsfolk and from where substantial donations and investments were channelled. Productive and industrial investment, however, is based more on business calculations. In recent years, Panyu has broadened its search for foreign investment to include not only its emigrants, but also other Asian and Western sources. As the primordial sentiment and kinship ties are losing appeal, all these detraditonalized *qiaoxiang* areas in Guangdong have to revamp or restructure their economic conditions in order to achieve modernization.

While most *qiaoxiang* areas in Guangdong are no longer reliant on overseas remittances, a considerable number of residents and households in Wenzhou still depend on their overseas kinsfolk for living expenses as well as building houses and shrines. With emigration resumed, Wenzhou represents what we can call an expanding *qiaoxiang* that is actively stretching linkages overseas. Along and within the far-flung networks, Wenzhou people have been stepping into Western Europe and North America and maintaining ties with their native soil through remittances and trade connections.

With the booming local private and household enterprises, Wenzhou appears not to need foreign investment as much as the old *qiaoxiang* areas in Guangdong do. Although the private-initiated enterprises did not receive much encouragement from the Chinese central government, the state did play a role in allowing foreign trade, thus helping forge the transnational business networks and *qiaoxiang* ties involving Wenzhou trading migrants. Inside China, the Wenzhou migrants have helped to expand the Wenzhou model by marketing the products made in Wenzhou to many parts of the country. In the future, it is likely the Wenzhou people outside China will play an increasingly important role in promoting Wenzhou products in the international market. This will help the Wenzhou model adapt and link to global capitalism – thus Wenzhou as a *qiaoxiang* will be expanding in economic terms.

NOTES

1. *Huaqiao* refers to the nationals of China temporarily residing abroad. For succinct analyses of the connotation and appropriateness of the term in different contexts, see Wang Gungwu 1992b, 2001a and Douw 1999.

2. The popularity of the term *qiaoxiang* can be easily identified in the Overseas Chinese magazines and newspapers as well as the websites run by the local governments especially in Guangdong, Zhejiang and Fujian provinces.

3. To show the changing identities of the ethnic Chinese outside China, Wang Gungwu coined the term 'Chinese overseas' to refer to everyone of Chinese descent living outside mainland China, Hong Kong, Macau, and Taiwan, whether or not they are PRC nationals. See Wang Gungwu 1992a.

4. Compare ZRGGQQB and QQGZH.

5. As Chen Ta observed in Chaozhou (Guangdong), Quanzhou, Haicheng and Xiamen (Fujian) in the 1930s, the families with South-east Asian connections relied heavily on remittances that made up between 75 and 80 per cent of their household income. See Chen 1939: 83, 95, 115.

    In Guangdong, the largest proportion of the donations were utilized to establish and expand primary and middle schools, while the remaining portions went to hospitals, ancestral halls, temples and victims of floods and earthquakes (Lin 1999: 35-37)

6. In fact, throughout the span between 1860 and 1949, the monies allocated for investment never exceeded 5 per cent of the total amount received from Overseas Chinese (Feng Yuan 1987).

7. Hainan Island was separated from Guangdong province in 1988 to form a new province. However, discussion of the diaspora from Guangdong has often included people originating from the island.

8. The Chinese emigration since 1978 has received scholarly attention recently and such emigrants were collectively called 'new migrants' (*xin yimin*) to differentiate them from Overseas Chinese (Wang Gungwu 2001b). The growing importance of new migrants brought about a shift in China's policy in the 1990s to appeal more to them instead of the established Chinese overseas communities (Thunø 2001).

9. This is not the place to discuss what modernization and urbanization mean in the context of China. Here, I follow the broad definition of the two terms: modernization means changing traditional systems and values while urbanization means working in non-agricultural activities. Basically, rapid urbanization has since 1978 been taking place in many towns and villages in China where many labor-intensive manufacturing plants were set up. On urbanization in China, see Guldin 2001.

10. 1997 is studied for Panyu as this is the year for which statistical data is available on the four groups. For the same reason, 2001 is studied for Wenzhou.

11. This is based on the interviews I did in Panyu in late 2000.

12. See the study on migrant workers in Nanhai, Panyu, Xiamen, and Quanzhou in Lever-Tracy et al. 1996: 273–285.

13 The information was collected with the help of the Overseas Chinese Affairs Office of Panyu as well as the Panyu associations around the world. Like the data concerning other Chinese overseas groups, the accuracy of the information is not totally reliable. It provides, however, a fairly correct picture of the diaspora distribution and the relative size of each community.

When overseas Panyu people are cited, I use the numbers in Appendix 1, because those in Appendix 2 only correspond with the towns and villages in Panyu. Regrettably the total number of Panyu people in Hong Kong and Macau is unobtainable and thus I have to use the numbers in Appendix 2.

14 Qingtian, famous for its pale-green soapstone, is situated immediately west of Wenzhou. Very often, the studies on Wenzhou's international migration include this locality, not merely because of their geographical proximity, but also based on the fact that both have the same Ouyue culture. In the 1950s, Qingtian was administered by Wenzhou *shi* and Qingtian people had to obtain permission from Wenzhou before they could go overseas (Wang Chunguang 2000), p. 20, footnote 1.

15 To illustrate more clearly, Giese gives as an example a former self-employed blacksmith with three children and a monthly income of RMB400-600 in the 1990s. See the same article, p. 213, footnote 5. For discussion on Chinese immigrants in various parts of Europe, see Benton and Pieke 1998.

16 See, for instance, Mackie 1995. Some case studies even reveal that, while doing business in China, Singapore Chinese are uncomfortable with the operation of *guanxi*, arguably commonly practiced by the Hong Kong and Taiwan businesspeople. See Chan and Tong 2000.

17 Although no particulars are provided in the appendix regarding welfare and other categories, it does not affect the argument here about the emergence and importance of production.

18 This has been a common practice for many Mainland Chinese companies that wanted to enjoy the special treatment given to Hong Kong companies when investing in Mainland China.

19 It seems that no consistent calculation has been made to demonstrate the trends and changes in the investments made by the Chinese diaspora. However, from the data scattered among the available sources, it is obvious that out of the total foreign capital received, the proportion of Chinese diaspora contribution was significant in any given year.

20 On the Wenzhou model, see Liu Yia-ling 1992 and Parris 1993. On the Zhujiang ,model, see Maruyo 1998, especially p. 79 for the discussion on the importance of foreign investment.

REFERENCES

Appadurai, Arjun and Carol Breckenridge (1989) 'On moving targets', *Public Culture*, vol. 2, pp. i–iv.

Benton, Gregor and Frank N. Pieke (eds) (1998) *The Chinese in Europe*. New York: St. Martin's Press.

Cai, Kejiao and Zhu Jianren (2002) 'Wenji huaqiao yu Wenzhou jinji fazhan' [The overseas Wenzhou people and Wenzhou's economic development]. *Wenzhou luntan* [Wenzhou forum] no. 89, pp. 23–26.

Cai, Xiaozhen (ed.) (2002) *Wenzhou tongji nianjian 2002* [Wenzhou statistical yearbook 2002]. Beijing: Zhongguo tongji chubanshe.

Chan, Kwok Bun and Tong Chee Kiong (2000) 'Singaporean Chinese doing business in China', pp. 71–85. In Chan Kwok Bun (ed.), *Chinese Business Networks: State, Economy and Culture*. Singapore: Prentice Hall; Copenhagen: Nordic Institute of Asian Studies.

Chan, Ming K. (1995) 'All in the family: the Hong Kong–Guangdong link in historical perspective', pp. 31–63. In Reginald Kwok Yin-Wang and Alvin Y. So (eds), *The Hong Kong–Guangdong Link: Partnership in Flux*. New York: M.E. Sharpe.

Chan, Sucheng (1986) *This Bitter-Sweet Soil: The Chinese in California Agriculture, 1860–1910*. Berkeley: University of California Press.

Chen, Ta (1939) *Emigrant Communities in South China: A Study of Overseas Migration and Its Influence on Standards of Living and Social Change*. Shanghai: Kelly and Walsh.

Cheng, Yuk-Shing, Lu Weiguo and Christopher Findlay (1998) 'Hong Kong's economic relationship with China', *Journal of the Asia Pacific Economy*, vol.3, no. 1, pp. 104–130.

Dolven, Ben (2003) 'A cauldron of free enterprise', *Far Eastern Economic Review* (3 July), pp. 24–25.

Douw, Leo (1999) 'The Chinese sojourner discourse', pp. 22–44. In Leo Douw, Cen Huang, and Michael R. Godley (eds), *Qiaoxiang Ties: Interdisciplinary Approaches to "Cultural Capitalism" in South China*. London and New York: Keagan Paul International.

——, Cen Huang and Michael R. Godley (eds) (1999) *Qiaoxiang Ties: Interdisciplinary Approaches to "Cultural Capitalism" in South China*. London and New York: Keagan Paul International.

Ethnic and Racial Studies, vol. 22, no. 2 (Special Issues: Transnational Communities) (March 1999).

Fang, Xiongpu (2000) 'Zhongguo qiaoxiang de xingcheng yu fazhan' [The establishment and development of *qiaoxiang* areas in China]. In Zhuang Guotu (ed.), *Zhongguo qiaoxiang yanjiu* [Studies of *qiaoxiang* in China]. Xiamen: Xiamen daxue chubanshe, pp. 278–288.

Feng, Yuan (1987) 'Luelun jiefang qian Guangdong sheng huaqiao huikuan' [A general discussion on money sent back by Overseas Chinese to Guangdong before 1949]. *Qiaoshi xuebao*, no. 1, pp. 36.

Fitzgerald, Stephen (1972) *China and the Overseas Chinese: A Study of Peking's Changing Policy, 1949–1970*. London: Cambridge University Press.

Giese, Karsten (1999) 'Patterns of migration from Zhejiang to Germany', pp. 199–214. In

Frank N. Pieke and Hein Mallee (eds), *Internal and International Migration: Chinese Perspectives*. Richmond, Surrey: Curzon Press.

GSH. See Guangdongsheng difang shizhi bianzuan weiyuanhui (ed) (1996).

Guangdong guiguo huaqiao lianhehui (QQGZH) (ed.) (1996) *Qiaolian qiaowu gongzuo ziliao huibian* [Collection of materials on Overseas Chinese affairs of All China Federation of Returned Overseas Chinese]. Guangdong.

Guangdongsheng difang shizhi bianzuan weiyuanhui (GSH) (ed.) (1996) *Guangdong shengzhi huaqiaozhi* [The Overseas Chinese of Guangdong Province]. Guangdong: Guangdong renmin chubanshe.

Guarnizo, Luis Eduardo and Michael Peter Smith (1998) 'The locations of transnationalism'. In Michael Peter Smith and Luis Eduardo Guarnizo (eds), *Transnationalism from Below*. New Brunswick: Transaction Publishers, pp. 3–34.

Guldin, Gregory Eliyu (2001) *What's a Peasant to Do? Village Becoming Town in Southern China*. Boulder, Colorado: Westview Press.

Hamilton, George G. (1996) 'Overseas Chinese capitalism', pp. 328–342. In Tu Wei-Ming (ed.), *Confucian Traditions in East Asian Modernity*. Cambridge, MA: Harvard University Press.

Hu, Hongwei and Wu Xiaobo (2002) *Wenzhou xuannian* [Contemplating Wenzhou]. Hangzhou: Zhejiang renmin chubanshe.

Jiang, Yuebo and Yang Weiming 'Zheli ren ren xiang dang laoban – kan Wenzhou zenyang jihuo minjian touzi 5' [All the people want to be the boss: how Wenzhou has stimulated private investment, part 5]. URL: www.cnhubei.com/aa/ca201072.html (accessed 24 February 2004).

Johnson, Graham E. and Woon Yuen-Fong (1997) 'The response to rural reform in an Overseas Chinese area: examples from two localities in the Western Pearl River Delta Region, South China', *Modern Asian Studies*, vol. 31, no. 1, pp. 31–59.

Kotkin, Joel (1993) *Tribes: How Race, Religion, and Identity Determine Success in the New Global Economy*. New York: Random House.

Lever-Tracy, Constance, David Ip and Noel Tracy (1996) *The Chinese Diaspora and Mainland China: An Emerging Economic Synergy*. London: Macmillan Press Ltd.

Li, Minghuan (1999a) 'To get rich quickly in Europe! – Reflections on migration motivation in Wenzhou', pp. 181–198. In Frank N. Pieke and Hein Mallee (eds), *Internal and International Migration: Chinese Perspectives*. Richmond, Surrey: Curzon Press.

—— (1999b) 'Xiangdui shiluo' yu 'liansuo xiaoying': guanyu dangdai Wenzhou diqu chuguo yiminchao de fenxi yu sikao' [Relative deprivation' and 'cumulative causation': analysing and contemplating contemporary migration out of Wenzhou]. *Shehuixue yanjiu* [Sociological research], no. 5, pp. 83–93.

Limlingan, Victor S. (1986) *The Overseas Chinese in ASEAN: Business Strategies and Management Practices*. Manila: Vita Development Corporation.

Lin, Jiajing (1999) *Jindai Guangdong qiaohui yanjiu* [The studies of the money sent back by Overseas Chinese in the pre-1949 period]. Guangzhou: Zhongshan daxue chubanshe.

Liu, Yia-Ling (1992) 'Reform from below: the private economy and local politics in the rural industrialization of Wenzhou', *The China Quarterly*, no. 130 (June), pp. 293–316.

Lui, Ping-Keung (2000) 'Hong Kong special administrative region: waves of Chinese immigrants and their children', pp. 257–285. In Peng Xizhe and Guo Zhigang (eds), *The Changing Population of China*. Oxford: Blackwell Publishers.

Luo, Jingxiang (ed.) (1995) *Panyu xianzhi* [The annals of Panyu county]. Guangzhou: Guangdong renmin chubanshe.

—— (ed.) (1998) *Panyu Nianjian* [Panyu yearbook]. Guangzhou: Guangdong renmin chubanshe.

Mackie, Jamie (1995) 'Economic systems of the Southeast Asian Chinese'. In Leo Suryadinata (ed.), *Southeast Asian Chinese and China*. Singapore: Times Academic Press, pp. 33–65.

Maruyo, Toyojiro (1998) 'The economy'. In Y.M. Yeung and David K.Y. Chu (eds), *Guangdong: Survey of a Province Undergoing Rapid Change*. Hong Kong: Chinese University Press, pp. 63–85,

McKeown, Adam (1999) 'Conceptualizing Chinese diasporas, 1842 to 1949', *Journal of Asian Studies*, vol. 58, no. 2 (May), pp. 306–337.

QQGZH. See Guangdong guiquo huaqiao lianhehui, 1996.

Pan, Lynn (ed.) (1998) *The Encyclopedia of the Chinese Overseas*. Singapore: Archipelago Press & Landmark Books.

Parris, Kristen (1993) 'Local initiative and national reform: the Wenzhou model of Development', *The China Quarterly*, no. 134, pp. 242–263.

Panyu Foreign Economic Relations and Trade Bureau (2000) 'Panyu's sources of foreign investment by country and territory'. Panyu: Internal Document.

Panyu Museum. 'Panyushi rongyu shimin guangrongce' [The honours roll of Panyu honorary citizens], 1993, 1994, 1996, 1998, 2000.

Panyuxian qiaowu bangongshi [The Overseas Chinese affairs office of Panyu] (ed.), 'Panyuxian huaqiao, GangAo tongbao zhi' [An account of Overseas Chinese, Hong Kong and Macau compatriots of Panyu origin]. Panyu: Internal Document. (No date not stated in the material)

Portes, Alejandro, Luis E. Guarnizo and Patricia Landolt (1999) 'The study of transnationalism: pitfalls and promises of an emergent research field', *Ethnic and Racial Studies*, vol. 22, no. 2 (Special Issue: Transnational Communities) (March), pp. 217–237.

Purcell, Victor (1980) *The Chinese in Southeast Asia* (2nd ed.). Kuala Lumpur and Oxford: Oxford University Press.

Redding, S. Gordon (1990) *The Spirit of Chinese Capitalism*. New York: de Gruyter.

Sinn, Elizabeth (1999) 'Cohesion and fragmentation: a county-level perspective on Chinese transnationalism in the 1940s'. In Leo Douw, Cen Huang, and Michael R. Godley (eds), *Qiaoxiang Ties: Interdisciplinary Approaches to 'Cultural Capitalism' in South China*. London and New York: Kegan Paul International, pp. 67–68.

Smart, Alan and Josephine Smart (1998) 'Transnational social networks and negotiated identities in interactions between Hong Kong and China'. In Michael Peter Smith and Luis Eduardo Guarnizo (eds), *Transnationalism from Below*. New Brunswick: Transaction Publishers, pp. 103–161.

Smith, Michael Peter and Luis Eduardo Guarnizo (eds) (1998) *Transnationalism from Below*. New Brunswick: Transaction Publishers.

Thunø, Mette (2001) 'Researching out and incorporating Chinese overseas: the trans-territorial scope of the PRC by the end of the 20th century', *The China Quarterly*, no. 168, pp. 910–929.

Tomba, Luigi (1999) 'Exporting the "Wenzhou Model" to Beijing and Florence: suggestions for a comparative perspective on labour and economic organization in two migrant communities'. In Frank N. Pieke and Hein Mallee (eds), *Internal and International Migration: Chinese Perspectives*, Richmond, Surrey: Curzon Press, pp. 280–294.

Tracy, Noel, and Constance Lever-Tracy (2000) 'Global champions for Asian Nations'. In Teresita Ang See (ed.), *Intercultural Relations, Cultural Transformation, and Identity: The Ethnic Chinese* (Selected papers presented at the 1998 ISSCO Conference). Manila: Kaisa Para Sa Kaunlaran Inc., pp. 257–283.

Wakeman, Federic (1966) *Strangers at the Gate: Social Disorder in South China, 1839–1861*. Berkeley and Los Angeles: University of California Press.

Wang, Benzun (2000) *Haiwai Huaqiao Huaren yu Chao Shan Qiaoxiang de Fazhan* [The Chinese overseas and the development of Chaozhou and Shantou qiaoxiang]. Beijing: Zhongguo huaqiao chubanshe.

Wang, Chunguang (2000) *Bali de Wenzhou ren – yige yimin qunti de kuashehui jiangou xingdong* [Wenzhou people in Paris: the translocal construction of a migrant community]. Nanchang: Jiangxi renmin chubanshe.

Wang, Gungwu (1992a [1991]) *China and the Chinese Overseas*. Singapore: Times Academic Press.

—— (1992b) 'The origin of hua-ch'iao'. In Wang Gungwu, *Community and Nation: China, Southeast Asia and Australia*. Kensington, Australia: Asian Studies Association of Australia in association with Allen & Unwin, pp. 1–10.

—— (2001a) 'Sojourning: the Chinese experience'. In Wang Gungwu, *Don't Leave Home: Migration and the Chinese*. Singapore: Times Academic Press, pp. 54–72.

—— (2001b) 'New migrants: How new? Why new?' Paper presented at the Fourth International Conference of the International Society for the Studies of Chinese Overseas (Taipei, 26–28 April).

Weidenbaum, Murray and Samuel Hughes (1996) *The Bamboo Network: How Expatriate Chinese Entrepreneurs Are Creating a New Economic Superpower in Asia*. New York: The Free Press.

Wencheng xianzhi (1996) [The annals of Wencheng county]. Beijing: Zhonghua shuju.

Wenzhou huaqiao shi (1997) [The history of Overseas Chinese of Wenzhou origin]. Jinri Zhongguo chubanshe.

Wenzhou shizhi bianweihui [Editorial committee of the annals of Wenzhou city] (1998) (eds) *Wenzhou shizhi* [The annals of Wenzhou city]. Beijing: Zhonghua shuju. Cited as WS.

Wenzhoushi difangzhi bianzuan weiyuanhui [The editorial committee of Wenzhou city annals] (WN) (1998, 2002) (ed), *Wenzhou nianjian* [Wenzhou yearbook]. Beijing: Zhonghua shuju.

Wickberg, Edgar (ed.) (1982) *From China to Canada: A History of the Chinese Communities in Canada*. Toronto: McClelland and Stewart.

WN. See Wenzhoushi difangzhi bianzuan weiyuanhui, 1998, 2002.

Wong, John and Sarah Chan (2003a) 'China's rising outward direct investment', EAI Background Brief no. 154.

—— (2003b) 'An assessment of China's outward direct investment', EAI Background Brief no. 155.

Woon, Yuen-Fong (1990) 'International links and the socioeconomic development of rural China: an emigrant community in Guangdong', *Modern China*, vol. 16, no. 2, pp. 139–172.

WS. See Wenzhou shizhi bianweihui, 1998.

Wu, Li (1995) 'Wenzhou diqu qiaoxiang yu feiqiaoxiang funu de jingji huodong – gean bijiao' [A comparative study of the economic activities of females in *qiaoxiang* and non-*qiaoxiang* areas in Wenzhou], *Huaqiao huaren lishi yanjiu* [Overseas Chinese history studies], no. 2, pp. 70–76.

Yow, Cheun Hoe (2002) 'The changing landscape of qiaoxiang: Guangdong and the Chinese diaspora, 1850–2000', PhD dissertation. East Asian Institute, National University of Singapore.

—— (2004) 'Poor and old: Xinyi as a *qiaoxiang* in the reform period'. Paper presented at the International Workshop 'Asian Diasporas: Revisiting the Chinese and South Asian Experiences' in Singapore, organized by Faculty of Arts and Social Sciences, National University of Singapore and the Chinese Heritage Centre (Singapore, 5–7 April).

Zhang, Zhicheng (1987) 'Wencheng xian huaqiao jianshi' [A brief history of the Overseas Chinese from Wencheng county]. *Zhejiang huaqiao ziliao* (Historical documents on Zhejiang migrants abroad). Hongzhou, pp. 11–30.

—— (1991) 'Wenzhou huaqiao lishi gaikuang' [A survey of the history of Overseas Chinese from Wenzhou]. *Wenzhou wenshi ziliao*, vol. 7, pp. 1–12

Zhonghua Renmin Gongheguo guiqiao qiaojuan quanyi baohufa (ZRGGQQB) [The law on protection of rights and interests of *guiqiao* and *qiaojuan*, People's Republic of China] (2000). Beijing: Zhongguo minzhu fazhi chubanshe.

Zhuang, Guotu (1998) 'The policies of the Chinese government towards Overseas Chinese (1949–1966)'. In Wang Ling-chi and Wang Gungwu (eds), *The Chinese Diaspora: Selected Essays*. Singapore: Times Academic Press, pp. 14–29.

—— (ed.) (2000) *Zhongguo qiaoxiang yanjiu* [*Qiaoxiang* studies in China]. Xiamen: Xiamen daxue chubanshe.

ZRGGQQB. See Zhonghua Renmin Gongheguo guiqiao qiaojuan quanyi baohufa, 2000.

Appendix 5.1. Overseas distribution of people of Panyu-origin, 1997

Continent	Country	Number
Asia	Singapore	30,724
	Malaysia	9,457
	Vietnam	3,354
	Brunei	3,354
	Philippines	2,232
	Thailand	1,553
	Japan	909
	Cambodia	122
	Indonesia	22
	South Korea	9
	Subtotal	**51,736**
Americas	Canada	39,753
	United States of America	11,401
	Peru	14,830
	Cuba	296
	Brazil	196
	Guatemala	183
	Venezuela	152
	Columbia	104
	Ecuador	91
	Panama	69
	Honduras	57
	Guyana	35
	Costa Rica	22
	Dominica	22
	Suriname	3
	Subtotal	**67,214**

Europe	United Kingdom	3,067
	Switzerland	835
	France	257
	Sweden	218
	Germany	191
	Netherlands	100
	Luxembourg	57
	Austria	17
	Subtotal	**4,742**
Australasia	Australia	3,067
	New Zealand	218
	Subtotal	**3,285**
Africa	South Africa	300
	Mauritius	87
	Madagascar	65
	Nigeria	26
	Somalia	4
	Subtotal	**482**
	Total	**127,459**

Source: Panyu Museum, Panyu

Appendix 5.2. Towns in Panyu and their relations with the Chinese overseas and compatriots in Hong Kong and Macau, 1997

Town	Chinese Overseas	Hong Kong and Macau Compatriots
Shiqiao	5,619	25,617
Dashi	5,352	24,537
Nancun	31,932	27,582
Xinzao	8,769	37,173
Hualong	14,400	54,000
Shilou	795	37,830
Shiji	5,550	73,248
Zhongcun	2,775	19,560
Dongchong	24	960
Huangge	0	1,341
Lianhuashan	24	1,647
Nansha	81	4,260
Wanqingsha	9	483
Hengli	0	2,400
Tanzhou	141	6,300
Dagang	516	2,124
Yuwotou	78	1,434
Lingshan	75	6,300
Shawan	6,120	39,120
Xinken	9	570
Lanhe	12	237
Total	**82,281**	**366,723**

Source: Panyu Museum, Panyu

Appendix 5.3. The first to fifth group of Panyu honorary citizens: Place of residence

	First (1993)	Second (1994)	Third (1996)	Fourth (1998)	Fifth (2000)
Hong Kong	22	19	13	24	31
Macau	4	1			
Taiwan	1			2	
Spain	1				
Australia	1				
Canada			1		
United States of America				2	2
United Kingdom				1	1
South Korea				1	1
Japan					1
Singapore					1
Total	**29**	**20**	**14**	**30**	**37**

Source: *Panyushi rongyu shimin guangrongce*, 1993, 1994, 1996, 1998, 2000.

Appendix 5.4. The first to fifth group of Panyu honorary citizens: Ancestral homeland (zujidi)

	First (1993)	Second (1994)	Third (1996)	Fourth (1998)	Fifth (2000)
Panyu	23	15	10	7	19
Nanhai	1	1		1	
Shunde	1			1	2
Guangzhou	1			1	
Dongguan	1	1		1	3
Baoan				1	
Zhongshan				1	
Xinhui		1		1	1
Kaiping				1	2
Taishan				1	1
Heshan			1	2	1
Sihui					1
Boluo			1		
Shantou				1	
Chaoyang				4	
Huilai					1
Haifeng					1
Wuchuan					1
Guangdong					1
Yongchun (Fujian)		1	1		
Yongding (Fujian)				1	
Fujian					1
Shanghai		1			
Suzhou			1		
Anhui				1	
Zhanghua (Taiwan)				1	
Gaoxiong (Taiwan)				1	
Japan					1
Korea				1	1
United States of America				1	
United Kingdom				1	
Spain	1				
Australia	1				
Total	**29**	**20**	**14**	**30**	**37**

Source: *Panyushi rongyu shimin guangrongce*, 1993, 1994, 1996, 1998, 2000.

Chapter 6

The Chinese in Italy at a Crossroads: The Economic Crisis

Antonella Ceccagno

According to official Italian data, the number of Chinese adults holding residence permits for Italy was estimated to be 29,000 persons in 1996 which by the end of 2002 had increased to 62,312 (Caritas and Migrantes 2003). In January 2003, after the legalization amnesty in July 2002 (Immigration law 189/2002) the number of regular Chinese adult migrants reached 100,109 persons and Chinese migrants now made up 4.6 per cent of all foreigners in Italy (Caritas and Migrantes 2004). A large number of these new Chinese migrants operate or work in garment workshops, performing contract work for Italian manufacturers. Over the years, these migrants have proven themselves to be dynamic, mobile and flexible. They have been able to adapt to local labour contexts without becoming stuck in the roles that were initially available to them, and they have been able to seize opportunities offered by new productive and commercial sectors.

In this chapter, I argue that over time the Chinese productive activities in Italy have contributed significantly to maintaining the competitiveness of some of the sectors in which *Made in Italy* products are famous such as clothing, leather goods, couches and shoes (this chapter specifically addresses the garment industry). In some instances, they have even contributed to the expansion of the sector and the area within which they operate, as it has been suggested for other migrant groups by Light et al. (1999). Even more significantly, in recent years a growing number of Chinese migrants have been able to blend strategies of migration and transnational capital accumulation, taking advantage of China's growing role in the global economy. That Chinese importers' businesses have, in the last few years have contributed heavily to redefining the modalities of the Chinese presence in Italy, is due to China's central role in economic globalization and to its growing capacity to produce goods of diverse quality at competitive prices for the European markets. In the first years of the twenty-first century, this has meant that the businesses of Chinese importers have been on the verge of making Italy one of the principal European wholesale centres – second only to Budapest – for manufactured Chinese goods.

In this chapter, I will discuss the major economic changes that have taken place during the last decades for the new Chinese migrants in Italy and argue that an entirely new situation has emerged as the result of economic expansion and market development in China and its active involvement and participation in the global economy. The impact of China's new international role is modifying expectations, opportunities, employment patterns and self-perception among the Chinese migrants, and is enhancing the already strong propensity of these migrants towards high mobility within Europe and between China and Europe. I intend to offer Italy as a case study of how global capitalism and globalization is changing migration from an economic settlement in the ethnic niche of garment/ leather with modest possibilities of expansion to full manufacturing and new employment patterns as importers and wholesalers of goods made in China.

Recently, however, both production and commercial activities managed by Chinese migrants in Italy have been affected by an acute crisis as a result of a number of factors. For the Chinese involved in productive activities, the crisis can be framed within the broader crisis of the manufacturing sector as a whole in Italy, and possibly due to competition from imported Chinese goods; while the crisis affecting Chinese wholesale and retail importers has principally been caused by the Italian government's intent to contain imported goods from China that are perceived to be in direct competition with *Made in Italy* products produced in Italy. As a result, regulations to limit the economic activities of the Chinese have been implemented by the Italian government. In this respect, Italy may be viewed as a case study of official migration control using economic sanctions to impede China's economic expansion and market development.

AN OVERVIEW OF THE ACTIVITIES OF THE CHINESE IN ITALY

Three major phases in recent Chinese migration to Italy can be identified in terms of the migrants' economic activities. The decade of the 1980s and the early years of the 1990s constitute the early phase of arrival and settlement of the first group of the new Chinese migrants. It was the phase in which the production in garments and leather goods by Chinese pioneers who had settled in Italy from the beginning of the twentieth century was reclaimed and expanded by a large number of new Chinese migrants. A increasing number of garment workshops engaged in single manufacturing operations such as sewing and hemming emerged.

Until the mid-1990s, almost all Chinese migrants who arrived in Italy became integrated into this ethnic economy. At that time, the prevalent model of upward social mobility among the Chinese was based on the expectation that in a short period of time one could establish a small business such as a workshop or a restaurant. Although the entrepreneurial dream did not become a reality for everyone, the goal of self-employment was a powerful drive behind the success and growth of a number of sub-contracting activities among the Chinese that contributed to focusing energy, projects and capital to such an end.

Moreover, in the first decade of settlement in Italy, many migrants were able to cater to the needs of their co-ethnics by entering the new and rapidly growing businesses in the ethnic Chinese service sector. These included restaurants, groceries, video rental shops, phone card dealers, beauty parlours, travel agencies and agencies providing translations and migration assistance. Such businesses, along with that of importing were mainly accessible to those Chinese migrants who had capital and contacts with Chinese previously settled in Europe and Italy.

The second half of the 1990s brought an increase in the numbers of new Chinese migrants and the businesses they operated, with a diversification of the migrants' geographical origin and legalization of the status of the large majority of Chinese migrants in Italy.

Moreover, while the large majority of Chinese operating manufacturing businesses still specialize in garments and leather goods, in the second half of the 1990s the areas of activities expanded to other manufacturing sectors at the forefront of the *Made in Italy* production: shoe-making, the production of furniture and of home appliances.

The most recent phase – from the end of the twentieth century – coincides with the growing number of imports from China and the opening of wholesale and retail businesses among the Chinese in Italy. In fact, a significant change has taken place among the Chinese in Italy: their activities have evolved from a situation where the large majority of Chinese operated businesses were active in productive activities (which presumably lasted till the late 1990s or the early 2000s) to the present situation where commercial activities outnumber productive businesses – at least in terms of number of businesses.

Chinese workshops in Italy

The years bridging the end of the old century and the beginning of the new one bear witness to a significant growth in self-employment among migrants in Italy generally. The Chinese occupy a prominent position in this trend. According to data from Unioncamere Infocamere (the Italian Federation of Commercial Chambers), in June 2003 there were about 135,000 independent businesses managed by immigrants (including productive and commercial activities) constituting an increase of 16 per cent compared to the same period in 2002. The Chinese were the owners of a little more than 14,500 of these businesses, or about 11 per cent of the total (Pepi 2003).1

Data including the number and the nature of Chinese operated businesses in Italy is now available for the first time, as well as data for some of the main settlement areas in Italy. This data shows a significant increase in the number of businesses at national level. As Table 6.1 shows, businesses headed by Chinese in Italy numbered 18,554 in 2004.

While in the last years non-productive activities have outnumbered manufacturing, the latter is still the main activity in most of the main areas of settlement of the Chinese in Italy. Table 6.2 shows that manufacturing is by far the main occupation in Tuscany – the Italian region with the highest concentration of Chinese businesses – where out of a total of 4,518 Chinese-headed businesses 3,644 are active in the productive sector.

The same holds true for the Emilia Romagna and Veneto administrative regions, where 1,394 out of 2,001 businesses and 1,007 out of 1,698 businesses respectively are in the productive sector. In Lombardy, the productive and commercial sectors have reached a balance with 1,820 manufacturing activities out of a total of 3,665. Even though data on Rome is not available, it is believed that Rome has the highest concentration of Chinese commercial businesses (import and commercial activities will be dealt with below).

Table 6.1. Businesses headed by Chinese (PRC) in Italy, September 2004

Economic macro-section	Productive micro-section	Number
Agriculture		27
Manufacturing activities	Clothing	5,661
Manufacturing activities	Leather goods	2,155
Manufacturing activities	Textile industries	575
Manufacturing activities	Food and beverage industries	342
Manufacturing activities	Furniture and other	132
Manufacturing activities	Other	107
Manufacturing activities	Total	8,972
Wholesale and retail commerce of goods		7,735
Hotels and restaurants		1,274
Real estate, rent, IT		176
Building firms		114
Transport, stockage and communication		82
Monetary and financial services		12
Other		162
Total		**18,554**

Source: Spinner 2004, based on data from Chamber of Commerce, Industry and Agriculture, Modena

Table 6.2. Businesses headed by Chinese (PRC) in selected Italian regions, September 2004

	Toscany (central Italy)	Lombardy (northern Italy)	Emilia Romagna (northern Italy)	Veneto (northern Italy)
Productive activities	3,644	1,820	1,394	1,007
- textile, clothing and leather goods	3,580	1,687	1,263	935
Other	874	1,845	607	682
Total	**4,518**	**3,665**	**2,001**	**1,689**

Source: Spinner 2004, based on data from Chamber of Commerce, Industry and Agriculture, Modena

Until the late 1990s, employment within the ethnic manufacturing workshops was the first and most important mode of incorporation of new Chinese migrants. Most of the Chinese businesses active in productive activities operate as contractors and subcontractors for Italian manufacturers. The production of clothing (and leather goods) is by far the main productive activity among the Chinese in Italy, as shown in Table 6.2 (previous page): amounting to 98 per cent of total manufacturing activities in Tuscany, 93 per cent in Lombardy and Veneto regions and 91 per cent in Emilia Romagna region.

In the early 1990s, the industrial districts of Prato/Empoli/Florence in Tuscany, including Milan, were pioneer areas of settlement and for the expansion of Chinese ready-to-wear contracting workshops. Towards the mid-1990s, many garment workshops were also opening in other industrial districts specializing in fashion production, such as Terzigno/San Giuseppe Vesuviano (in south Italy, in the Naples area) in the Campania region[2] and, some years later, in the Carpi garment district (Emilia Romagna region) and the Veneto region. Towards the end of the century, however, Chinese workshops began expanding to many other areas of the country which had little or no previous history of garment production.

The growing role played by the Chinese in the Italian garment industry is the result of a combination of interests. Over the years ethnic networks became able to facilitate a soaring supply of cheap ethnic labour as the Chinese entrepreneurs met the Italian manufacturers' desire to be extremely flexible, operating in an informal economy and exploiting ethnic labour).[3] This encounter allowed the Chinese migrants to (mainly) replace Italian contractors and subcontractors in some cases (for example in the Carpi district) and to occupy semi-vacant spaces in others (for example in the Prato district) while simultaneously creating conditions for an expansion of garment activities (Ceccagno forthcoming; Waldinger 1996).

One of the most striking new features of Chinese migrants in Italy is the expansion from performing only simple manufacturing tasks for Italian suppliers to actually managing entire productive processes. Beginning in 2000, a limited number of Chinese entrepreneurs have also been able to expand their businesses from performing single manufacturing tasks for Italian suppliers to entering the areas of design, cutting, manufacturing and selling that only a few years earlier would have been inaccessible to them.

Chinese-operated workshops enhance the competitiveness of the Made in Italy position

The evolution described above needs to be understood against the background of the productive segment where Chinese migrants have made inroads: the fashion industry that is central to the Italian economy. In fact, in 2002 the clothing-textile industry in Italy was composed of about 58,000 industrial firms and a further 10,000 family-run businesses that employed 687,100 workers for a gross total of 45,911 million euros (60 per cent came from exports). The impact on the total Italian manufacturing sector went beyond 10 per cent for both the gross total and for exports. That same year, clothing and knitwear contributed to half of the commercial profit of the Italian clothing-textile industry (Smi-Ati Federazione Imprese Tessili e Moda Italiane 2005).

At the end of the century, Italy remained among the top global exporters in the fashion industry and was second after China as an exporter of fashion clothing. Nonetheless, in Italy, as in other major European countries, the textile-clothing industry (and in particular the garment and knitwear sectors) experienced a crisis caused by increasing competition from countries with low labour costs. Consequently, the garment sector underwent a phase of profound structural and organizational transformation and has for some years been searching for viable solutions to react to this crisis. Firms have attempted to recover price competitiveness first by outsourcing production to countries which offer lower labour costs (but also outsourcing to the south of Italy) (Dei 2001).

In this context, Chinese fashion businesses have been perceived and exaggerated by the Italian media as 'unfair competition', but as I argue below Chinese businesses are beneficial to the national garment industry (and most probably to the other productive sectors where they have entered). In the last 15 years, Chinese contracting garment workshops have made it possible for *Made in Italy* products to continue to be competitive. Relying on a certain amount of hidden or grey labour, which varies from area to area, compressing private life and care of children to adapt to production and working up to 16 or 20 hours a day when necessary, Chinese workshops have offered the Italian manufacturers a high degree of flexibility at low cost. Resorting to Chinese contractors and subcontractors represents the main response of Italian manufacturers to the major changes brought by the globalization of markets and capital.

Furthermore, the Chinese workshops have contributed to Italian manufacturers' competitiveness by being willing to move to the very districts where manufacturers cluster. Whereas previously manufacturers often had to rely on subcontractors located distant areas, they now use regional contractors and subcontractors who are ready to accept orders that arrive at any hour of the day. Moreover, the presence of Chinese labour also compensates for the lack of intergenerational continuity caused by young Italians' unwillingness to work as contractors in the garment industry.

Another striking feature is the expansive role played by the Chinese migrants in the Italian garment industry. The industrial district of Prato stands out as an example. Over the years, the quality of garments produced in Chinese workshops has become significantly higher and this has contributed to an expansion in the number of suppliers from outside of the Prato district who rely upon Prato-based Chinese workshops and to attracting more famous manufacturers (Ceccagno 2003a). The active role played by the Chinese in the expansion of the local production of garments and knitwear is also highlighted by the growing number of new Chinese ready-to-wear manufacturers, who now rely on an impressive network of buyers – they have clients, including Chinese wholesalers, who come from many European countries. In 2003, the production of garments and knitwear increased to the point that – also as an effect of the crisis and reduction in production within the textile industry proper – these businesses represented about 28.3 per cent of the textile and garment industry firms located in the Prato district and 25 per cent of the gross total (Camera di commercio of Prato 2004).

Prato is therefore a place where the contribution of Chinese to local productive activities is clearly visible: this town used to be a textile district that specialized exclusively in the production and export of textiles. In the last few years, however, thanks to the presence of Chinese garment workshops, the local textile chain of production has expanded to include the last phase of manufacturing, still making the area of Prato into a real fashion district (Ceccagno forthcoming).

The Italian economic crisis

As early as 2003, the major Italian economic institutions had warned that the Italian economy was facing a serious crisis. Specifically, Antonio Fazio, Governor of the Bank of Italy, had identified three principal causes for the drastic reduction in future Italian exports: (1) the composition of production, heavily geared towards sectors lacking in innovation; (2) low productivity, due to the fragmented nature of the Italian manufacturing system; (3) the emergence on the international markets of firms operating in the same sectors of specialization as Italy but located in countries where the costs of production are lower, productivity is growing at a fast rate and there is an increasing improvement in the quality of the products (Fazio 2003, 2004). Even in 2004, Fazio was reporting about a constant decrease in Italian exports to the global market[4] and identified the decreasing size of Italian firms as the principal cause for Italy's loss of competitiveness in this market. The small, flexible and dynamic enterprises today find themselves in a crisis, because of their inability to facilitate 'the activities of research and technological innovation, which are crucial for competing on global markets'. (Fazio 2004)

The crisis of the Chinese operated manufacturing activities

The crisis that is affecting many Italian firms obviously also has an impact on Chinese workshops: internal competition has stiffened (also due to the continuous arrival of undocumented and irregular workers from China), the margins of profit have generally been reduced while the entrepreneurial risks have increased for the owners. The smaller firms in particular encounter great difficulties in trying to remain in the market, and are characterized by a high failure rate. This situation was highlighted by a study conducted in Prato (Caserta 2003): out of the total number of Chinese-owned firms still active at the end of 2002, only 10 per cent were more than five years old. The failure rates underscore the fragility of this type of activity, especially in a period of crisis when Italian manufacturers are trying to cut costs to the maximum extent.

A growing number of Chinese contractors blamed the crisis they are experiencing on imports from China. Their businesses risk being disrupted by competition from products made in China and marketed by both Chinese migrants and Italians They also denounced a new dangerous trend: these days even smaller Italian manufacturers – when they do not rely on imported products – increasingly relocate their production to China or elsewhere, thus accelerating the decline in domestic contracting by both Chinese and Italians.

According to a research survey conducted in 2003 in the Florence area (the largest leather goods production area in Europe), many warehouses which used to house a number of different Chinese family businesses were already closing down, or were used only partially, to the point that the authors estimated an ongoing decrease in the overall number of Chinese-operated businesses in the area (Fondazione Michelucci 2004).

The acute perception of economic crisis has pushed many workshop owners – who not long ago appeared to be established and able to diversify their production activities – to travel to other European countries, searching for alternative opportunities for economic success. Many now believe that opportunities for quick economic upward mobility should be looked for elsewhere: moving out of the productive sector where they have traditionally been active, towards the growing business of importing from China.

Chinese importers for the European market

Most Chinese migrants are constantly in contact with their place of origin and therefore have been witnesses to the changes that have brought China from being a developing country looking for foreign investments in the early 1980s to becoming the biggest recipient of foreign investments and contributing 6.6 per cent of world exports (Siddivò 2005).

New production capabilities and low production costs in China, and in particular in their areas of origin, have pushed some Chinese migrants – who in Italy had acquired manufacturing know-how and experience in fashion – to foster in their places of origin the production of garments to be marketed in Italy and Europe. Chinese migrants' imports of clothing, footwear, bags, toys, furniture and home appliances from China emerged quietly during the second half of the 1990s and over the years the success of the first entrepreneurs has pushed many Chinese to seek their fortune in this field. According to collected data, in 2003 in Rome some 400 Chinese importers managed wholesale/retail stores in the area around Piazza Vittorio.5

The majority of Chinese migrant importers in Rome market products purchased in China. However, a small subset claims to have started workshops in China with products specifically for the European market. According to local authorities who were interviewed in September 2003 in Wenzhou – the core of the area from where the majority of the Chinese settled in Italy originate – about 5 per cent of the migrants who export local manufactured goods to the markets of southern Europe are also the owners of the factories that produce them.

These Chinese products are even marketed outside of Italy. In fact, the wholesalers who for a few years have been heading to Rome to purchase goods from the Chinese importers of Piazza Vittorio are not just Italians or Chinese living in Italy, but also Chinese nationals or Europeans from Austria, France, Germany, Greece, England, Portugal and Spain; this is despite the fact that in some of these countries – such as France and Spain – there are Chinese migrant importers who carry out the same types of business activities as those found in Italy. By contrast, the countries of

Eastern Europe are excluded and rely instead on Hungary as a hub for this type of import activity.

Italy's competitive advantage compared to that of neighbouring countries seems to be the prices, the variety of models – always fashionable – and, in particular, the ease of customs crossings (which also has positive consequences for migrant importers, both financially and in terms of the speed of importing). According to the Chinese interviewed, Naples' customs has by far been the most popular and the most advantageous port of entry of the past few years, a place where controls have been limited and where it has been possible to bring in great quantities of goods while paying reduced duties, thanks in part to the practice of sub-invoicing (for example declaring a value of 10 while importing a value of 100).

The most striking development is that some of the garments imported from China now are ready-to-wear items. This is a significant step, which seemed unreachable until very recently. At the end of the twentieth century, the Chinese in Italy were able to commission from China the production of items that normally would be on the market only after a long period of time. Now, the entrepreneurship of migrants originating from Wenzhou and its interior, along with the drive for communication which goes hand-in-hand with globalization, has made it possible to cross the frontier of ready-to-wear garments. In fact, thanks to the frequent flights between Europe and China and to an extremely flexible organization of work in China, an importer can commission a certain number of clothing items from Wenzhou (or from other Chinese cities), knowing that in about five days they will arrive in Italy. According to the expert at the local import-export organization in Wenzhou, interviewed in the fall of 2003, 15 per cent of the clothing items produced on site is shipped by air – within the timetable for ready-to-wear – while the remaining 85 per cent of the local production headed for Italy is sent by ship.

The areas of production of goods to be transported to Europe are mainly located in the city of Wenzhou and in the rest of the Zhejiang province (mainly textiles, jeans and sweaters, but recently also footwear); and in the provinces of Fujian (mostly sport footwear) and Guangdong (textiles, toys, etc.). According to data gathered in September 2003 in the area of Wenzhou, there are supposed to be about 700 to 800 'small-sized' private firms (in other words, employing about a hundred workers) producing clothing items exclusively for export, and which emerged as a result of export businesses managed by Chinese migrant importers in Europe.

The role of migrant importers/exporters seems to vary among the different European countries. According to officials interviewed in China in September 2003, about half of the exports from Wenzhou for Europe are managed by migrant-importers. However, this percentage reaches about 90 per cent of the exports destined for Italy, France and Spain. These are very preliminary data that only have indicative value; no other study of this phenomenon has been conducted in Europe or in China.

HOW THE BUSINESS OF THE CHINESE MIGRANT HAS BEEN CHANGING

The success of Chinese importers and wholesalers in Italy has offered Chinese migrants in Italy a glimpse of new opportunities up for grabs. This has led a certain number of Chinese migrants to leave contracting work for Italian firms to open their own retail marketing activities in Italy as well as in other European countries.

Europe has always been perceived by Chinese migrants as a large chessboard along which one can travel in order to seize opportunities for legalization of residency status and for enrichment (see Ceccagno 2003b; Pieke et al. 2004). This opportunity is no exception. The import business from China to Italy has stimulated the mobility of a number of Chinese in Europe who have moved to other European countries with the aim of drawing upon the competitive advantage conferred by their direct relationship with importers. For example, about 50 Chinese migrants, who had accumulated a modest capital over many years of work heading a workshop in Prato, have transferred to Germany where they have opened retail stores selling clothes they import from the importers of Rome. Moreover, from interviews conducted in Rome, similar experiences have emerged: the owner of a wholesale store in Rome tells of her husband who has opened a store in Greece where he sells merchandise bought from importers in Rome; importers in Rome tell of an increasing number of Chinese migrants who move to Athens and Salonicco in Greece, where the market for Chinese products – imported through Rome – is in full expansion.

As a whole, a new situation has emerged which can be sketched as follows:

- *Pure Importers*: those who do not directly market what they import. According to the few available indications, this category consists of a limited number of Chinese migrants who usually work alongside Italians and sell directly to large Italian commercial chains.

- *Importers–Wholesalers:* the vast majority of Chinese importers belong to this group; they import goods and sell them in shops. As we have seen, a limited number of importers-wholesalers also head one or more factories in China where the goods that will be subsequently imported in Italy and distributed throughout Europe are produced. In some cases, the importers–wholesalers are also retailers.

- *Wholesalers:* they are Chinese nationals who do not have enough power to import directly; they purchase imported goods from their compatriots. In some cases, these wholesalers start their business on the tailwind of a relative or a friend who is established in the importer–wholesaler activity, even if they do not necessarily remain connected to that sole channel for their supply. Moreover, these wholesalers often open their own shops in other Italian cities lacking importers–wholesalers and can become a reference point for the Chinese retailers settled in that area.

- *Retailers*: retail shops managed by the Chinese have by now reached even small Italian towns. The supply can be diversified: some stores purchase only items imported from China from Chinese importers or from wholesalers settled in major towns; others also purchase clothing manufactured in Italy from the Chinese ready-to-wear businesses or from Italians contracting its manufacturing to Chinese-operated workshops.

As we have seen, many Chinese active in productive activities in Italy fear this new development and perceive migrant importers and marketers of goods made in China as direct competitors. Others are seeing it as a new economic opportunity. In these cases, the diverse functions of production and importing combine and blend, and the distinction between those Chinese active in production and those who market imported goods is gradually being blurred. Now there are entrepreneurs who produce ready-to-wear garments in Italy, but at the same time are also active as manufacturers in China and importers for Italy and Europe. In the Prato area, for example, an entrepreneur settled in Italy for over 15 years employs about 60 Chinese (plus some Italian fashion designers) spread in a few sweater workshops. This same entrepreneur has opened a sweater workshop in China (in Rui'an, Zhejiang province) that manufactures exclusively for Italy, from where the garments are then marketed throughout Europe. Similarly, a recent preliminary survey conducted among 53 Chinese operating ready-to-wear in Prato reveals that about 40 per cent of the total quantity of fabric used in their workshops is imported from China.[6]

All in all, import and commercial activities in Europe are by now much more appealing to Chinese migrants than merely operating a business as a contractor for Italian manufacturers in Italy. Being a contractor is increasingly less profitable, more exposed to competition and tax audits, and one in which work time and living time blend together. This evolution is the direct result of globalization and of the ever steadier role of China as an exporter to international markets. Thanks to rapid changes in their country of origin, a growing number of Chinese migrants have increasingly been able to rely on production in China and accordingly to move around to market opportunities developing in other European countries.

The implications of these developments

The import business from China shows the potential for further expansion: the range of products to be imported is widening and the growing commitment and success of Chinese importers settled in Italy could lead to the centrality of Italy in Europe, or at least in part of it, as producer and distributor of fashion apparel managed by the Chinese migrants. Until the summer of 2003, we could have imagined an evolution toward the polarization of this business in Europe into two principal hubs (which do not exclude the existence of minor centres in other European capitals): Rome as the distribution point for south-western Europe and Budapest for north-central and north-eastern Europe.

The critical element of this new situation lies in the competitiveness that develops for products imported from China – garments and footwear first of all, but not only – and those manufactured in Italy by both Italian and Chinese operated contracting firms (who in large part take advantage of the labour in workshops managed by the Chinese). In fact, imports of products from China, the quality of which is increasingly similar to that of *Made in Italy*, are perceived by many in Italy as a serious threat to Italian products – particularly to those who do not benefit from a name brand that is world-famous. The success of Chinese wholesale stores actually shows that, in this changing international situation, even the Chinese workshops that for about 20 years have guaranteed Italian firms flexibility and the outsourcing of social costs have now themselves become radically less competitive.

Italy's reaction to the impact of the global economy and the consequences for the Chinese migrants

This situation has led exponents of the Italian government to complain about the unfair competition from the products arriving from China. In 2003, coinciding with the Italian presidency of the European Union, Giulio Tremonti, the Italian Minister of Economy, expressed his concern that products imported from China and other Asian countries were threatening jobs in a number of different manufacturing sectors, including many of those in which Italy has traditionally been outstanding. On the occasion of the G7 meeting in Bercy, Paris, he proposed limiting the opening of free commerce by introducing restrictive formulas. According to an interview granted by Tremonti:

> Europe should do what America, the land of liberalism, has been doing successfully for some time. That is, it should protect its internal market and its national production not only with customs taxes, but also with indirect tools, such as alimentary, sanitary, and working condition controls over products originating from the Far East. (Oldani 2003, see also Vialetti and Fiocca 2003)

This statement was echoed by associations representing Italian industrial firms from the sectors most involved in the export business (such as leather goods, footwear, textiles, glasses, gold jewellery and leather working). An advertisement that took a half-page in some Italian newspapers demanded customs controls for products that enter Italy and Europe with the trademarks *Made in Italy* and CE (European Community).[7] A little over a month later these complaints translated into guidelines for Italian customs agencies to improve controls over merchandise originating in China. These guidelines were never discussed and made officially public in Italy; data on the dimensions of the control policy is therefore not available.[8]

At the end of 2003, the major consequences of customs controls weighed most obviously on importers settled in Rome. According to statements by a number of Chinese importers, many shipping containers were held for long periods of time by customs, and products manufactured in China for the Christmas season arrived in Rome only after the holidays.

In the following few months the situation appeared to have deteriorated further. The importers–wholesalers interviewed in March 2004 in Rome expressed increasing levels of frustration over the import freeze, which, according to them has became even more stringent in the month of February.

> Compared to last December the situation has changed, but for the worse. Before, by paying a little more it was possible to be released from customs; now it's impossible to get anything out. The port of Naples is full of our shipping containers. In January [2004] there was a period of releases probably because they didn't know where to put them. Then the freeze started again, worse than before. (Interview file LC, Rome, no. 16, 27 March, 2004)

The mood was increasingly desperate, the tension was palpable and the diffidence so diffused that interviews with the importers–wholesalers of Piazza Vittorio in Rome, which had been conducted with relative ease just a few months earlier, had by then become considerably more difficult. Many of those interviewed reiterated that their presence in many ways had been very advantageous for Rome and for Italy. Almost all claimed with pride China's central role in the world economy, a role that allows them to distinguish themselves from other migrants who live in Italy, and which gives them the pride and the strength to believe that, whatever happens, in China, in Italy or elsewhere in Europe they will find a way to continue their work as transnational individuals who have learned to blend strategies of migration with translocal capital accumulation.

The informants told of Chinese migrants who had already moved to other European countries, or who were thinking about it in case the customs freeze continued. The country of destination would mainly be Spain, which today is considered an important market with great prospects, or alternately Greece as the emerging southern European country.

Most of the interviewees stated that many of them were already moving or had the intention of moving to other countries where controls were less strict – the main hit destination being Spain – and declared that imports from China to Italy would not actually decrease because of the freeze imposed by Italian customs. In fact, goods entering Europe in Barcelona or other ports in Spain would later reach other European countries, including Italy, as in the past had happened for merchandise entering Italy.

The new attitude of the Italian government seems to have brought a decrease in the quantity of goods directly imported from China. Even though data on the subject is not available, one manager of China Ocean Shipping Group, interviewed in Naples in April 2004, declared that 80 per cent of goods arriving from China to the Naples' harbour underwent control of the shipment (instead of simple control of the documents) and that as a result only 40 containers a day from China were able to pass customs control in 2004 instead of the 150 in 2003 (Sacchetti 2004).

Today, controls at the Italian main entry ports do not seem to have brought about a reduction in the Chinese commercial business activity in the country. Statistical data on Chinese commercial businesses show that by September 2004, 7,735 Chinese businesses were operating wholesale or retail shops in Italy (see Table 6.3).

Table 6.3. Selected commercial activities of the Chinese in Italy and in some Italian regions, September 2004

Geographical area	Wholesale and retail commerce	Transport, stock and communication	Total
Italy	7,735	82	7,817
Lombardy	1,312	19	1,331
Toscany	723	17	740
Veneto	505	8	513
Emilia Romagna	470	9	479

Source: Spinner 2004, based on data from Chamber of Commerce, Industry and Agriculture, Modena

The majority of Chinese businesses are still in Rome (statistical data is not available), but significant numbers are now also active in Lombardy (1,312 such businesses), in Naples (data is not available, but in Naples a Chinese-owned and operated wholesale market called Cina Mercato is hosting 76 stands based on the model of the Four Tigers' Market in Budapest), in Tuscany (723), Veneto (505), Emilia Romagna (470) and spreading also into other parts of Italy. Further research could verify whether merchandise sold in these shops arrives directly from China or, as foreseen by the interviewed migrants, the bulk of the imports in southern Europe has moved from Italy to other European ports.

CONCLUSION

Chinese migrants with powerful ethnic networks have made inroads into the Italian garment industry, activating a growing number of ethnic contracting and subcontracting businesses. Italian manufacturers contract out the production of garments, and increasingly also the production of other goods for which *Made in Italy* is famous, to Chinese-operated workshops. As we have seen, this kind of arrangement has been beneficial to Italian industry in the new globalized framework as it has enabled Italian manufacturers to contain competition from countries where the costs of production are lower. Productivity has been growing and the quality of products has constantly improved.

However, during the 20 years of the presence of new Chinese migrants in Italy, the widespread popular opinion in Italy has been that Chinese businesses engage in 'unfair competitive practices' that take away work from Italians. This perception is linked to the national experience *vis-à-vis* international migration. First of all the presence of migrants in Italy is a fairly recent phenomenon. In the last century, the garment industry in many European countries has during survival and expansion phases counted on the presence of successive waves of migrants (Rath 2002; Green 1997), but in the Italian fashion industry, Chinese migrants have entered in significant numbers as a rather new phenomenon. Second, the perception of Chinese migrants as a threat was also due to the massive positioning of Chinese migrants within an ethnic economy that over time has produced a growing number of small entrepreneurs within the context of an Italian landscape where the vast majority of migrants were employed by Italians. As a consequence an assessment of the positive role played by Chinese migrants in the fashion industry has never taken place in Italy.

Recently, China and its rising economic and commercial power in the globalized world is the central issue. Italian worries concentrate on goods imported from China – especially after the end of the Multi-Fibre Agreement in January 2005 – and on the role played in this growing business by Chinese migrants. As we have seen, the Italian government first tried to draw the attention of the European Community to the issue and then, starting from September 2003, activated a not widely advertised control on imports from China. Intensive control at the Italian customs prevented imported goods such as easily 'perishable' garments from entering the market for long periods of time and as such should be considered equal to limiting free commerce. These practices applied to migrant importers, are having the effect of moving the entry ports from Italy to other southern European countries where controls are less stringent.

Sentiments similar to those widespread in Italy have recently also emerged in Spain. Popular reactions to imports from China have taken place in Spain in September 2004 when Spanish workers in Elche, a shoe-producing town in the coastal province of Alicante, set fire to containers of shoes imported from China by Chinese migrants (Portal Democracia National 2004).

These experiences in Italy and in Spain – while substantially different, the first one being conducted by the national government and the second one being a popular and limited reaction – lead to some reflection generally on the effects of globalization on national economies, and in particular on the effects of the Chinese increasing their export practices on Europe.

Different European countries nurture different perceptions of the dangers of imports from China for their economies and these perceptions are probably directly linked to the relevance to the national economy of those sectors subject to imports.

The importance of fashion and household products to the Italian economy helps explain why imports from China are perceived as disruptive in Italy (much more so in a period when in Italy is experiencing an economic crisis). Conversely, countries mainly active in less mature sectors and therefore less exposed to competing imports from counties that can count on low labour costs seem to be less concerned with the political and/or social concerns that have been mounting in Italy and Spain in the last years.

The case of Italy poses questions of restriction and protection policies *vis-à-vis* fundamental changes that are taking place as a result of globalization. Up to now the issue of migration as a result of globalization has mostly been discussed in terms of control by nation-states of in-migration, and only recently did European countries start to think of a concerted policy for frontiers control. However, the link between migration and globalization is now taking other shapes. Facing China's rising economic, commercial and political power, at least one European country is now recognizing that migration control should be contemplated also in terms of economic sanctions (and, more and more also in terms of the prevention of disruptive social protests against migrants from China and their economic activities) and acting accordingly.

NOTES

[1] According to other sources, in June 2004, 71,843 individual businesses were operated by foreigners in Italy; Chinese migrants owned 10,199 of these, or about 14 per cent of the total, being second to Moroccan migrants operating 14,554 businesses constituting a little more than 20 per cent of the total (Caritas and Migrantes 2004).

2. In 2003, there were 1,171 Chinese businesses in Campania region, including both productive and commercial activities (Chamber of Commerce of Naples in Sacchetti 2004).

3. Similar to Italian-operated entrepreneurial activities, a large portion of the Chinese economy remains irregular, but the degree of irregularity varies depending upon the areas and regions where the Chinese firms have settled.

4. 'The rate of Italian exports to international markets, which was at 4.3 per cent in 1995 and 4.2 per cent in 1996, has constantly decreased in the past seven years, reaching 3.7 per cent in the year 2000, and in 2003 around 3.3 per cent'. (Fazio 2004)

5. Information on this subject was collected in 30 interviews based on a questionnaire prepared by the author, 18 of which were administered in Chinese by Laura Cassanelli in Rome from October 2003 to April 2004, while 12 interviews in Chinese and Italian were conducted by the author in Wenzhou, Rome, Prato, Olbia and Carpi from June 2003 to March 2004.

6. Data from Prato, January 2005.

7. See for example *la Repubblica*, 9 October, 2003, p. 31.

8. Information on customs control and on a new severity in port inspections have been inferred from news in local pages of national newspapers (see for example the local Naples pages in la Repubblica, 18 and 19 September, 2003 and in particular from De Matteis 2003 and from interviews conducted among Chinese importers in Piazza Vittorio in Rome.

REFERENCES

Camera di Commercio di Prato (2004) *1994–2004: Da X Anni Regista del Sistema Economico Pratese* [1994–2004: ten years of data on Prato's economic system]. Prato: unpublished volume.

Caritas and Migrantes (2003) *Immigrazione. Dossier statistico* 2003 [Immigration. statistical records 2003]. Roma: Anterem.

Caritas and Migrantes (2004) *Immigrazione. Dossier statistico* 2004 [Immigration. statistical records 2004]. Roma: Anterem.

Caserta, Dario (2003) 'Imprenditoria straniera: caratteristiche strutturali e tendenze evolutive' [Foreign enterpreneurship: structural characteristics and trends]. In *Rapporto sull'imprenditoria Straniera in Provincia di Prato* [Report on foreign entrepreneurship in Prato province]. Prato: unpublished report, pp. 3–13.

Ceccagno, Antonella (forthcoming) 'Compressing personal time: ethnicity and gender among the Chinese in Italy', *Journal of Ethnic and Migration Studies*.

—— (2003a) 'Le migrazioni dalla Cina verso l'Italia e l'Europa nell'epoca della globalizzazione' [Migrations from China towards Italy and Europe in the era of globalization]. In Antonella Ceccagno (ed.), *Migranti a Prato. Il Distretto Tessile Multietnico* [Migrants in Prato; the multiethnic industrial district]. Milano: Franco Angeli, pp. 25–68.

—— (2003b) 'New Chinese migrants in Italy'. *International Migration*, vol. 41, no. 3, special issue, pp. 187–213.

De Matteis, Giantomaso (2003) 'Napoli, porto franco della Cina' [Naples, China's free port] *la Repubblica*, 18 September, p. I.

Dei (2001) 'Il tessile-abbigliamento toscano nel contesto nazionale ed europeo' [Tuscany Textile-Garment industry in the Italian and European context]. In Monica Baracchi, Daniela Bigarelli, Matteo Colombi e Armando Dei (eds), *Modelli territoriali e modelli settoriali. Un'analisi della struttura produttiva del tessile-abbigliamento in Toscana* [Territorial models and sectoral models. An analysis of the productive structure of the textile-garment industry in Tuscany]. Torino: Rosenberg and Sellier, pp. 13–23.

Fazio, Antonio (2003) 'Giornata Mondiale del Risparmio' [World Savings Day]. URL: www.bancaditalia.it (accessed 28 April, 2006).

Fazio, Antonio (2004) 'L'economia Internazionale e l'Italia' [The international economy and Italy]. URL: www.bancaditalia.it (accessed 28 April, 2006).

Fondazione Michelucci (ed.) (2004) *La Lontananza Vicina, la Vicinanza Remota* [Simultaneously nearby and distant]. Firenze: unpublished report.

Green, Nancy (1997) *Ready-to-Wear, Ready-to-Work. A Century of Industry and Immigrants in Paris and New York*. Durham and London: Duke University Press.

Light, Ivan, Richard B. Bernard and Rebecca Kim (1999) 'Immigrant incorporation in the garment industry of Los Angeles', *International Migration Review*, vol. 33, no. 1, pp. 5–25.

Mania, Roberto (2004) '"E" il boom delle persone-imprese' [Single-person enterprises are booming], *la Repubblica*, 17 March, p. 29.

Oldani, Tino (2003) "La crisi viene da oriente" [The crisis comes from the East], *Panorama*, August, 28, pp. 36–41.

Pepi, Giambattista (2003) 'L'immigrato si mette in proprio' [The immigrant becomes self-employed], *Il Sole 24 ore*, 24 November.

Pieke, Frank N., Pál Nyíri, Mette Thunø and Antonella Ceccagno (2004) *Transnational Chinese. Fujianese Migrants in Europe*. Stanford: Stanford University Press.

Portal Democracia National (2004) 'Los incidentes de Elche y algunas explicationes', 21 October, pp. 1–5. URL: http://democracianacional.org/portal Accessed 28 April 2006.

Rath, Jan (ed.) (2002) *Unravelling the Rag trade. Immigrant Entrepreneurship in Seven World Cities*. Oxford and New York: Berg.

Repubblica, la (2003) 18, 19 September, p. III; 9 October, p. 31.

Sacchetti, Maurizia (2004) 'Migranti cinesi in Campania' [Chinese migrants in Campania]. In Massimo Galluppi and Franco Mazzei (eds), *Campania e Cina* [Campania and China]. Napoli: Edizioni scientifiche italiane, pp. 177–224.

Siddivò, Marisa (2005) 'Il coraggio di riflettere' [The courage of reflection]. In Giorgio Trentin (ed.), *La Cina che arriva* [The forthcoming China]. Roma: Avagliano, pp. 61–78.

Smi-Ati Federazione Imprese Tessili e Moda Italiane (2005) 'Made in Italy: Textile, Clothing, Fashion Chain' URL: www.smi-ati.it/documenti/il_ns_settore_inglese_v03.pdf (accessed 20 August 2006).

Spinner (acronym for a research group) (2004) *Analisi Statistica sulle Economie Etniche e la non Regolarità di Impresa in Emilia Romagna* [Statistical analysis of ethnic economies and their irregularity in Emilia Romagna]. Bologna: unpublished report.

Vialetti, Giuseppe and Mariateresa Fiocca (2003) "Il neocolbertismo", [The neo-colbertism] *Aspenia* n 23, pp. 215–229.

Waldinger, Roger (1996) *Still the Promised City? African-Americans and New Immigrants in Postindustrial New York.* Cambridge MA and London: Harvard University Press.

Chapter 7

Influx of New Chinese Immigrants to the Philippines: Problems and Challenges

Teresita Ang See

INTRODUCTION

China's economic reforms in the early 1980s, which led to its opening up to the outside world, started a new trend of immigration from China to all parts of the world. Although a majority of migrants opted to go to developed countries, quite a number also made their way to South-east Asia. The Philippines, in particular, is one of the popular destination countries of the so-called new immigrants from Fujian province. After all, almost 90 per cent of ethnic Chinese in the Philippines hail from Fujian province, and these new immigrants would therefore have ready-made ties – kinship, classmates/alumni, business, and related ties – with them. The increased immigration from China to the Philippines was further facilitated after the Philippines established formal diplomatic relations with the People's Republic of China (PRC) in 1975. Moreover, the early 1980s was also the period when President Ferdinand E. Marcos was desperate for foreign investments. He issued a presidential decree that sanctioned foreign investments into the Philippines from communist and socialist countries, including the PRC.

Most of the new immigrants who made it to the Philippines in the 1980s, however, were not the big investors that the government wanted to encourage. They were mainly distant or immediate relatives of the earlier immigrants who made it to the Philippines. Subsequently, aside from kinship ties, new ties of friendship, schoolmates, and village or town-mates started to entice more and more immigrants from the PRC. Many of them, unfortunately, entered and stayed on in the Philippines illegally because since 1940, the Philippines had outlawed immigration from the PRC except as investors, retirees, or students (Fernandez and Domingo 1970). In the 1990s, more immigrants arrived from China. They are, again, different from the earlier immigrants in the 1970s and 1980s who had kinship and other ties with the ethnic Chinese community here. Some of them, in fact, came from provinces like Liaoning, Shandong, Jiangsu, and other places outside of Fujian and Guangdong, the southern coastal areas where most Philippine-Chinese hailed from.

This chapter explores the issue of the new Chinese immigrants from the PRC in two sections. The first section gives an overview of the general situation and discusses the problems and challenges the new immigrants pose for Philippine society in general and for the Chinese-Filipino community in particular. The chapter argues that the situation and problems of the new Chinese immigrants to developing countries like the Philippines are quite different from those who immigrate to developed countries like the United States and Europe. In the second section, the chapter explores the China factor in the issue. While earlier immigrants to the Philippines came mainly in order to improve their lives due to reasons of poverty as well as to join their families, the influx of new immigrants into developing countries like the Philippines, which are much poorer than the PRC, were for entirely different reasons. The question is – which not only the Chinese government but also researchers in China, have so far merely glossed over: if China is now enjoying phenomenal growth, why are its citizens still bent on leaving the country for good? Though there are some migrants who used the Philippines as a transit point to other countries, they are extremely few because of the ban on immigration of the Chinese since 1940, making their stay in the country illegal unless they are investors or retirees.

This chapter argues that it seems too simplistic to say that the new immigrants leave China mainly because there is still an economic imbalance between China and the developed countries, or that they leave the country for developed destinations to improve their lot, and that the Chinese government need not be overly concerned about the problem. Most of the studies on new immigrants that the author has encountered, especially those written by Chinese researchers, focus more on the supposed positive value of the new immigrants to their new countries of destination and regard the problems that they create as of no great importance, citing the fact that the number of Chinese immigrants is quite small compared to the number of immigrants worldwide.[1]

Naturally, we cannot pass a general judgement that most of the immigrants who came here were irregulars or illegal. There are a number of professionals who have contractual employment and have given great service to the community. These include the Chinese-language teachers hired by the Chinese-Filipino schools, the secretaries and clerks at many of the local Chinese organizations and the employees of the four Chinese-language daily newspapers. Without these new immigrants, the functions of these institutions would be adversely affected because few of the local-born Tsinoys have enough competence in Chinese-language communication. Nevertheless, these professionals are few in number compared with the irregular, undocumented immigrants who, despite having a livelihood back in their hometowns in China, still brave the adverse and hostile climate in the Philippines, with the illusion that life is better and the grass is greener on the other side.

While it is understandable that centuries ago, the Chinese, especially those who immigrated to the Philippines from impoverished villages in Fujian, were forced to pull out their roots to seek greener pastures and improve their lots elsewhere, it is surprising that they continue to do so, especially to developing countries like the Philippines, which does not have much to offer them in terms of improving their situations. This new group of immigrants creates an entirely new problematic situation for Philippine society as a whole and for the Chinese-Filipino community in particular. Because immigration to the Philippines has been banned since the 1940s, except for investors and retirees, many of these Chinese entered the Philippines and stayed on in the country illegally – either as undocumented immigrants or immigrants with falsified or illegal papers. While the problem of integration and identity among the early pre-war immigrants to the Philippines has been smoothly resolved, the new immigrants have created new problems and challenges – politically, economically, socially, and culturally – for the well-integrated Tsinoy community. One of the biggest problems is that because of the very nature of their illegal entry into and/or subsequent illegal residence in the Philippines, many of the new immigrants have become involved in various forms of criminal activities, especially illegal drugs trafficking. These have an adverse backlash for the Tsinoy community and create a very negative image, not just for these new immigrants but also for the entire Tsinoy community and most importantly, for China, too.

In short, before the twentieth century, Chinese immigrants, especially those who came to the Philippines, were forced to leave their country as a consequence of poverty, famine, political chaos, and peasant uprisings. They suffered hardships, adverse conditions and often had to take extreme measures for their survival. It is difficult to imagine that in the last two decades of the twentieth up to these early years of the twenty-first century, while China is enjoying a phenomenal growth compared to its neighbours in South-east Asia, out-migration from China continues to cause new problems to countries like the Philippines.

GENERAL SITUATION

Definitions and numbers

By 'new Chinese immigrants', we mean those who came to the Philippines from the PRC since the late 1970s to the present. They are usually referred to in China as *xinyimin* (new immigrants), but in the Philippines, the terms *xinqiao* and *jiuqiao* (old immigrants) are more popularly used to refer to the new immigrants (after the 1970s) and the earlier immigrants (before the 1970s), respectively. Among the local Chinese Filipinos, the *xinqiao* are often referred to as TDK (an acronym for *Tai Diok A* 'mainlanders' in Hokkien), not without derogatory or pejorative connotations.

The term 'undocumented' Chinese refers to those who entered the Philippines with fake documents. Entry to the country was therefore illegal. The term 'illegal aliens' or 'illegal Chinese' encompasses a bigger group that includes both the 'undocumented' and those who entered with legal documents but subsequently stayed on in the country through illegal means or used fake and spurious documents in order to stay on in the country.

The terms 'Tsinoy' and/or 'Tsinoy community' refer to the ethnic Chinese community in the Philippines who are already Filipino citizens or those whose roots are already in the country. The term was coined and popularized in the early 1990s precisely to differentiate them from the new Chinese immigrants who often hog the media headlines as a consequence of illegal activities.

An interview with the executive director of the Bureau of Immigration Roy M. Almoro, reveals that the number of illegally overstaying Chinese in the Philippines is still speculative. Ballpark figures of about 80,000 to 100,000 are often cited, culled arbitrarily from the number of deportations carried out each year and from the discrepancy between the number of arrivals and departures. Of these, 70 to 80 per cent are said to be PRC citizens.

Chinese who have permanent residency numbered about 120,000 before 1975. In 1985, this number was drastically reduced to just about 25,000. Nearly 96,000 Chinese obtained Filipino citizenship through presidential decree from 1976 to 1985. Former President Ferdinand E. Marcos issued an Executive Order in 1975 that allowed mass naturalization by administrative means on the eve of the establishment of diplomatic relations with the PRC. President Marcos did not want the substantial number of Chinese nationals to be legally under the jurisdiction of a communist regime. Of the more than a hundred thousand applications, about 90 per cent were finally able to obtain Filipino citizenship. Today, the number of PRC migrants with Chinese citizenship has gone back to the pre-1975 figures of about 100,000. Less than half of these numbers can be said to have legitimate or legal papers that allow them to reside in the Philippines (either through the investment or retirement scheme or as foreign students). Those who availed themselves of the amnesty programme offered by the government in 1992 were able to legalize their stay subsequently, although some used falsified documents to take advantage of the legalization program (Arquiza 1996).

Background of the xinqiao

Go Bon Juan has made a comparison of *xinqiao* and *jiuqiao* (Go 2002: 309–319). I will not dwell on this matter further, but summarize what he discussed to give a background of the *xinqiao* in contrast with the *jiuqiao*. The differences lie in their reasons for migration, hometown of origins, means of immigration (transportation used), 'quality' of the immigrants (like level of education, manners and civility), and relations with the local Chinese. From the comparison given, readers can discern that the patterns, reasons, and means of immigration to the Philippines are quite different.

First is the observation that the old immigrants (or *jiuqiao*) were products of an old China beset by famine, abject poverty, backwardness, and political chaos and, thus, immigration was desirable and understandable. In contrast, the *xinqiao* are products of the new China, a growing world power with a modern rapidly developing economy. The *jiuqiao* were forced by circumstances to leave the country mainly as a means of survival and to be reunited with their families, particularly in developing countries like the Philippines. In contrast, the *xinqiao* have opted to leave voluntarily, many with some money for investments and for settling down. Others leave merely to get *huaqiao* status, which they have hoped will give them certain privileges and serve them better back home. Some of the women I interviewed opted to join their husbands in the Philippines just for the privilege of having a second child, because the first-born was a female.

Although the *xinqiao* have higher educational achievement or are better educated, they are still looked down upon by the local ethnic Chinese as uncouth, ill-mannered and uncivilized. Many tend to ignore Philippine law enforcers and openly flaunt rules and regulations such as 'no smoking', 'no littering or spitting', 'turn off mobile phones' and the like. Spitting just anywhere is a habit that the local Chinese would like to find corrected but seems impossible. A few examples on the blatant disregard for law are given here in a subsequent section. Even young students in Chinese-language schools tend to dissociate or distance themselves from classmates who are *xinqiao*. They complain that these classmates are quite spoiled, are bullies and unruly, prone to cursing, and even in high school, many have been disciplined for gambling and smoking. The schools' prefect of discipline revealed that disciplinary problems among these young students are several times more difficult to deal with than those of their local students. These experiences were shared in a forum on '*Xinqiao* and the Problems of Illegal Aliens' organized by Kaisa Para Sa Kaunlaran on 24 November 2002, where the participants shared their encounters with the *xinqiao*, some good but mostly not too positive. At the conclusion of the forum, it was agreed that Kaisa should explore the possibility of bridging the gap between the *xinqiao* Chinese and the Tsinoys, as well as help the *xinqiao* understand the local culture not just that of the Tsinoys but most importantly of mainstream society.

New legislations affecting Chinese nationals

Due to the increasing number of overstaying Chinese and new Chinese immigrants in recent years, the Philippine government has adopted new legislation and administrative measures as stopgap policies to ease or help solve the problem. Some of the more significant ones are cited here to highlight the fact that the Philippine government does exert effort to address the problem created by the *xinqiao* illegally staying in the country.

The presence of illegal immigrants has been a perennial headache. Former Immigration Commissioner Miriam Defensor Santiago initiated the amnesty programme in 1988 to legalize those who had been in the Philippines for 20 to 30 years, through Executive Order 324, signed as an administrative act of President Corazon Cojuangco Aquino.[2] Upon the recommendation of then Immigration Commissioner Santiago, E.O. 324 legalized the stay of immigrants who entered the Philippines before 1984. After about three months of implementation, Congress suspended the programme in 1989 on the grounds that amnesty programmes can only be granted by the legislature. A little over 3,000 applications were approved under E.O. 324 before its suspension (Son 1989).

On 24 February 1995, lawmakers passed Republic Act 7919, granting legalized status to immigrants who can prove that they entered the country prior to 30 June 1992 and have continuously stayed there. Also covered are those immigrants who applied for legalization under E.O. 324 and whose applications were granted before or after 21 November 1988. The integration fee is set at PhP 250,000 (about US$6,000 at an exchange rate of US$1 is to PhP42 then) payable within three years for the principal applicant or head of the family or PhP200,000 in a single payment. The spouse pays a PhP50,000 fee, and each legitimate child below 18 pays PhP25,000.[3] More than 16,000 illegal immigrants have applied for amnesty, generating close to PhP2 billion in integration fees for the government (Arquiza 1997). In June 2001, Republic Act 9139 was signed into law. It allowed the acquisition of citizenship by administrative proceedings rather than judicial means for non-Filipino citizens who were born and residing in the Philippines, subject to certain requirements dictated by national security and interest.

Any amnesty programme, as experiences of other countries have shown, will work only if the Immigration tightens its controls on the entry of immigrants and strictly enforces the rules against overstaying foreigners after the amnesty period. Unfortunately, R.A. 7919 became an excuse to open the doors wider to corruption and the influx of illegal immigrants. Many immigrants who came to the Philippines after 1992 were able to avail themselves of the legalization law through various underhanded means: by bribing immigration officials and employees to issue them fake immigration stamps or to have their records from the Bureau of Immigration pulled out to obliterate proof of when they entered the country. Others who did not avail of R.A.7919 were still able to stay on by producing fake birth certificates or fake Filipino citizenship papers. Sad to say, some of these applicants were even assisted by officers of some local Chinese organizations who helped process a large number of these fake papers or attest to their entry before 1992. Money certainly exchanged hands in this scheme (Arquiza 1996).

The biggest drawback in this scam is that the papers of all applicants, whether legitimate or not, have now become open to question. Because of the large number of defective applications, even those that are in order are now tainted with suspicion, making the legitimate immigrant residents as vulnerable as the illegal residents. This defeats the purpose of the amnesty programme. When the alien legalization programme ended, immigrants reverted to the old practice of extending their visas to allow them to overstay, even if they were aware that this was in violation of the law.

Other immigrants applied for permanent residency through the special investor's visa (SIRV) or retirement visa. A non-Filipino citizen is supposed to invest at least US$75,000 to obtain an SIRV and US$50,000 to obtain a retirement visa. But, again, because of corruption, permanent residency has been obtained even in the absence of any actual investment. The investment is, at best, 'on paper only'. There are several ways this can be done:

- The amount 'invested' is supposedly used to buy a condominium unit. Sometimes, the unit is truly owned by the investor but sometimes, the title is given back to the real owner or worse, sold to the next applicant after the residency is obtained.
- In some instances, applicants get a bank certificate stating that they have sizable deposits, which, in reality they do not have. Or else, the applicant borrows money with interest, puts it into the bank as his own and then returns the amount after the residency is obtained. In other cases, relatives remit the amount needed and get back the money, with interest, after the residency is obtained.
- This also applies to stocks. An applicant gets a broker to issue the stocks in his name and then gives back the certificate to the broker or owner, after paying a certain fee and after the residency is obtained. The stocks sometimes are reissued to a new applicant.

Problems created by Chinese immigrants and/or illegal immigrants

The above legislation shows that even in a developing country like the Philippines, which is much less developed than the sending country, China, immigration problems exist and the government has made several attempts to try to legalize the status of the illegal immigrants who have overstayed in the country through time. The illegal or undocumented status of the *xinqiao* makes them vulnerable to corrupt Immigration agents who make the immigrants pay to prevent them from being deported. In addition to problems of extortion and corruption, the presence or the influx of new Chinese immigrants has brought about problems and complications to the

Tsinoy community and to Philippine society. Most of these problems are often blared in media headlines.

In March 1997, former Senator Anna Dominique 'Nikki' Coseteng revealed through a privilege speech at the Senate the existence of a syndicate of Bureau of Immigration (BI) personnel engaged in human smuggling. 'For a fee,' Coseteng said, 'Chinese or Indian nationals are allowed to slip into the country despite the lack of proper documents'. She says undocumented immigrants usually paid PhP120,000 per person to be allowed in and a BI intelligence consultant quoted a figure of PhP200,000. Other insiders from the Tsinoy community and travel agencies said undocumented immigrants were willing to pay as much as PhP250,000 to PhP300,000 each. The extent of corruption is an open secret and these illegal immigrants become permanently vulnerable to extortion. On the Chinese side, particularly the Chinese Embassy's official position – all these irregularities in the entry and residency of Chinese nationals would not be possible without the connivance of corrupt immigration officials and employees who allow immigrants to stay even if they are aware that the residency has been obtained fraudulently (Lacson 1996).

The Philippines has recently become a favourite destination as a transit point for migrants who use the South Pacific and Latin American countries as transit points to the United States. Nauru is a popular destination and on several occasions, transit passengers were arrested at the Ninoy Aquino International Airport due to fake documents.[4] Quite a number of these migrants are Chinese who themselves have been victimized by illegal recruiters in their country. Some of these Chinese hock everything they own to try to find an entry to a developed country. Fresh in our mind were the deaths of Fuzhou peasants inside a container van bound for London and new Chinese immigrants who were caught in freezing high tide while picking up cockles in the English coast. Stories such as these abound so much so that they became fodder for literary novels and short stories.[5] Many immigrants, however, who used the official route to enter these developed countries, are actually not the impoverished people who wanted to find better opportunities abroad. Some of them are sons and daughters of Chinese officials who want to take the opportunity to build themselves another nest while they are still in power. As mentioned later, a large number of them often enter a country as students or as tourists and later just stay on as entrepreneurs or employees (Cheng 2002: 161; Chin 2002: 244-45; Nyíri 2002: 327).

So disturbing has the surge in illegal Chinese migration been that the Bureau of Immigration and Deportation conducts periodic 'raids,' euphemistically called 'inspection sorties,' into places where Chinese nationals are known to be engaged in business.6 The Retail Trade Law bans foreigners from retail business, the occupation of most of the overstaying Chinese. The presence of the new immigrants and the problem of the big number of overstaying Chinese are conducive not just to corruption but to legalised preying on the immigrants. Many immigrants insist that the Bureau of Immigration remains among the most corrupt government agencies. Raids conducted by the immigration agents on immigrant communities have gained an infamy: immigrants – especially the Chinese and Indians – are well aware of the money that immigration agents raise from immigrants they have rounded up for allegedly staying illegally in the country and/or engaging in retail trade. In fact, shopping at the malls in or near Chinatown has become hazardous for any Chinese-looking individual, whether Filipino citizen or not, because the infamous 'raids' are often conducted by the immigration agents in the most popular shopping areas operated by the Chinese in Manila (Bordadora 2000).

The manner in which the raids are conducted and their aftermaths have caused great concern not just among the *xinqiao*, but also among the Tsinoys themselves. The raids are a gross violation of the human rights of the people arrested, especially since many are innocent and are put in jail for several months until they can prove themselves innocent of the charges. Immigration agents, assisted by the police, pick up anybody who looks Chinese. Even shoppers, minors, students playing computer games in the mall after classes and innocent bystanders were rounded up. A newly married couple on a honeymoon trip to the Philippines did last minute shopping and missed their flights when they were detained after one of the raids. 'These people are treated worse than convicted criminals when all that they did was to make the mistake of choosing the Philippines as their destination,' complained some of the local organizations. These are the oft-told stories that appear in the Chinese newspapers whenever a crackdown on illegal immigrants occurs. What is puzzling is that the frequency of the raids and the arrests do not seem to be a deterrent to these new immigrants, nor a strong enough reason for them to give up and return to their homes in China, as evidenced by their continued presence in the country. In fact, the frequency of crackdowns against illegal immigrants has even reached a point wherein those arrested consider their arrest as an 'investment'. In the 2002 forum on '*Xinqiao*' mentioned earlier, some participants revealed that they don't fear arrest as it gives them a chance to befriend the immigration official who arrested them, and after paying a substantial amount (PhP100,000 to PhP200,000) that agent becomes a 'friend' of the illegal immigrant and a permanent contact when-ever things go wrong again or if rearrested (Casas 1995).

Tourists, students, and investors who illegally stay in the Philippines and/or illegally engage in some work, like retail trading, without work permits, are not the worst problem. A major problem caused by corrupt BI agents is allowing members of Chinese criminal syndicates to enter the country. Whenever China, Taiwan, or Hong Kong crackdown on criminal syndicates or triads, these organizations find their way to the Philippines, and even the Chinese press cite the Philippines as a safe haven for Chinese who are wanted criminals in their country (Casas 1995).

A report submitted by the non-government organization Kaisa Para Sa Kaunlaran to the Chinese government in 2002, and then again in 2003, through the Chinese Embassy and the Overseas Chinese Affairs Director, respectively, detailed the extent of damage done by the illegal drugs trafficking ran by PRC nationals. Included in the reports were facts such as that 100 per cent of laboratories manufacturing illegal drugs raided by the Philippine Drugs Enforcement Agency were owned and ran by Chinese nationals. Of the cases filed in court, involving drug hauls of a hundred kilos and above, close to 90 per cent involved Chinese nationals. Worse is the alarmist report compiled by the office of the National Intelligence Coordinating Agency and submitted to Congress and later distributed to selected organizations. The title of the report was 'China's Weaponless War'. Its main thesis was that the illegal drugs trade proliferating worldwide is a deliberate ploy by China to undermine other countries. The contents of the report were garnered mainly from the Internet. Discerning people would recognize the biased sources, but many are convinced by such information because it is a fact that the menace of illegal drugs in the Philippines does involve mostly Chinese nationals, from the mainland principally but also from Hong Kong and Taiwan. The Chinese book *Drugs Nest* (Qiu 2004: 75–76), which describes the notorious network of China's drugs trafficking (from Asia to America) mentions links with the Philippines, too. Headlines in Philippine newspapers often state that those arrested in one illegal drug bust after another are Chinese nationals. Many do not discriminate between ethnic Chinese and newcomers, labelling them all as Chinese (Botial and Laude 2004; Adraneta and Mendez 2004; Alquitran 2004).

The worst incident was in 2001 when seven Chinese nationals were arrested and charged in court for the kidnapping of 29-year-old Jacky Rowena Tiu of San Fernando, La Union, a province more than 300 km north of Manila. Both the Tsinoy community and Philippine society were very much alarmed and shocked by the kidnapping. The Tsinoy community, especially, was enraged by the fact that it was a Chinese gang that preyed on a Tsinoy victim. 'Isn't it bad enough that the Tsinoys are already so much traumatized by their vulnerability to kidnapping by Filipinos, and now to have Chinese preying on them too?' the Tsinoys asked. Some even feared that from illegal drugs the Chinese syndicates might have also shifted to kidnapping. Fortunately, the first attempt was foiled because the criminals were later caught with the PhP10 million (US$ 210,000) ransom (Bagares 2001b).[7]

The present position enjoyed by the Tsinoy community from the Filipinos, one of respect and admiration, often tinged with envy, is a hard fought battle that took decades and years. With the new immigrants being headlined for illegal activities so often, the image of the Tsinoy community in general is being damaged. Though the mainstream media have started to be more discriminating in their reports, due to efforts of non-government organizations like the Kaisa Para Sa Kaunlaran, in general Filipinos still make little distinction between the local Tsinoys who have been in the country for generations and the newcomers. One bad apple sadly reflects on the whole basket.

The issue has also created unrest, dissension and division in the Tsinoy community, as may be gleaned from the heated arguments that appeared in articles and letters published in the Chinese-language dailies by the *xinqiao* and the *jiuqiao*. If the media does not differentiate between the local born Tsinoys and the new immigrants, it is even less likely that they appreciate that there may indeed be differences between the *xinqiao* and *jiuqiao*. In this matter of involvement by the *xinqiao* in criminal activities, even the *jiuqiao* themselves have resented the havoc created by the *xinqiao* to their image, one of a generally law-abiding community. This image was painstakingly built up through generations, but the unsavory image projected by those *xinqiao* who have been involved in criminal activities unfortunately reflects on the entire group. The Jacky Rowena Tiu kidnap-for-ransom incident mentioned above was a case in point. For weeks, there were bitter recriminations from the local Tsinoy community against a Chinese Embassy official, who, without investigation and validation, mysteriously decided to write a *note verbale* to the Department of Foreign Affairs attesting to the innocence of two of the suspects arrested in the kidnap-for-ransom incident, demanding that they be released immediately. This intervention in a criminal case created uproars in the Tsinoy community, especially since it is common knowledge that the Chinese Embassy has always been reticent and reluctant to intervene on behalf of its nationals even in less notorious cases.[8]

Another big source of conflict between the Tsinoy businessmen and the new immigrants is the unscrupulous and unethical practices the latter are more prone to. 'As long as there is profit to be made, the method of making such profit is not a consideration at all,' these new immigrants say.[9] Many of the *xinqiao* have no compunction in taking shortcuts that lead to greater profits, something which the local Tsinoys are unwilling to do, especially since these shortcuts are mostly illegal. The unscrupulous and unethical practices give rise to unfair competition even with the local Tsinoys. In this case, 'money, or profit, is certainly thicker than blood'. For example, in the shopping malls where a lot of these new immigrants congregate, goods are sold so cheaply (cheaper than what they would have been even back home in China) that people wonder where they could have been sourced. A blouse and skirt set sells for less than US$2, denim pants for US$3, children's clothes for a dollar. The secret was unravelled only when some of the buyers reportedly discovered packets of shabu (methamphetamine hydrochloride or 'the poor man's cocaine') inside the clothes. The buyers conclude that ostensibly, the clothes themselves cost nothing at all because the main goods are the illegal drugs hidden in the shipment of clothes.[10] One graphic example of how unscrupulous the *xinqiao* can be is a newcomer who was driving within one week of his arrival in Manila. When asked how he could do so when he does not know local traffic rules, nor is he familiar with Metro Manila roads, he answered, 'Everything in the Philippines is easy, as long as you have money'. He said he always have ten PhP100 notes in his pocket. When apprehended for a traffic violation, he just gives one note and in most cases, the traffic officer does not even ask to look for a license. For bigger traffic violations, he will just pass on two notes and the same thing happens. In a country where the traffic enforcer receives only between PhP200 to PhP300 in daily wages, the bribe offered is rarely turned down.

The many cases of bribery and corruption – of immigration agents, police officers, traffic enforcers, and other government agencies in the country, like the Bureau of Customs and the post office (where some of the goods are coursed through) – erode the moral fibre of Philippine society. It is easy enough for the Chinese immigrants to be defensive and say it is not the briber's fault but the recipient's fault. But the very fact that the people who offer the bribes are Chinese adds an unsavory racial dimension to the problem. Many Filipinos simply generalize that all Chinese are corrupt and these are bolstered by the stories of bribery mentioned above.

The Chinese nationals' inability to speak Filipino has not deterred them from putting up stalls in the sidewalks of commercial centres and markets, including even the national Rizal Park at the Luneta, to sell various Chinese-made goods and merchandise. They are able to sell their products with the use of calculators, sign language or small writing pads where they write the prices of their wares. Filipino vendors have often complained about the heavy losses they have suffered at the hands of their Chinese competitors. In most areas, Filipino vendors pay a little less than one US dollar daily to sell their wares. The Chinese vendors, on the other hand, give an additional PhP100 (US$2) bribe to the policeman tasked to drive away the vendors. Hence, it is the Filipino vendors who are being driven away or pushed way inside marketplaces while the Chinese vendors can stay out in front. This elicits a lot of resentment from the Filipino vendors. Hence, they do not sympathize with the Chinese who are arrested whenever immigration agents conduct raids and arrest them. For the local Tsinoy and Filipino traders who have legitimate retail businesses of their own, illegal Filipino vendors are bad enough for their business, but now they have to contend with Chinese immigrants too.

In 2004, the Philippine population is 83 million and considering the Philippine land area that is just 300,000 square kilometres the population density nationwide is high. In the National Capital Region, with a population of more than 10 million and a land area of 636 square kilometres, the density is as high as 17,000 people per square kilometre (National Statistics Office 2004). Hence, any new immigration is a burden for Philippine society. Some of the new immigrants the author interviewed revealed that the reason they left China is because their parents want them to learn English so that when they go back to China, they can find more lucrative jobs. Others cite China's one-child policy. A couple who would like to have another child are forced to immigrate, so that when they go back home to China, they not only have two children but they also will have the Overseas Chinese or *huaqiao* status and the privileges this status entails. This was revealed to me by the wife of Zhang Du, one of the suspects in the kidnap-for-ransom case mentioned above. There is no consideration at all that China's one-child policy indicates that the society and government are overburdened by the population. Furthermore, they never even consider why the Philippines should shoulder this tenuous burden that their own country finds problematic. In China, villagers fight one another bitterly and even kill each other for incidents of encroachment on their lands. These are just small villages, which they fiercely defend against encroachment. But how come the new immigrants think nothing of encroaching on another country, which can ill afford to absorb them?

The China factor

2005 marked the centennial of the movement against the Chinese Exclusion Act. Among the activities launched in 1905 to fight the imposition of the onerous law was a boycott of American goods. One hundred years ago, Chinese immigrants fought to be allowed to enter the United States (Alejandrino 2003), a hundred years hence little has changed since the Chinese still exhaust every move possible to get an entry ticket to the great American society and to other parts of the world outside China

The first part of this chapter discussed the situation and the problems created by the new immigrants *vis-à-vis* Philippine society. It is sad that the problems and the situation of the Chinese immigrants have again surfaced and are again causing headaches for some countries, like the Philippines. The second part explores the situation as it relates to China and the Chinese government and people. It should also be worthwhile looking at how China has treated these immigrants, and see how the Chinese, including its officials and its academicians, view the problem. I will emphasize here that this chapter is written from the context of being a social activist who is constrained to raise the problems for public awareness and discussion. It is, in no way meant to malign China or the Chinese government. The realities, as they apply to the situation of the new Chinese immigrants, the Chinese-Filipinos and the Philippine government are raised here to help us understand the problems and seek enlightened solutions for them.

China's attitude toward immigrants in historical times

Historically, we have seen that China did not give much protection to the so-called sons of the yellow emperor scattered all over the world. The Philippine experience is one of the best examples. After the first massacre of 1603 when more than 20,000 Chinese were killed, the Spanish colonizers feared retribution from the Chinese emperor. They sent envoys to explain the tragedy, but the response from the emperor was that these people who migrated overseas were unfilial and disloyal sons who deserved their cruel fate and that the Chinese emperor did not consider their deaths a big loss to the empire (Felix 1969). Five other massacres occurred during the Spanish occupation; the second one in 1639 cost more than 30,000 Chinese lives, but China maintained the same attitude and did not intercede on the victims' behalf.

The oft-repeated sayings like 'orphans of the Pacific' (*haiwai guer*), 'poor countries do not have foreign relations' (*qiongguo wu waijiao*), 'poor people have to stoop down when entering the house of richer neighbors' (*jiren lixia*) explain the humiliation and degradation the early Chinese immigrants went through when they sought refuge and better opportunities abroad. The Chinese emperor hardly ever acted on their behalf in those years of sufferings because China itself, at the time, could not lift its head up before the community of nations. In fact, throughout the 333 years of Spanish occupation of the Philippines, despite repeated attempts by the Chinese immigrants to get consular protection from China, it was not until the very last year of Spanish rule, in 1899, that the Chinese government deemed the Chinese immigrants useful and important enough to be worthy of representation and therefore sent its first consul, Tan Kang, to the Philippines (Tan 1972).

It is only when the Chinese government, in different historical periods, needed the Chinese overseas that they were considered treasures and assets. The Republicans called them the 'mother of revolution,' the new China and Taiwan both exploited them as sources of funds for reconstruction and investments.

China's attitude toward immigrants in modern times

That was the situation in historical times but, to a great extent, the same holds true in modern times. When China needs funds and investments from the Chinese overseas, then they call them 'treasures' and 'assets' and makes propaganda overtures and enticements to attract them to help China. But when things go wrong in the Chinese communities overseas, the government could not care less because the official view is that these ethnic Chinese are citizens of their countries of residence and that they cannot interfere in the internal affairs of these countries. For example, to the huge disappointment of the Tsinoy community, both China and Taiwan held the same view about non-interference in internal affairs in the last 10 years that a kidnapping problem beset the ethnic Chinese in the Philippines. The Tsinoy community expected China to use its political clout and Taiwan its economic clout to intercede on their behalf when they became most vulnerable to kidnapping. It was a rude awakening for them to realize that China would only adhere to the principle of non-interference in the internal affairs of another country (See 1997: 107–121). But, when China needs the investments from the Overseas Chinese, then it ignores the fact that these people are already citizens of another country. It is worse than 'interference in internal affairs' because what China is trying to attract are the resources and assets of another country's citizens. There is a crude and derogatory remark popular among local Chinese that describes this situation more precisely: '*Tua-kiao po diao diao, Sio-kiao bo chap siao*' (in Hokkien). It means that for big-time investors, China can give all the protection needed but for small investors, China could not care less.

While China can make Filipino citizenship of the Tsinoys an excuse for non-interference, they should not do the same for the new Chinese immigrants. The Chinese government hardly lifts a finger for them even now. As we've seen in the earlier section, despite the humiliation and degradation many of the new immigrants are subjected to, the Chinese government has not actively interceded on their behalf nor proactively tried to address the problem. Repeated 'raids' by the immigration agents in congested shopping malls and markets have often resulted in illegal arrests, maltreatment and abuse of the illegal Chinese immigrants, but rarely do we see the Chinese Embassy interceding for them officially. They, in fact, would rather depend on the local Chinese leaders to intercede on behalf of the immigrants who broke Philippine laws in the first place. This creates a dilemma for the Tsinoy leaders, who know that Philippine laws were broken, but still have to exert efforts to intercede on behalf of the culprits. Officials of Chinese organizations have made representations to the Chinese government to suggest that China launches an information campaign in the villages where these illegal immigrants originate and let them realize that they should obtain legal papers to enter and stay in the country. Unless they do, they will not be welcome and are bound to suffer the humiliating and degrading treatment being accorded the Chinese new immigrants in the Philippines, especially if they are undocumented.[11]

The local Chinese organizations in the Philippines are aware that the Fujian government has even imposed jail terms and fines of up to RMB5,000 for illegal emigrants caught in or outside China and that the security bureaus of five provinces have been ordered to tighten border controls. James K. Chin wrote that as of early 1992, the Overseas Chinese Affairs Office under the State Council, the Ministry of Foreign Affairs, the Ministry of Public Security, the Ministry of Foreign Trade and Economic Cooperation and the Ministry of Labour drafted jointly a document on illegal emigration. The Police Departments of five provinces, Fujian, Zhejiang, Guangdong, Yunnan, and Guangxi were ordered to tighten their control over the border regions and coastline (Chin 2002). However, the unabated influx of new immigrants gives rise to speculation of corruption and laxity in the implementation of these rules. More importantly, these organizations have also asked China to undertake very stringent measures to prevent China's wanted criminals from making their way to the Philippines. The shipments of raw materials for illegal drugs manufacture originated mainly from China's coastal areas and there must be widespread corruption also that allows these shipments to slip through China's noose and make their ways to the Philippines.

Why they immigrate

There are two contrasting views about why some Chinese choose to leave their country now. On one hand was the view that as long as an economic imbalance exists, then the Chinese will move from less developed China to the more developed countries in North America, Europe and Australia. Zhuang Guotu, of the Nanyang Research Institute of Xiamen University, echoes this view: 'Large-scale migration is a by-product of the imbalance in the world's economy; it is a phenomenon in social development that cannot be prevented'. He added that the Chinese government does not need to vigorously eliminate and can in no way prevent the trend of out-migration. He recommended that the Chinese government should not support or encourage illegal migration, but it does not need to look at the problem as a serious one, nor does it need to address the problem too assiduously (Zhuang 1997: 1–6).

Zhu Huiling of the China Overseas Exchange Association, in writing about the 'Push and Pull factors in twenty-first century Chinese migration' believes the same thing: 'China will push more people abroad due to the differences between China and the developed countries socially and economically'. Both papers emphasized that compared to the trends of world migration only a very small percentage of the Chinese population goes abroad. And of the new immigrants, 85 per cent go to developed countries and most are educated professionals and technicians. Only 15 per cent go to developing countries. Zhu believes that the migration of the Chinese intellectuals fill up a vacuum to replace the aging intellectual class in the US (Zhu 2002: 28-34). Of the choice of destinations – North America is the favourite, followed by Australia and West Europe, then South-east Asia. Latin America and the Pacific islands countries often act as transit points to the United States or other developed countries. Zhuang Guotu also reported that 60 per cent of the immigrants, or 400,000 out of the 600,000, are students, most of whom have received higher education. The illegal immigrants number about 200,000 and these are the ones who have lower educational levels. 'The *Xinqiao* (including those from Hong Kong, Macau and Taiwan) belongs to China's intellectual class. The 'quality' of these new immigrants is certainly much higher than the old immigrants of the 1940s'. (Zhuang 1997: 6).

While it is easy to say that most (supposedly as high as 60 per cent) of the immigrants who left China are from the intellectual class or are students in pursuit of higher degrees, many of the recent studies on migration to developed countries also debunk this theory. 'As Chinese business in Eastern Europe picked up, students increasingly turned to trading as soon as they arrived and often abandoned their studies or had no intention to study at all,' he adds. (Nyíri 2002: 327).

The opposing view – that Chinese immigration in fact often moves from the more developed to the less developed – is borne out by the Philippine situation. Among the reasons cited by the immigrants to the Philippines include the view that it is easier to get a livelihood or earn money there. An article in the leading Philippine newspaper, *Philippine Daily Inquirer*, says it more succinctly:

> Why are they abandoning their own green pastures in favor of a place whose economic development is nowhere near that of their homeland? There must be strong reasons for making that sacrifice. They probably believe there are better business opportunities here than in their homeland. Their optimism about future economic prosperity remains strong in spite of the kidnappings, inadequate public infrastructure, corrupt government officials and all the problems of governance that many Filipinos have cited as excuses for leaving the country for supposedly greener pastures elsewhere in the world. ... They probably believe the expected rewards from that move will more than compensate for the sacrifices they have to make in living and working in a society with a social and political culture totally different from theirs. (Palabrica 2002)

A professor at Fudan University in Shanghai, Ge Jianxiong, gives more details about the trends and patterns of Chinese migration. His findings also support the idea that Chinese migration usually involves moves from developed to less developed areas. He observes that

> ... history bears out the fact that immigration moves out from the more densely populated to the sparsely populated areas and from the economically more developed areas to less developed areas and not the other way around. (Ge 1997: 131)

We should recall that even the Europeans who moved to the US in the seventeenth to eighteenth centuries moved from more developed areas to try to seek new opportunities in the undeveloped areas of the Americas. In modern times, this view – that it is not really lesser development that drives the immigrants out of China – is reinforced by people who write about Chinese migration to the U.S. (Chin 1999)

The latter view also holds true for the children of corrupt officials in China who need to siphon off money abroad and put it into a nest egg where it can be safe from the vagaries of political instability and changes in China. Somehow, the Chinese officials themselves do not believe that China's reform and liberalization will last or outlast them. While they still enjoy power, they decide to do something about pulling strings to put their children abroad as their safety nets for the future. They follow the dictum, 'Make use of your power while you are still in position'. Hence, these immigrants are not poor peasants seeking better opportunities abroad. The local population in the US, Canada and Australia are often shocked at the profligacy of these young, spoiled, immigrants born with rich, powerful parents providing for them. Wherever these people migrate to real estate prices rise and creates another kind of controversy and resentment among the locals (Beech 2002; Qiu 2004). This phenomenon is true even in developing countries like Burma. Bertil Lintner writes: 'The presence of almost unlimited amounts of drugs money, which have to be laundered, has pushed up prices of real estate beyond the means of most ordinary Burmese. Not surprisingly, this new wave of Chinese migration has re-ignited old anti-Chinese sentiments among Burmese, feelings reflected in cartoons and short stories in local Mandalay publications'. (Lintner: 2002)

To bolster the argument that it is not necessarily true that people move from poorer to richer countries, one can look at the case of the Chinese who went back to serve China after the war. In the early post-liberation days of the new China, especially in the early 1950s, the Philippines was far ahead of China in development, but many of the Chinese there and in other parts of South-east Asia in fact reversed the migration by giving up their more comfortable lives to go back to help their native country (Wang 1995: 12–30; Zhou 1999). The dedication and commitment of the Chinese people to their country and their trust and confidence in their leaders at that time led them to contribute and make sacrifices for China, a phenomenon that is sorely lacking today.

CONCLUSION

The problem of illegal immigrants has existed since colonial times. During the Spanish occupation, the number of Chinese was restricted to 6,000, but at any one time, the number of Chinese often reaches ten times that. During the American regime, the American Exclusion Act of 1902 was extended to its territories. Hence, Chinese immigrants were restricted only to teachers, students, priests, tourists and merchants or sons of merchants. The Chinese still managed to come into the country by using 'paper names', applying as sons of merchants already there even if not related. To this day, the Chinese can overstay with impunity because of corrupt immigration agents and a sorely anachronistic and unreasonable immigration law. This also gives the illegal Chinese immigrants a window of opportunity to stay on in this country and gives China a convenient excuse to turn a blind eye to what is happening. While it is a convenient excuse to blame the corrupt immigration officials for the state of affairs *vis-à-vis* illegal immigrants, China and the Chinese immigrants must also bear responsibility for the resurrection of old problems brought about by these immigrants. These problems that existed centuries ago were addressed and resolved before, but with the influx of new migrants, the problems have since recurred in new forms and dimensions.

As far as China is concerned, it is also an unhealthy development to just gloss over, or in fact, entirely disregard the adverse impact of the new immigrants on developing countries. While it is true that, statistically, only a small percentage of the population leaves China, the problem is not just a matter of how big or small they are in absolute numbers. It is unfair, especially for developing countries, to continue to absorb the burden of new immigrants and conclude that the Chinese government does not need to address the problem zealously. Likewise, it is also unreasonable to compare the problems posed by the *xinqiao* with those of the *jiuqiao* – the times are different, the nature of immigration and immigrants are different, the motivating factors are different. There is no comparison at all – between the *jiuqiao* who never had a choice and the *xinqiao* who have more choices but still opt to leave their country – just as there is no comparison between the new China and the old China. Who would have imagined that the same problems brought about by China's abject poverty and backwardness would again arise as byproducts of Chinas modernity and development?

This is not to say that all new immigrants are problematic. A majority is low-key, law-abiding and hard-working. Most are proprietors of small business enterprises. Others are employed in various tasks where Chinese language ability is a requirement. The Tsinoy community depends on them as teachers, workers in the Chinese-language press and secretaries in Chinese associations. But because of the illegal status of their residency, they pose problems, since by the very nature of their illegal stay, they become vulnerable to extortion and illegal activities. It is a problem that the Chinese immigrants, the Tsinoy community and the Chinese government must address so that a viable solution can be found.

Zhou Enlai said in late 1956: 'In our country, the industrialists and the traders have to be law-obedient. Overseas, they also have to obey other countries' laws. This is very important, especially for the citizens of new China. Our every word and action should be that of a model citizen, to be worthy of being children of the new China'.[12] In a related manner he said in 1959: 'Earning money must be governed by principles, we should not covet wealth obtained illegally'.[13] This exhortation was true 50 years ago, and this should be applied even more stringently now that China is more prosperous and developed. In this era of globalization, it behoves the Chinese government to take responsibility for its citizens who migrate overseas. They give face to the new China just as the early, impoverished immigrants gave face to the old China. Stringent measures should be taken by China to prevent the lawbreakers and those with a criminal background from leaving the country and sowing havoc in other shores. The task is of some urgency especially as these illegal immigrants adversely affect not just China's relations with these new receiving countries but also the image of the ethnic Chinese who have lived there for generations and have worked hard to build a positive image of good and responsible citizenship.

NOTES

1. Overseas Chinese history studies (*Huaqiao huaren lishi yanjiu*) is a regular journal of the Overseas Chinese History Research Institute under the All-China Federation of Returned Overseas Chinese (*Qiaolian*). It usually has an article or two on the phenomenon of new Chinese immigrants.

1. *Tulay* (Monthly Chinese-Filipino Newsdigest) (1988) 'CID starts legalization', vol. 1, no. 3, p. 1.

2. *Tulay* (Monthly Chinese-Filipino Digest) (1995) 'R.A. 7919 to legalize aliens' status', 6 March.

3. *Manila Times* (2003) 'Airport immigration officials foil attempt to smuggle Chinese', 3 October; *Philippine Daily Inquirer* (2000) 'RP a transit point for Nauru-bound Sinos', 20 June.

4. There have been a number of books, novels, short stories and essays detailing this phenomenon of illegal migration and the tales of hardships these people go through (Cao 1995; Liu 1996; McCarthy 2000).

5. *Manila Times* (2003) 'Immigration agents caught 430 illegal aliens this year', 23 July; *Manila Times* (2003) '282 illegal aliens arrested; 244 deported', 23 April.

6. *Tulay* Fortnightly Chinese-Filipino Digest (2002) 'GMA assures Jacky Tiu of government assistance', vol. 14, no. 17, 5 February.

7. *Chinese Commercial News* (2001), pp. 24–26; pp. 28–29 December; *Chinese Commercial News* (2002), 9 January; *Sino-Fil Daily* (2001), 28 December; *World News* (2001), 28 December; *World News* (2002), 2 January.

8. Discussion forum (2002) on the problems of new immigrants convened by Kaisa Para Sa Kaunlaran, 24 November, 2002 at the Kaisa office in Intramuros, Manila, attended by new immigrants and members of the organization.

9. In the course of revising this paper, I interviewed the officers of the Association of Stall Owners of the 168 Mall (July 8, 2006) who explained that their goods are cheap because they import them directly from factories in China. They denied that shabu was ever found among the goods that they sell. They, however, admitted that the report of the buyers finding shabu hidden in the clothes purchased had happened in another mall.

10. There have been a number of meetings convened by the Federation of Filipino-Chinese Chambers of Commerce, the Federation of Filipino-Chinese Associations, Amity Club and Kaisa Para Sa Kaunlaran among others, with the Chinese ambassador and visiting leaders of the Chinese government to discuss government policies on the new Chinese immigrants and stringent measures that can be adopted to curtail drugs trafficking and manufacturing by these Chinese nationals. But the problems continue unabated.

11. Zhou Enlai's speech at the welcoming party in Burma on 18 December 1956 and at a meeting with Indonesia's foreign minister on 9 October 1959 (Government of the People's Republic of China, undated pamphlet).

12. Ibid.

REFERENCES

Adraneta, Katherine and Christina Mendez (2004) 'QC shabu lab falls'. *Philippine Star*, 2 March.

Alejandrino, Clark L. (2003) *A History of the 1902 Chinese Exclusion Act: American Colonial Transmission and Deterioration of Filipino-Chinese Relations*. Manila: Kaisa Para Sa Kaunlaran, Inc.

Alquitran, Non (2004) 'Drug busters bare most wanted'. *Philippine Star*, 24 February.

Arquiza, Rey (1996) 'Gov't alerted on fake documents of illegals from mainland China'. *Philippine Star*, 11 August.

—— (1997) 'Amnesty program ends: task force to go after illegal aliens'. *Philippine Star*, 1 July.

Bagares, Romel (2001a) 'Chinese kidnappers have only just begun'. *Philippine Star*, 24 December.

—— (2001b) 'Kidnappers from China now operating in RP'. *Philippine Star*, 23 December.

Beech, Hannah (2002) '"Smuggler's Blues"'. On Lai Changxing, China's Most Wanted'. *Time Magazine*, 14 October, vol. 160, no. 14, pp. 34–40.

Bordadora, Norman (2000) 'Envoy says Manila cops arrested wrong Chinese: they're not intruders, they're shoppers'. *Philippine Daily Inquirer*, 20 February.

Botial, Jerry and Pete Laude (2004) 'Cops seize P2M shabu in buy bust'. *Philippine Star*, 17 February.

Cao, Guilin (ed.) (1995) *Touduke* [Stowaway]. Beijing: Xiandai chubanshe.

Casas, Gemma (1995) 'Syndicate sabotages alien amnesty'. *Today*, 12 September.

—— (1995) 'RP remains favorite hub of alien criminals'. *Today*, 8 October.

Cheng, Xi (2002) 'Non-remaining and non-returning: the mainland Chinese students in Japan and Europe since the 1970s'. In Pál Nyírí and Igor Saveliev (eds), *Globalizing Chinese Migration: Trends in Europe and in Asia* (Research in migration and ethnic relations series). Aldershot, England: Ashgate Publishing Ltd., pp. 158–172.

Chin, James K. (2002) 'Gold from the lands afar: new Fujianese emigration revisited'. In Pál Nyírí and Igor Saveliev (eds), *Globalizing Chinese Migration: Trends in Europe and in Asia* (Research in migration and ethnic relations series). Aldershot: Ashgate Publishing Ltd., pp. 242–253.

Chin, Ko-lin (1999) *Smuggled Chinese: Clandestine Immigration to the United States*. Philadelphia: Temple University Press.

Depasupil, William (2003) 'BI deports 12 Chinese traders', *Manila Times*. 23 December.

Felix, Alfonso (ed.) (1969) *The Chinese in the Philippines, 1570–1770*, vol. 1. Manila: Historical Conservation Society.

Fernandez, Eduardo F. and Oscar A. Domingo (1970) *Philippine Immigration Law and Procedure*. Mandaluyong: SMA Printing Corporation.

Ge, Jianxiong (ed) (1997) *Zhongguo yiminshi* [History of Chinese migration], six volumes. Fuzhou: Fujian renmin chubanshe.

Go, Bon Juan (2002) 'Old and new migrants from China: comparative dimensions'. In Pal Nyírí and Igor Savaliev (eds), *Globalizing Chinese Migration: Trends in Europe and in Asia* (Research in migration and ethnic relations series). Aldershot, England: Ashgate Publishing Ltd., pp. 309–319.

Government of the People's Republic of China (undated pamphlet) *Speeches of Zhou Enlai*.

Lacson, Liza (1996) 'BI officials in cahoots with human smuggling gang—solon'. *Philippine Star*, 21 December.

Lintner, Bertil (2002) 'Illegal aliens smuggling to and through Southeast Asia's Golden Triangle'. In Pál Nyírí and Igor Savaliev (eds), *Globalizing Chinese Migration: Trends in Europe and Asia* (Research in migration and ethnic relations series). Aldershot: Ashgate Publishing Ltd., pp. 108-119.

Liu, Ningrong (1996) *Zhongguo renshechao* [Wave of Chinese snakeheads]. Xianggang: Jiushi niandai zazhi she.

Mah, Karen and Jane Moorse (2000) 'Chinese illegal aliens: what motivates them'. *Philippine Star*, 28 October, pp. 8-9.

McCarthy, Terry (2000) 'Out of China – Journey to the west'. *Time Magazine*, Vol. 155, No. 18, 8 May, pp. 20–25.

National Statistics Office, Republic of the Philippines (2004) 'Census and Statistics Report 2004'. URL: http://www.census.gov.ph (accessed 21 April 2006).

Nyírí, Pál (2002) 'Afterword'. In Pál Nyírí and Igor Savaliev (eds), *Globalizing Chinese Migration: Trends in Europe and Asia* (Research in migration and ethnic relations series). Aldershot: Ashgate Publishing Ltd., pp. 320–337.

Palabrica, Raul (2002) 'Puzzling inward migration'. *Philippine Daily Inquirer*, 11 August.

Qiu, Ping (2004) *Duxiao – Fujian guanchang Da Kuilan* [Druglord: Fujian official Da Kuilan]. Hong Kong: Xiafei'er chuban youxian gongsi.

See, Teresita Ang (1997) 'Chinese in the Philippines: Changing views and perceptions'. In Teresita Ang See (ed.), *Chinese in the Philippines – Problems and Perspectives*, vol. 1. Manila: Kaisa Para Sa Kaunlaran, Inc., pp. 107–121.

—— (2000) 'Preying on aliens'. *Tulay Fortnightly* (Chinese-Filipino Digest), vol. 12, no. 20, pp. 8–9.

Son, Johanna (1989) 'Senate urges scuttling of alien legalization program'. *The Manila Chronicle*, 24 November.

Tan, Antonio S. (1972) *The Chinese in the Philippines, 1898–1935: A Study of Their National Awakening*. Quezon City, Philippines: R.P. Garcia Publishing Company, Inc.

Wang, Gungwu (1995) 'Southeast Asian Chinese and the Development of China'. In Leo Suryadinata (ed.), *Southeast Asian Chinese and China: The Politico-Economic Dimension*. Singapore: Times Academic Press, pp. 12–30.

—— (2001) *Don't Leave Home: Migration and the Chinese.* Singapore: Times Academic Press.

Zhou, Nanjing (ed.), (1999) *Huaqiao huaren baikequanshu* [Encyclopedia of Chinese overseas]. 9 vols. Beijing: Zhongguo huaqiao chubanshe.

Zhu, Huiling (2002) '21 shiji shangbanye fada guojia huaqiao huaren shehui de fazhan taishi' [The development of the Overseas Chinese communities in developed countries in the first half of the twenty-first century]. *Huaqiao huaren lishi yanjiu* [Overseas Chinese history studies], no. 2, pp. 28–34.

Zhuang, Guotu (1997) 'Dui jin 20 nian lai huaren guoji yimin huodong de jidian sikao [Some reflections on international Chinese migration during the last 20 years], *Huaqiao huaren lishi yanjiu* [Overseas Chinese history studies], no. 2, pp. 1–6.

PART III

China's Rise as a Global Power and Transnational Issues

Chapter 8

Liuxue and *Yimin:*
From Study to Migranthood

Wang Gungwu

Let me begin with two statements. The first is that Chinese students are not migrants. The second, less categorical than the first, is that some students do want to become migrants and this seems to be happening today. For the past five decades, hundreds of thousands of Chinese students from Mainland China, Taiwan, Hong Kong, Macau as well as scores of overseas communities, have been leaving home for studies abroad. They see knowledge as being increasingly global and are now prepared to go almost anywhere to learn what they want and get the qualifications they need. When many do not return home but seek to work in the countries where they received their further training and education, their decisions raise questions about whether this tide of young people marks a distinct form of migration. Would they lead to migratory results? These are not matters that can be decided in a few years. But the possibility that they amount to 'delayed' or 'future' migration, or some other form of migration altogether, is there, and this is a subject that deserves attention.

We already know that students from some countries in Asia and Africa go to and ultimately settle down in North America, Australasia as well as the European states that had colonial empires. For some time, this has also been a European phenomenon. Some European students who have gone to study in the United States and Australia have stayed on, and their decisions about settling abroad could provide comparative material for the study of the Chinese and other Asians following similar routes.[1] Furthermore, when students ultimately become migrants, questions about the complex nature of modern migration itself arise. Such questions help us not only to understand what certain Chinese are doing in foreign places, but also to refine our concepts of migration.

The chapter will be divided into two parts. The first will deal with the four key words in the title: *liuxue*, *yimin*, study and migranthood. The second will examine the three major trends that have led many more young Chinese to study abroad after the end of the Second World War.

Let me begin with the four key words. *Liuxue* is the common word used for studying abroad. I thought that it was an ancient Chinese word related to the idea of *qujing*, a word that described Chinese Buddhist monks who went by sea or land to India to learn about their faith from the original source. *Qujing* meant 'bringing back the sutras'.[2] The term underlined the sacred duty of devoted monks who risked their lives to travel thousands of miles for their faith. I was, therefore, surprised to learn that *liuxue* was never the word used for these Chinese monks, but that it was originally coined by the Japanese, *ryugaku*. It was first used to describe young Japanese who accompanied an embassy to China in the year 775 and stayed on to study there. The phrase used was *ryugaku jugyo* (*jugyo* or *shouye* meant to receive instruction) and the implication was that the student remained for a while to study with his teacher.[3]

It is interesting that *liuxue* did not arise from the experiences of Chinese monks, the most famous being Faxian, Songyun, Xuanzang and Yijing, who travelled to India and Pakistan, and also to Sri Lanka, Nepal, Bangladesh and Buddhist lands of the Malay archipelago. They were away for long periods, sometimes more than 20 years, but the records never revealed what they learnt or who they studied with, only which sacred texts they brought home (Faxian and Songyun 1869; Faxian 1923; Xuanzang 1904).

In modern times, the Japanese used the term *ryugaku* for the students who went to the West the way their predecessors had gone to China from time to time since the Tang dynasty.[4] It was therefore appropriate to use the same term, *liuxue* in Chinese, to apply to the hundreds of Chinese students who set forth to study Western Learning, either directly in the West or indirectly in Japan. And, indeed, the numbers who went to Japan at the turn of the twentieth century were very large, larger than those who went to Europe and North America put together.[5] Thus the *liuxue* phenomenon had nothing to do with migration. All who went to *qujing* and *ryugaku* or *liuxue* did what they had to do and brought what they learnt back home.

Yimin, the second word, is now accepted as the Chinese word for migration and migrant. It is an ancient word, but it had only been used to describe officially approved movements of people from one area to another, normally for economic or strategic reasons, when whole villages and communities were forced to move for their own good or for the good of the country.[6] There simply was no concept of voluntary migration of individuals or their families in East Asia. Thus, for China, both *yimin* and *liuxue* (or *ryugaku*) are old terms that have been adopted to describe contemporary realities of the past century.

The third word 'study' is the simplest. It is equated here with *liuxue* (remaining to learn) with the emphasis on the idea of *liu*, 'remaining'. It applies to individual students who stay abroad for some time to receive the fullest possible instruction and master a particular branch of knowledge or acquire a superior profession. It does not apply to those who make brief visits to institutions of higher learning to take short courses or complete their research projects, or to those who do short stints of teaching. Nor would it normally include those sent officially on major missions to bring home modern scientific truths comparable to the Law or dharma. Most of these students are young, but there may also be older ones, particularly postgraduate students acquiring new qualifications or refining and advancing the knowledge they already have. In most cases, this kind of 'remaining' would mean living five or more years away from home, with some having their wives and children join them.[7]

The fourth word 'migranthood' needs more explanation. It is especially significant for this chapter and this should become clear later. The simple definition of migranthood is 'the condition or quality of a migrant'. The word 'migrant' has historically applied to cheap and unskilled labour and used to describe their migratory patterns. Today, the word broadly covers everyone who leaves home without intending to return, thus becoming the usual targets of every country's immigration policy, departments and officials. When students stay on after completing their studies and change their legal status to become immigrants, citizens or permanent residents, it does not mean they have become migrants. Instead, they are using their qualifications as professionals and masters of their particular disciplines to sustain a migrant-like existence. This is what I call 'migranthood'. It is not necessarily a decision to settle permanently, but to position themselves in the space between that of a student and that of a settled migrant. Within that area, they can identify with many other conditions. For example, they could choose to feel that they are in a state of exile or that of a refugee; or they could also resort to the ancient art of long-term sojourning, or acquire the skills of a modern transnational.[8]

Although originating from different circumstances, exiles, refugees, or sojourners tend to focus on their homes and dream of returning home. Transnationals, on the other hand, put the stress on their freedom to move physically and cross politically defined borders. Migranthood could include elements of all these conditions. But it is more varied and subjective, often reflecting a chosen state of mind that makes the condition appear indeterminate. It does not promise any homecoming, nor does it need to result in any further movement of persons or change of place of residence. It is a migrant-like condition that may never be comfortable, but it may remain stable for long periods of time.

TOWARDS MIGRANTHOOD

There are a few early examples of the phenomenon, but this chapter will focus on more recent changes when long periods of study abroad lead to migranthood. Where the Chinese are concerned, what studying overseas means has itself been changing, and so has the meaning of migrating. Chinese people, however, have had no difficulty in recognizing the reality of the two new phenomena of studying abroad and migrating even before they used the words *liuxue* and *yimin*. The first clear example, in fact, came from ordinary people and was the product of private enterprise. This was when Rong Hong (Yung Wing) and his two friends were taken by their missionary teacher to the United States in 1847 (LaFargue 1987; Qian and Hu 2004; Rong 1909; Shu 1989; Wang Qisheng 1992). It was a path-breaking act that predated by a few years the frenzied rush of thousands of Chinese miners, merchants and labourers to the goldfields of the American West Coast. Those thousands of men had also taken risks as expressions of private enterprise. They certainly did not think of themselves as migrants because most of them only planned to be temporarily away to seek their fortune and eventually return to China.

The tradition of sojourning in South-east Asia dates back at least several centuries.[9] But the only early example of something comparable to studying abroad was that of the few Christian boys from Guangdong who between 1818 and 1843 had gone to the Anglo-Chinese College in Malacca founded by the Scottish missionary Robert Morrison. But theirs was a purely seminary education to enable them to engage in future missionary work in China and was not meant to lead to other career possibilities (Harrison 1979). Once that college was closed in Malacca and its successors established in Macau and Hong Kong, there were no other cases of Chinese going to South-east Asia to study anything for the next century and a half. Only in the last decade have there been examples of large numbers of Chinese students being sent to study in Malaysia and Singapore.

The three boys who went to the United States soon after the Malacca College was closed, and following the opening of the Treaty Ports in China, had wider educational choices. In any case, they were never conscious of the idea of migration. After he graduated from Yale University, Rong Hong was naturalized as an American, returned home to help China's technical and military modernization and also help other Chinese study in the United States. He was always confident about being Chinese even though he married an American, was disappointed in his many efforts to help China, and then lived the rest of his life in the US (Gu 1984; LaFargue 1987).

Chinese migration in Asia had been, of course, a reality for over two thousand years. The Chinese went overland to tribal lands in the south and west and to the Korean peninsula, and a few others went overseas to Japan and the region we now call South-east Asia. Being temporarily away from home was the accepted idea even though some Chinese never went home. This remained true down to the twentieth century. What was exceptional and totally new during the nineteenth century was that a few missionaries had welcomed Chinese to study in their colleges outside of China. There were other exceptional cases. The most famous was one that took place two decades after that of Rong Hong. This was Gu Hongming (Ku Hung-ming) of Kedah (in Malaysia, the state next to Penang), who was sent to school in Scotland when he was only ten years old. He finally returned to British Malaya 13 years later, but did not like what the British were doing and left again. This time, he went to China, reidentified with Chinese tradition with enthusiasm and then spent the rest of his life working there. Thus, four generations after his ancestors left China, he returned and stayed, thus justifying the idea of being a truly long-term sojourner and representing the kind of Chinese who never really left home (Kong 1996).

The *liuxue* phenomenon became official when the Chinese government sent an educational mission to the United States. Between 1872 and 1881, 120 young boys were sent to study, but the experiment was a failure and most of them were brought back without obtaining any qualifications. More successful were the naval engineers and others sent for training to Britain, France and Germany (Wang, Y. C. 1966; Jerome Chen 1979). They were then followed by thousands of more mature students and scholars who went to study in Japan. Japan had just defeated China in a most humiliating way, but it had the chance to become the most influential force in China's modernization. But its ambitions to expand into Chinese territory turned the Chinese against Japan. Instead, America stepped in and, thereafter, more Chinese went to the United States to study even though its immigration policy was degrading and offensive.

Significantly, at a time when Chinese migration was barely possible in the United States, Chinese students were let in, if not always welcomed. That clearly reinforced the difference between *yimin* and *liuxue*. Of course, among the old sojourners (the *lao huaqiao*) who had migrated earlier, some of their very few local-born children were also admitted to universities, but they went into those institutions as of right. The difference was that, while the vast majority of *liuxuesheng* returned to serve China after completing their studies, most of the local-born Chinese would try to join mainstream American society (Kung 1962; Lee 1960; Wong and Chan 1998; Yi 2001).

For most of the twentieth century, many Chinese studied abroad. There was no set pattern. The numbers were uneven, sometimes a mere trickle as with those who went to Britain, France and Germany, and occasionally amounting to a flood as with countries like Japan in the 1900s. The figures were steadier with the United States for which special institutions were created, notably the establishment of Tsinghua College. Much depended also on the conditions in China. The country suffered from civil wars, foreign harassment leading to incremental invasions of Chinese territories and the full-scale Sino-Japanese War from 1937 to 1945. Under those conditions, young Chinese began to develop a new nationalism that ensured that the vast majority were determined to return home to serve China with the education they had received. The question of migranthood was not apparent during the first half of the twentieth century (Chiang 2001; Wang, Yi 1966; Wang, Gungwu 1995).

The situation changed greatly after the end of the Second World War and this has led to a very different situation during recent decades. Before the Second World War, up to 90 per cent of the Chinese overseas, sojourners and settlers, were found in South-east Asia. Almost none of them had gone to study abroad in the countries in which they resided.

Even with the remaining 10 per cent, who had gone elsewhere and among whom many had stayed on to settle down, the majority were labourers and merchants and their descendants. Only a very small fraction of this remainder consisted of Chinese studying abroad, and they did that mostly in the United States. No one would connect these students with the act of migration. But that began to change after the 1950s. Both the West as the receivers of students and China as the sender of its best and brightest have undergone transformations during the past 40 years. The two parallel pressures to study abroad and to migrate have risen to sizeable levels. It should not be surprising if the two should be seen as intermingled in new and unforeseen ways. A survey of the main trends will help us to determine if the two will eventually converge or if recent developments might lead us to redefine the concept of migration itself.

There are three trends leading to greater numbers studying abroad that deserve special attention.

1. The earliest might be described as the colonial and postcolonial strand. This was somewhat overshadowed by the second.
2. This second trend was the product of the Cold War conditions of the 1950s to 1970s.
3. The third trend has become dominant more recently. It is one in which economic determinants linked to globalization are central to its significance.

The first two were politically driven and they have now been superseded by the technological and business trend that has encouraged and enabled more students to turn to migranthood. Although the reasons for studying abroad may have changed, the outcome is similar. For example, some of the Chinese who left home to study abroad for political reasons could also end up staying behind primarily for economic advancement. In other words, the political conditions at home may have improved, but not the economic opportunities. The three trends will be treated separately in order to outline the different routes from study to migranthood.

Colonial students largely from European colonies in South-east Asia, including many Chinese, had been studying in metropolitan training colleges and universities in increasing numbers since before the war. Some may not have seen themselves as studying abroad because, in one sense, they were not abroad but had simply gone as imperial subjects to study in their 'mother' country. In any case, they were all expected to return to serve in the empire, whether it was British, French, Dutch or American, and the colonial Chinese were among those who indeed wanted to do just that.[10] But, in so far as a few did stay abroad to find work and ultimately settle down, these might provide some early examples of a kind of migranthood. But there have not been studies of these early cases for us to compare with.

The picture changed dramatically after the decolonization process began. On the one hand, erstwhile colonials and nationals of newly independent states, who understandably still preferred to study in their former empire's colleges and universities, had become genuine *liuxuesheng*. On the other, political conditions in some of the new states were not always conducive to the products of imperial education. This is noticeable when these graduates were of Chinese descent in South-east Asian states like Indonesia, Malaysia and the Philippines, in the West Indies and in new states like Mauritius and Fiji. Wherever possible, some of these Chinese later returned to the countries where they had received their higher education, notably to Britain, France, the Netherlands and the United States, but also to Canada, Australia and New Zealand (Andressen 1993; Hodgkin 1966; 1972).

For Chinese, this could be described as remigration but, where periods of education had been key factors in the decisions to move, it was really closer to delayed migranthood. There had been a time lapse between study and remigration and these Chinese often remained mobile after the move. A further factor was that, after the 1950s, the position of Chinese overseas was made more precarious by the Communist victory in China and the Cold War in Asia. Among those students from the former colonies were those who could not, or did not wish to, return to China, even more sought to study abroad with a readiness to convert to migrant status. This was made easier by factors that had less to do with post-colonial political sympathy than with the changes in the higher education industry in countries like Britain and Australia and the demand for skilled graduates no matter where they came from (Greenaway and Tuck 1995; Jolley 1997; McNamara and Harris 1997). These changes helped to underline the later importance of economic determinants after the 1980s.

This first trend began as part of a more general phenomenon that affected other students like those from India, Pakistan, Egypt and Palestine, to take some notable examples. For most Chinese students, the changes were primarily the result of post-colonial developments in South-east Asia. But in time the push factor gave way to the pull factor as the Chinese students who continued to study abroad found it more advantageous to remain. But whatever the reason for not going home, the decision to settle initially in the country where they had studied did not automatically make them migrants. Technically, many had to be reclassified from student (or former student) to migrant when they applied to stay and take up employment. And there were often other conditions that had to be fulfilled before they each could obtain an employment permit and then permanent resident status. Legally and administratively, they would have become a migration statistic. But, not being refugees or exiles, or consciously acting as sojourners eager to go home when an opportunity eventually arose, what they actually entered into is a state of migranthood.

Australia provides some notable examples. Over the past decades, several Malaysian associations and smaller groups of Indonesian Chinese consisting of many former students have been organized. Adding to the variety, there were many students among the refugees from the former colonies of French Indo-China states following the Vietnam War. In contrast, there has not been migrant Chinese labour since the turn of the twentieth century. Thus large numbers of the new Chinese today were once students, but who have chosen to stay. They are keenly concerned about what migrant rights there are or ought to be, but not all of them are comfortable to be grouped with all other newcomers as migrants. Their condition could be said to hover between an assertion of ethnicity and distaste for assimilation. But they are resigned to the fact that they are considered as some kind of eventual migrant, one of the manifestations of migranthood. Several have distinguished themselves as scholars who study the Overseas Chinese phenomenon, together with the descendants of earlier settlers who have been challenged by recent developments to search deeply for their roots not only in China but also in the migrant trajectories of their ancestors in Australia itself.[11]

The second strand began as a different wave of studying abroad that was largely the product of war, especially of the Cold War. There was a comparable refugee phenomenon in Europe, but the impact of the Second World War on various groups of Chinese was particularly strong. It had begun with the last years of the civil war in China when many of China's brightest university graduates were sent overseas. When the Chinese Communist Party won that war, some of them chose not to return to China. With the fall of the Nanjing government and the establishment of the People's Republic of China in 1949, large numbers of refugees fled to Hong Kong.

These included scholars and merchants and their families, most of whom were better educated than the usual migrant labour of earlier periods. At the same time, many more similarly well-educated Chinese followed the Nationalist regime to Taiwan. Here the Cold War played its part. As with the Korean students who were welcomed to some of the best American universities following the Korean War, the children of nationalist officials and professionals in Taiwan were also encouraged to study in the United States (Xu 2001).

In this way, throughout the next two decades, the number of young people sent to study abroad increased rapidly. Significantly and unlike in the past, the majority of these students did not return to Taiwan. This was partly because the United States, as the new superpower defending half the world against communist revolutions, was keen to train a new generation of an anti-communist elite. But it was also partly because most Taiwan-born students hated the Chiang Kai-shek regime and many of those born on the mainland had not lived long in Taiwan and did not really feel that Taiwan was their home. Whatever the reason, this gave birth to the idea of a Chinese 'brain drain', something new for any Chinese government (Chen 1996; Xia 1994).

The idea of *liuxuesheng* not wanting to return, the growing number of post-graduates students forming enclaves of Chinese in university and corporate communities and the difficulties of adapting to the American environment thus led to a new genre of Taiwan literature written in Chinese. This was a multi-layered genre that sought to capture a wide range of experiences, but many writings depicted the college-educated Chinese, mostly now from Taiwan, struggling with their nostalgia for a 'China' that had ceased to exist or was about to be transformed altogether. Among the best known were writers like Eileen Chang (Zhang Ailing) who had started her writing career earlier in Hong Kong and Shanghai, Bai Hsien-yung, son of a famous Guomindang general, and Nieh Hua-ling, whose partnership with her husband had created a haven at Iowa University for generations of Chinese writers.[12]

There were others who were born of families who had been in Taiwan for centuries. Chen Juo-hsi (Chen Ruoxi) had the most unusual experiences. She chose to return to the mainland after studying in America and fell victim to the Cultural Revolution. She then returned to the United States, nominally as a migrant or remigrant but, after a few years, decided to return to Taiwan.[13] At each step, her acts were greatly influenced by political concerns that made her indecision more poignant than that of the others. Among other things, she describes the indecision thus:

> Many Overseas Chinese intellectuals share an internalized psychological conflict ... known as the 'Chinese emotional knot' ... and still hold on to a 'resident visitor' mentality. (Chen, Ruoxi 1993)

The best writer among those who scrutinized the lives of the *liuxuesheng* was Yu Li-hua. Almost all her short stories and novels dealt with them and she describes their lives, from the time they decided to stay to make their careers in the USA, with great sensitivity. From the writings of this group of fiction authors, we meet a condition of life that always remained transitional and one that approximates that of migranthood. All these writers wrote from personal experiences reflecting a state that resembles that of the refugee or the exile but also reminds us of earlier concepts like sojourning and can even be described as resembling that of the transnational (Cheng 2003; Yin 2000). Their condition was in no way comparable to that of the much larger numbers of Chinese from Hong Kong, Taiwan and elsewhere who migrated in response to the relaxation of US immigration policy after 1964.

For the two decades of the 1960s and 1970s, Chinese students were also going to North America and Australasia from other parts of the world affected by the Cold War, notably from South-east Asia. Their concerns were less about returning. Although many did go home to their respective adopted countries, many others went abroad to study with a readiness to migrate and make their new homes in the West. When these descendants of earlier Chinese migrants made themselves remigrants, their ability to adapt to Western migrant societies, and particularly for those familiar with European languages, helped to make that adjustment less painful. But even they would experience from time to time the condition of doubt and discomfort about staying or leaving, and wanting to have it both ways. That produced a state of mind similar to the kind of migranthood that the Taiwan Chinese experienced. Of course, for Taiwanese and those from Hong Kong and South-east Asia, communication lines to and from their respective places of origin have been good; thus the condition of migranthood with regular and increasingly effective access to families at home was made tolerable.

Since the early 1980s, even larger new waves of students from Mainland China have gone to the West, mostly to the United States. And I should also mention that the significant numbers of Chinese students of all ages now studying in Malaysia and Singapore are beginning to make an impact among the local Chinese. These student waves make a new story.14 The writings generated by the students so far are more straightforward than those of the Taiwan writers a generation earlier. Those in America are notable for warning the Chinese who are planning to study abroad of the pitfalls or explaining what needs to be done in dealing with a superpower, addressing both the dangers of confrontation as well as of appeasement. There are early signs that some of these students and graduates are contemplating long stays abroad that would lead them to a state of living akin to migranthood and to what their counterparts from Taiwan had experienced. But on the whole it is still too early to tell whether they will feel that way for long. China is not Taiwan or Hong Kong, and even more different from the other states where there are disillusioned Overseas Chinese. What is fascinating is to observe how most of them will have to deal, sooner or later, with the decision to stay or return. As it appears at the moment, the chances are good that many of them would also have to contemplate a condition of migranthood.

Finally, the third trend is the product of economic and technological globalization. The scientific advances and the expansion of the global free market after the end of the Second World War have been spectacular. For those Chinese studying abroad under these changing conditions, references to older ideas about migration may well be inappropriate. The global demand for high-tech skills may not apply to all such students, but the number of Chinese who are responding to that demand is rising exponentially. This has enabled some of these foreign-educated Chinese to free themselves from traditional state boundaries. The movement of skilled and talented people would remind one of the High Middle Ages in Europe. As suggested by Tanaka Akihiko, this means that the world is facing a 'New Middle Ages', during which scholarly elites would share a common civilization and move around as 'wanderers' (Tanaka 2002). I hesitate to predict the end of the nation-state as we know it, especially where China is concerned. But the possibility that the new business and scientific networks would make the idea of migration for the college-educated obsolete is now there. These skilled professionals would move whenever their jobs required them to do so.

I can only speculate about this here. The first two trends have given us glimpses of how difficult it is for students to become migrants. It was never merely a question of legality and acceptance by the indigenous and the earlier settlers. The global search for modern skills is likely to intensify and the supply of Chinese, like that of the Indians, to meet that demand will continue to be high. Two developments are likely. Under new conditions of globalization, the new foreign-educated elites of Chinese descent, especially those from the mainland, may find it easier to see China not as a mere country but as a continental hub in a multipolar world, something they could serve or serve from. If that should gradually become a reality, then migranthood could become an accepted position after completing their higher studies. It would then be a recognized place where the weighty choice between serving China and Chinese communities or serving the world could be made. On the surface, this might appear to be a return to the art of sojourning. The key difference lies in that sojourning always implied a readiness to return to China. Migranthood makes no such commitment. It is both flexible and unpredictable where notions of home and nationality are concerned. The other development is for the new reality to force the rewriting of all hateful immigrations policies. Most of them have an abominable history that began as efforts to demean the Chinese just over a hundred years ago and extended to cover everyone else. The time has come to remove what had first been devised to protect the economically and racially privileged. The example of the student attaining a state of migranthood could be a prelude to a new kind of mobility and personal responsibility. It is not an easy condition to live with but, as it spreads among more of the educated, it could make the punitive attitudes toward migrants unnecessary in the future.

NOTES

[1] Students from Europe and the Mediterranean regions may have agonized about whether to go home or to remain in the United States, but this has not attracted research. In sharp contrast, there is a vast literature about European immigration, settlement, political participation, and assimilation. There were, of course, academics and other professionals who had good careers in the United States and then returned to Eastern Europe and the Middle East to become senior politicians or civil servants. These have been written up, but they are exceptions. An excellent example of one who did not return but was consciously involved in affairs back home in dramatic ways is that of Edward Said with his autobiography *Out of Place: a Memoir* (Said 1999). He did not live to write the later part of his personal story. Had he done so, he would seem to have lived a life that approximated one of migranthood.

[2] *Qujing* was first used in Yang Xuanzhi (d. 555?), *Luoyang qielanji* [Record of the Buddhist monasteries of Luoyang] (a work completed in 530) with reference to the monk Songyun of Dunhuang who had gone to India as Faxian as others had done before him. Their main mission was to bring back more of the original texts of the Buddhist classics. Later, Japanese Buddhists used a similar term, *kyuho* or *qiufa*, that meant 'seeking the Law or dharma' to describe what Xuanzang had done during the

Tang dynasty. In Chinese, *qiufa* is found in another book by Yijing (635–713), *Nanhai jigui neifa zhuan*. This has been recently translated (Lahiri 1986).

3   *Zoku Nihongi* for the sixth year of the Hoki reign-period (755) used the phrase *ryugaku jugyo* for the students who accompanied Japanese embassies to Chang'an, the capital of the Tang empire (Morohashi 1986: vol. 7, 1093).

4   The large number of Japanese students sent to study abroad during the second half of the nineteenth century is recorded in Tezuka (1992) and Koyama (1999).

5   On Chinese students in Japan see Saneto (1970) and Reynolds (1993).

6   The early references to *yimin* in *Zhou Li* [The rites of Zhou] and *Meng Zi* [Mencius] are quoted throughout Chinese history to emphasize the readiness of rulers to move the population about in response to economic and strategic needs. The best known are the words of King Hui of Liang in *Mencius* (1970: 50).

7   The classic example is still that of Xuanzang whose journey and stay lasted over 15 years. The stress is less on study than on remaining away, and the time spent on the latter is captured vividly in Sun (2003). There is a growing literature in the People's Republic of China and Taiwan on and by overseas students. On the question of 'remaining', useful insights may be found in Chen (1996).

8   I have written elsewhere to suggest that 'sojourning' is a neutral and useful term for what is evolving today, but recognize that it should be distinguished from being in exile and being given refugee status. Unlike being a transnational, sojourning away from a specific place called 'home' is less conscious of national identity (Wang 1993; 1996).

9   Chinese monks from southern Tang China (including northern Vietnam) stopped in Sri Vijaya (East coast of Sumatra) to prepare themselves for further study in India, *Yijing* (Lahiri 1986). No other references to Chinese studying in South-east Asia have been found until the nineteenth century.

10   I have only second-hand knowledge of the behaviour of students from the Netherlands East Indies, the Philippines and French Indo-China, but the scattered accounts I have seen about them conform quite closely to the pattern found among Malaysian students. See *Bulletin of the Malayan Students' Union* 1955 and an early study of Malaysian students in Britain (Abraham 1965).

11   There is a growing literature on ethnicity and assimilation among the Chinese in Australia and the United States. See Chan et al. 2001; Shen 2001; Stratton and Ien 1998.

12   The three writers have been much written about. I shall merely mention some of the more accessible writings about them in Yu (2001); Yuan (1991); and Yu (1993).

13   For Chen Ruoxi's own writings, her own *Selections* from 1976 remain the freshest.

14   'Zhongguo liuxuesheng liuxue xinjiapo liu dazhuyi shixiang' (2004) The Ministry of Education announced in June 2003 that there were 11,058 students from China studying in Malaysia. The Chinese were the largest number among the foreign students.

REFERENCES

Abraham, Collin, E. R. (1965) *Malaysian Students in Great Britain and the Republic of Ireland*. The Hague: Institute of Social Studies.

Andressen, Curtis (1993) *Educational Refugees: Malaysian Students in Australia*. Clayton: Centre of Southeast Asian Studies, Monash University.

Bulletin of the Malayan Students' Union 1955. London: Malayan Students' Union, vol. 1, no. 1.

Chan, Henry, Ann Curthoys and Nora Chiang (eds) (2001) *The Overseas Chinese in Australasia: History, Settlement and Interactions*. Taipei and Canberra: Interdisciplinary Group for Australian Studies, National Taiwan University and Centre for the Study of the Chinese Southern Diaspora, Australian National University.

Chen, Changgui (1996) *Rencai wailiu yu huigui* [Brain drain and returned students]. Wuhan: Hubei jiaoyu chubanshe.

Chen, Jerome (1979) *China and the West: Society and Culture, 1815–1937*. London: Hutchinson.

Chen, Ruoxi (1976) *Selections*. Taipei: Lianjing Publishers.

—— (1993) 'Prologue: Chinese overseas writers and nativism'. In Hsin-sheng C. Kao (ed.), *Nativism Overseas: Contemporary Chinese Women Writers*, Albany, N.Y.: State University of New York Press, pp. 9–24.

Cheng, Xi (2003) *Dangdai Zhongguo liuxuesheng yanjiu* [A study of contemporary Chinese students abroad]. Hong Kong: Xianggang shehui kexue Publishers.

Chiang, Yung-chen (2001) *Social Engineering and the Social Sciences in China, 1919–1949*. Cambridge: Cambridge University Press.

Faxian (1923) *The Travels of Fa-hsien (399–414 A.D.), or Record of the Buddhist kingdoms*. Herbert A. Giles, tr. Cambridge: Cambridge University Press.

Faxian and Songyun (1869) *Travels of Fah-Hian and Sung-Yun, Buddhist Pilgrims: from China to India (400 A.D. and 518 A.D.)*. Samuel Beal, tr. London: Trubner & Co.

Greenaway, David and Jacqueline Tuck (1995) *Economic Impact of International Students in UK Higher Education*. London: Committee of Vice-Chancellors and Principals of the Universities of the United Kingdom.

Gu, Changsheng (1984) *Rong Hong: Xiang Xifang Xuexi de Xianqu* [Rong Hong: a pioneer student in the West]. Shanghai: Shanghai renmin chubanshe.

Harrison, Brian (1979) *Waiting for China: the Anglo-Chinese College at Malacca, 1818–1843, and Early Nineteenth-century Missions*. Hong Kong: Hong Kong University Press.

Hodgkin, Mary C. (1966) *Australian Training and Asian Living*. Perth: University of Western Australia Press 1966

—— (1972) *The Innovators: the Role of Foreign Trained Persons in Southeast Asia*. Sydney: Sydney University Press.

Jolley, Ainsley (1997) *Exporting Education to Asia*. Melbourne: Victoria University Press, Centre for Strategic Economic Studies.

Kong, Qingmao (1996) *Gu Hongming pingzhuan* [Gu Hongming: a critical biography]. Nanchang: Baihuazhou wenyi chubanshe.

Koyama, Noboru (1999) *Hatenko 'Meiji Ryugakusei' retsuden: Daiei Teikoku Ni Mananda Hitobito* [An unprecedented phenomenon, students abroad during the Meiji: people who studied in the British Empire]. Tokyo: Kodansha.

Kung, Shien-woo (1962) *Chinese in American Life: some Aspects of their History, Status, Problems and Contributions*. Seattle: University of Washington Press.

LaFargue, Thomas E. (1987) *China's First Hundred: Educational Mission Students in the United States, 1872–1881*. Pullman: Washington State University Press.

Lahiri, Latika, tr. (1986) *Chinese Monks in India: Biography of Eminent Monks who went to the Western World in Search of the Law during the great T'ang Dynasty*. Delhi: Motilal Banarsidass.

Lee, Rose Hum (1960) *The Chinese in the United States of America*. Hong Kong: Hong Kong University Press.

McNamara, David and Robert Harris (eds) (1997) *Overseas Students in Higher Education: Issues in Teaching and Learning*. London: Routledge.

Mencius (1970) D.C. Lau, tr. Harmondsworth: Penguin Books.

Morohashi, Tetsuji (1986) *Dai kan-wa jiten* [The great Chinese-Japanese dictionary]. Tokyo: Taishukan, Revised Edition.

Qian, Gang and Hu Jingcao (2004) *Liu Mei youtong: Zhongguo zuizao de guanpai liuxuesheng* [Young students in America: the earliest official Chinese overseas students]. Shanghai: Wenhui.

Reynolds, Douglas R. (1993) *China, 1898–1912: the Xinzheng Revolution and Japan*. Cambridge, MA: Council on East Asian Studies, Harvard University.

Rong, Hong (1909) *My life in China and America*. New York: Henry Holt.

Said, Edward (1999) *Out of Place: a Memoir*. London: Granta Books.

Saneto, Keishu (1970) *Chugokujin Nihon ryugaku shi* [History of Chinese students in Japan]. Tokyo: Kuroshio.

Shen, Yuanfang (2001) *Dragon Seed in the Antipodes: Chinese-Australian Autobiographies*. Carlton, Vic.: Melbourne University Press.

Stratton, Jon and Ien Ang (1998) 'Multicultural imagined communities: Cultural difference and national identity in the USA and Australia'. In David Bennett (ed.), *Multicultural States: Rethinking Difference and Identity*. London: Routledge, 1998, pp. 135–162.

Shu, Xincheng (1989) *Jindai Zhongguo liuxue shi* [A history of Chinese studying abroad] [1933]. Hong Kong: Zhonghua.

Sun, Shuyun (2003) *Ten Thousand Miles without a Cloud*. London: HarperCollins.

Tanaka, Akihiko (2002) *The New Middle Ages: the World System in the 21st century*. Jean Connell Hoff, tr. Tokyo: International House of Japan.

Tezuka, Akira (1992) *Bakumatsu Meiji kaigai Tokosha soran* [Japanese traveling overseas during the late Tokugawa and Meiji period]. Tokyo: Kashiwa Shobo.

Wang, Gungwu (1993) 'Migration and its enemies'. In Bruce Mazlish and Ralph Buultjens (eds), *Conceptualizing Global History*. Boulder, CO: Westview Press, pp. 131–151.

—— (1996) 'Sojourning: the Chinese experience in Southeast Asia'. In Anthony Reid (ed.), *Sojourners and Settlers: Histories of Southeast Asia and the Chinese*. St Leonard's, NSW: Allen & Unwin, pp. 1–14.

Wang, Qisheng (1992) *Zhongguo liuxuesheng de lishi guiji, 1872–1947* [Historical tracks of Chinese students abroad, 1872–1947]. Wuhan: Hubei jiaoyu chubanshe.

—— (1995) *Liuxue yu Jiuguo: Kangzhan shiqi haiwai xueren qunxiang* [Study abroad and national salvation]. Guilin: Guangxi shifan daxue.

Wang, Y. C. (1966) *Chinese Intellectuals and the West, 1872–1949*. Chapel Hill: University of North Carolina Press.

Wong, K. Scott and Chan Sucheng (eds) (1998) *Claiming America: Constructing Chinese American Identities during the Exclusion Era*. Philadelphia: Temple University Press.

Xia, Chenghua (1994) *Lü Mei huaren liuxuesheng dui Zhonghuaminguo zhengzhi taidu zhi yanjiu* [Political attitudes towards the Republic of China among Chinese students in America]. Taipei: Haihua wenjiao jijinhui.

Xu, Zechang (2001) *Cong Liuxuesheng dao Meiji huaren: yi ershishiji Zhongye Taiwan liu Mei xuesheng weili* [From overseas student to American-Chinese]. Taipei: Haihua wenjiao jijinhui.

Xuanzang (1904) *On Yuan Chwang's Travels in India, 629–645 A.D.* Thomas Watter, tr. edited after his death by T.W. Rhys Davids and S.W. Bushell. London: Royal Asiatic Society.

Yi, Haining (2001) *From 'Yellow Peril' to 'Model Minority': the Educational History of Chinese Americans, 1850-1990*. Ann Arbor, MI: University Microfilms International.

Yijing, *Nanhai jigui neifa zhuan* (1959) [Biographies of those who returned with the Dharma through the Southern Sea]. In *Datang xiyu qiufa gaoseng zhuan*. Taipei: Taiwan yinjingchu.

Yin, Xiao-huang (2000) *Chinese American Literature since the 1850s*. Urbana and Chicago: University of Illinois Press.

Yu, Bin (2001) *Zhang Ailing zhuan* [Biography of Zhang Ailing]. Guilin: Guangxi shifandaxue chubanshe.

Yu, Shiao-ling (1993) 'The themes of exile and identity crisis in Nie Hualing's fiction'. In Hsin-sheng C. Kao (ed.) *Nativism Overseas: Contemporary Chinese Women Writers*. Albany, NY: State University of New York Press, pp. 127–150.

Yuan, Liangjun (1991) *Bai Xianyong lun* [On Bai Xianyong]. Taipei: Erya Publishers.

'Zhongguo liuxuesheng liuxue xinjiapo liu dazhuyi shixiang' [Six important matters for Chinese students in Singapore to note] (2004). *Huanqiu shihbao* (Beijing) 11 June; Report in *Lianhe Zaobao* (Singapore) 25 Oct.

Chapter 9

Home as a Circular Process: The Indonesian-Chinese in Hong Kong

Wang Cangbai and Wong Siu-lun

INTRODUCTION: HOME AND MIGRATION

Home is perhaps one of the most common human notions that is taken for granted, because of its apparent universality. Ironically, it is also among the most controversial concepts in the glossaries of social sciences today that need urgent redefinitions and alternative understandings. Conventionally, home is treated as a 'stable physical centre of one's universe – a safe and still place to leave and return to (whether house, village, region or nation), and a principal focus of one's concern and control' (Rapport and Dawson 1998: 6). The notion of home is also very often 'associated with pleasant memories, intimate situations, a place of warmth and protective security amongst parents, brothers, and sisters, and loved people' (Sarup 1996: 2). As such, 'home' becomes synonymous with consistency, stability, certainty and permanence.

In a post-modern world, however, a concept of home as universal, stable and geographically confined is increasingly being challenged, and this is especially true for migrants who move from one social and physical setting to another. It has been demonstrated by a number of researchers that in a globalized world, home is becoming unprecedentedly uncertain and ambiguous, resulting in the emergence of various new types of homes for migrants. For example, based on her research on the Filipino domestic workers in Hong Kong, Constable (1999: 203) discovered that these migrant workers find themselves in an ambivalent state of 'at home but not at home'.

They 'develop a plural vision that allows – perhaps requires – them to create a new place to fit in both in Hong Kong and in the Philippines ... In circumstances of change and mobility, plural vision no longer permits the self the illusion of a unified, bounded, or coherent whole' (Constable 1999: 224). Similarly, Fouron (2003: 239) finds that 'home' for the Haitian immigrants in the United States is a 'transnational social field' across both Haiti and the United States, but 'neither of which can emerge as the permanent and definite home since neither one can ever fully satisfy their goals, aspirations, and expectations'.

As far as Chinese migrants are concerned, 'home' is also becoming vague and confusing. In the past, the so-called Chinese sojourners had a clear-cut concept of home as their village of origin, where their ancestors were buried and where they were supposed to return to, either physically or spiritually. It was not uncommon that bodies, or at least bones of the Chinese migrants who died overseas, were sent back to China for proper burial (Sinn 1989: 71). However, contemporary Chinese migrants 'tend to maintain multiple abodes in various places, being unsure in their mind of where they would call "home"' (Wong 1999: 147), exemplified in the returned HongKongnese migrants from Canada who conceive Hong Kong to be 'home but not home' (Chan 1996) in that they have difficulty in fitting into Hong Kong after years of living overseas despite the fact that they all grew up in Hong Kong. Another example is the high-tech Taiwanese migrants who regard both Hsinchu, Taiwan and Silicon Valley, USA as their home and as a result develop a 'transnational home identity' across the Pacific Ocean (Chang 2002: 142–144).

Given that 'home' is becoming diversifying and uncertain, is it still possible for migrants to go 'home'? Three major propositions are identified in the current migrant literature. One asserts that home is completely impossible for migrants. Whenever people have left their first and original social milieu, they will be unable to come back home again and are doomed to be left in a state of 'impossible homecoming' (Chambers 1994: 1), because with the acceleration of globalization, migrants are 'increasingly confronted with an extensive cultural and historical diversity that proves impermeable to the explanations we habitually employ' (Chambers 1994: 2–3). The second proposition argues that even though homes are not completely impossible, they are 'broken mirrors' that could only be restored in mind as 'imaginary homelands' (Rushdie 1991: 10–11). In this case, home is not restorable for any geographical location, but exists in the hearts of migrants, like 'a moveable feast' that migrants could 'bring along like a suitcase' and set up wherever they decamp (Harman 1988: 89–90). The last proposition goes even further by arguing the 'undesirability of home'. As Said (1984: 170) claims, 'In a secular and contingent world, homes are always provisional. Borders and barriers, which enclose us within the safety of familiar territory, can also become prisons, and are often defended beyond reason or necessity'. Therefore, only by being released from home can migrants become truly liberal and strong.

As discussed above, a pessimistic attitude with a sentimental colouring dominates the existing migrant studies that encompasses regretting the loss of a romantic home and worrying over the hazy future of home seeking. In our view, there are four problems with contemporary debates of home. First, in these discussions, home is treated as a linear process that starts from a traditionally defined tangible home, goes towards a gradually uncertain home in the process of movements and ends with an impossibility of homecoming. However, the paradox of 'a loss of a fixed home and an irresistible desire to overcome it' (Rapport and Dawson 1998: 9) is largely overlooked. Second, most studies overemphasize the contradiction between the 'old typed home' and 'new typed home', assuming that they are completely incompatible. The possible 'contradictory consistency' between the old and new homes is beyond the fields of view of most studies. Third, 'home' in existing literature is treated as a singular entity and is discussed in general terms. Despite the fact that some simple classifications of home have been made in some writings such as home as a 'physical location' versus home as 'a place of emotional attachment' (Constable 1999: 206–207), or home as 'a private domestic space' versus home as 'a larger geographical place' (Espiritu 2003:2), these classifications are not adequate for an analysis of global migrants who transcend broad time and space; more subtle and pertinent categories are called for. Finally, most studies attribute the uncertainty of home to cultural hybridity as a result of globalization (Chambers 1994; 2–3: Rutherford 1990: 25). How home is transformed and reconstructed in the discourse of changing power relations is not given enough attention.

To fill the gaps identified above, we propose to study home as a circular process with multiple dimensions to unveil a more complex and sensitive picture of home for Chinese migrants. Somerville's (1992) comprehensive and plausible classification of 'home', in our opinion, can serve as a good starting point for further analysis along this line. He classifies 'home' into the following seven dimensions identified by signifiers of shelter, hearth, heart, privacy, roots, abode and paradise respectively:

> Home as shelter connotes the material form of home, in terms of physical structure which affords protection to oneself ... Home as hearth connotes the warmth and cosiness which home provides to the body ... Home as heart ... the emphasis is on emotional rather than physiological security and health ... Home as privacy involves the power to 'control one's own boundaries' ... Home as roots means one's source of identity and meaningfulness ... Home as abode corresponds to ... the minimal definition of home, that is, anywhere that one happens to stay ... Finally, home as paradise is an idealization of all the positive features of home fused together. (Somerville 1992: 530–533)

Among the seven dimensions of home in Somerville's classification, the signifiers of root, heart and abode, we believe, are the most relevant ones for Chinese migrants. The relevance of root is not difficult to understand given the significance of place of origin (*jiguan*) in the self-identification of Chinese people and in defining the meaning of home for Chinese. Heart and abode represent the most subjective dimension and the most minimal definition of home respectively, and are thus chosen as the other two essential signifiers. Therefore, in this study, we propose to consider 'home' as a triad composed of dimensions of origin, emotion and function, symbolized by root, heart and abode respectively. We will examine how 'home' splits along these three dimensions and how these three dimensions compete with each other to define 'home'.

Our argument is that whenever migrants leave their original home, unavoidable ruptures within home begin to appear along the three dimensions identified. Home thus becomes divided and unstable, and the rupture deepens as the migrant journey continues, creating unsettled anxiety in the hearts of migrants. To overcome this anxiety, migrants make great efforts to reconstruct a home for themselves through borrowing traditional social and cultural elements, without being regulated by internal and external power relations. Consequently, in a world of globalization, home for migrants is a circular process starting from a 'consistent home' to a 'divided home' and finally arriving at a 'symbolic home', or more accurately, a 'consistent home in a symbolic sense', in which migrants fulfil their innermost desires for a cohesive home defined in the most traditional way and find their ends in their beginnings.

DATA AND METHODOLOGY

To explore the question of home, we believe a proper way is to study migration trajectories from a longer historical perspective than is usually found in current studies. In this chapter, we will trace the migration history of one group of Chinese migrants: the Indonesian-Chinese. The term 'Indonesian-Chinese' is used in this study as a shorthand label for Chinese people who were born in Indonesia, migrated to the People's Republic of China (PRC) in the 1950–1960s and remigrated to Hong Kong in 1960s to 1980s.

Partially because of Chinese nationalism triggered by the establishment of the PRC in 1949, and partially because of a desire to continue their Chinese education, about 100,000 ethnic Chinese from South-east Asia, mainly students and teachers went to the PRC in the early and middle 1950s. Another 200,000 ethnic Chinese migrated/returned in the early 1960s as a result of the expulsion policies against Chinese in a number of South-east Asian countries (Godley 1989; Godley and Coppel 1990b; Mao and Lin 1993: 206). Most of these migrants, after 20 years in China, exited to Hong Kong and Macau when the Chinese government changed its policies in 1972 and granted exit permits to those who wished to leave China (Burns 1987: 666; Chin 2003b: 65). At present, no accurate figures relating to the South-east Asian Chinese in Hong Kong are available due to the lack of official statistics. However, it is well recognized that Indonesian-Chinese constitute the vast majority of this group of ethnic Chinese, whose number varies between 100,000 to 200,000 persons according to different sources of estimation (Godley and Coppel 1990a: 94; Li 1987:25; Chin 2003a: 293–294).

From the 1980s onwards, Indonesian-Chinese in Hong Kong began forming associations according to different principles. We have identified a total of 48 South-east Asian Chinese associations in Hong Kong, with Indonesian-Chinese associations constituting the vast majority. Among these associations, 32 are made up of classmate associations (*xiaoyouhui*), 13 are based on locality while one is a research institute and two are composite associations.[1] Among all these South-east Asian Chinese associations, the Indonesian-Chinese classmate associations based on previous enrolment in a common Chinese-language high school in South-east Asia are dominant in terms of both members and activities. Since the Palembang *Chinese School's Alumni Association (HK) [PCSAA (HK)] [Jugang (Xianggang) xiaoyouhui]* is one of the first established and best-organized Indonesian-

Chinese classmate associations (Wang 1999) it will serve as the focus of this study. Simultaneously, we consistently have placed the Palembang Chinese against the overall picture of the South-east Asian Chinese in Hong Kong in order to improve and balance our investigations.

 The data for this chapter is partly drawn from a larger study conducted in the period from 1998 to 2003 by Wang Cangbai (Wang 2004). In that larger work, an ethnographic approach with qualitative orientation is applied and a holistic method is employed which involves semi-structured interviews, participant observation and archival studies. In that larger work, a total of 60 people were interviewed, among whom, 12 are females, and 48 are males. Because of the dominance of entrepreneurs in the composition of Palembang Chinese School's Alumni Association (HK)'s executive council and their dominant influence on the association (Wang 1999: 61–62), the interviewees were first selected from the entrepreneurs in this community and then extended to the Palembang Chinese in other occupations. 40 persons were interviewed, among which, 24 are businessmen, and the remainder are administrative or clerical staff in banks, travel agencies or in various private companies, high school teachers, doctors and engineers. In addition to in–depth interviews, numerous informal conversations with members of this community were carried out. These interviews and conversations make up the core part of our research material. To obtain a clearer and more balanced story of the Palembang Chinese, the scope of interview was extended to Palembang Chinese living outside Hong Kong and to the members of other Southeast Asian Chinese associations in Hong Kong. The former includes 15 interviews with the Palembang Chinese in Guangdong, Beijing, Jakarta and Palembang respectively, who are either former teachers, student leaders at Palembang Chinese schools or children of the leaders in ethnic Chinese communities in Palembang. The latter includes 5 interviews with South-east Asian Chinese activists in Hong Kong. A semi-structured method was applied in the interviews, and the language for interviews was Standard Chinese (*putonghua*). The average length of each interview was two to three hours, but some were over ten hours. The interviews were recorded and transcribed for analysis.

 An indispensable part of the fieldwork is participant observation. Wang Cangbai has kept close contact with key informants and constantly attended the activities of the Palembang Chinese, including community-wide gatherings, amenity activities, wedding parties, discussions on current events in Indonesia and trips to South China and Indonesia.

Archival analysis and library research is also an important integral part of this research. This chapter uses extensively the publications of the PCSAA. From its establishment in 1987 to the end of 2001, the PCSAA has published 12 issues altogether of the *Journal of the Palembang Chinese Schools' Alumni Association* (HK) [Jugang (Xianggang) xiaoyouhui huikan]. Edited by a committee composed of association members, the journal publishes articles written by Palembang Chinese, both in and outside of Hong Kong, and photographs. Copies of the journal are distributed free to a wide range of localities including Indonesia, Singapore, Australia, the United States, France and many big cities in China besides Hong Kong. Except for a small number of works that are written in Bahasa Indonesian and English, the rest are in Chinese.

'NO HOME BACK HOME'

Most of the Indonesian-Chinese who migrated to the PRC were actually born in Indonesia and had never been to China. For example, among the 40 Palembang Chinese in Hong Kong interviewed, 36 were born in Indonesia, one was born in Malaysia and only three were born in China. Furthermore, most were second-generation ethnic Chinese in Indonesia. Consequently, it is only valid at a spiritual level to compare them with other returning migrants in that they only 'returned' to China as their cultural centre and ancestral home.

However, many Indonesian-Chinese found the PRC to be 'no home back home' (Davison 1968: 499), because they had virtually no connections with their ancestral villages in Southern China. As one interviewee explained:

> Although, I am a Fujianese, I was not born there, and I have never been to Fujian. Though I have some distant relatives there, we do not know each other ... Yunnan is the only place where I have lived in China. I do not know any other places.

In fact, most of the ethnic Chinese from South-east Asia who went to the PRC in the 1950s did not settle in their ancestral villages, but went to major cities for tertiary education. A majority then settled in urban areas after graduation (Godley and Coppel 1990a, 1990b). Even for the returnees who came back in the early 1960s, many were allocated to state-run Overseas

Chinese Farms which were not necessarily close to their ancestral villages (Fitzgerald 1972: 70; Lu and Quan 2001: 102–104).

However, although aware of a possible disconnection with their ancestral villages before going to China, the Indonesian-Chinese did not worry about this aspect very much, and this separation, we believe, was not the main reason for their 'unhomeliness' in China. What really mattered to them was the status of 'Other' applied to them by diverse forces of ideological pressure, cultural orthodoxy and political control.

In spite of the fact that the Indonesian-Chinese regarded themselves as Chinese, as a whole they were not perceived by the majority society as 'one of us', but were identified as a special group in need of continuous socialist education, transformation and supervision. One way to indicate their alienation is to briefly examine the cultural and political meanings of the term *guiqiao*, which was first introduced in a central government document in 1957 as an official category for these 'returnees' (Lu and Quan 2001: 2). In Chinese, the word *gui* [return] has a more subtle meaning than just spatial movements, implying also a kind of conversion of allegiance and a pledge of obedience, especially for those who had departed from the orthodoxy but came back again. Second, the word *qiao* [sojourner] is not a neutral term in Chinese official discourse. It entails the negative meanings of being an outcast or person living in exile. This is largely due to the fact that China was a traditional agrarian society. Staying on the land until death had been taken as the normal state of life and was a respected virtue. The landless and jobless peasants and artisans were considered potential threats to the stability and strength of the empire, and Chinese who went abroad were equated with rebels. Rootedness was thus not only the official ideology but also an important part of mainstream Chinese culture. Though times have changed, the cultural residues still exist (Wang Gungwu 1981:118–112; Zhang 1998: 55–57). In the 1950a and 1960s, the Indonesian-Chinese were thus transformed into a culturally distinct 'Other' by the use of such a categorizing scheme.

This 'Other' status was also reflected in the *qiaowu* policy of the PRC, whose core spirit was the so-called Eight-Character Principle towards returned Overseas Chinese: 'to treat equally but make appropriate preferential arrangements' (Mao and Lin 1993: 54). This policy encouraged differential treatments toward the 'returnees' in various aspects, sometimes good, and sometimes bad, depending on the political atmosphere and the presumed value of the returnees for the 'national interest' (Chang 1980: 283). While during the first years of their return the methods for control featured positive treatments, such as privileged treatments in daily life – in view of their potential contribution to China's domestic economic development and regional security because of their wealth and connection with China's neighbouring countries. These changed to discrimination and persecution during the Cultural Revolution given their 'questionable history' and their 'complex' overseas relations. Therefore, it is not surprising to find that the *qiaowu* policy had 'veered from left to right, and alternated between severity and leniency' (Fitzgerald 1972: 54) and had 'otherized' the Indonesian-Chinese from time to time.

In fact, for most of the Indonesian-Chinese, their China experience was characterized by alienation and discrimination. Many of our interviewees complained that they were not trusted and had few chances to be promoted in their work, and only a very small number were able to become party members or join the army. Many of the Indonesian-Chinese and their dependants were persecuted during political campaigns. For example, during the Cultural Revolution, some of them were imprisoned as 'spies' or 'counterrevolutionaries', and more were attacked as 'worshippers of things foreign' and unjustly treated. Private property, such as houses and remittances were confiscated, and their normal communications with overseas relatives were inspected though not completely prohibited (Godley 1989; Zhuang 2001: 244–304).

The Indonesian-Chinese had relocated themselves to China, because they believed that they were Chinese set apart from the indigenous Indonesians around them and that they would feel at home in China. However, ironically, in the assumed cultural centre and ancestral home:

> no matter how much effort they put into their daily lives and work in the hope of becoming real Chinese, most of them failed to change the image they left in local society as being *huaqiao* or *Nanyang ke* [guests from South-east Asia] though they had been learning and working in mainland China for a long period. ... this local perception of their difference stranded the overseas Chinese in mainland China in an identity limbo. (Chin 2003b: 76)

In short, they had come home, but they were still searching for a genuine home. In the word of an Indonesian-Chinese writer, they had become 'orphans at home' (Bai 1983).

A divided home

The plight of homelessness was not alleviated after the Indonesian-Chinese arrived in Hong Kong. It was difficult for them to identify with local society due to cultural barriers, structural disadvantages and misrecognition by the local society. Only a small number of the Indonesian-Chinese could speak Cantonese, since the majority were from southern Fujian province and spoke minnan dialect, although they could also speak Standard Chinese after having lived in the PRC for decades. In a society where 'Cantonese Chauvinism' (Guldin 1997: 27) had long existed, they faced both a language barrier and cultural exclusion. In addition, although more than 10 per cent were China-trained professionals (doctors, engineers and university teachers), their qualifications were not recognized by the British colonial administration (Mu 1980; 1984). Like their ancestors in Indonesia, they had to start from scratch in a new environment (Godley and Coppel 1990a: 97–98; Li 1987: 25).[2] It was therefore not uncommon that in the early years of their arrival, the majority of the Indonesian-Chinese found employment of the most menial kind (Mu 1979; Fei 1982). Even today after years of struggle, only 5 to 10 per cent of the Indonesian-Chinese have managed to rank among the higher social class through becoming entrepreneurs or professionals, while the rest belong to the group of low-ranking employees.[3]

It was also difficult for the Indonesian-Chinese to identify with other Chinese immigrants from the PRC in spite of the fact that they all suffered similar prejudice in the former British colony. This is because, as just noted, they were not regarded as *really* Chinese. In addition, unlike other PRC immigrants who could fulfil their need for home by joining existing native place associations in Hong Kong or through paying regular visits to their hometowns in southern China, the Indonesian-Chinese did not have this option. They hardly knew their ancestral native place and had limited affection for it or its people.

Finally, they were also unable to return to Indonesia because they had no travel documents to go anywhere until they became permanent residents in Hong Kong, which took seven years of uninterrupted stay. As a result, during the 1970s and most of the 1980s, few of them could visit their families in Indonesia. Even after they had secured permanent residency and proper travel documents, they found it difficult to re-establish family relationships, because in their long absence much had changed and returning permanently to Indonesia had become a non-viable option. Many of the interviewees intentionally hold an estranged attitude toward their family members in Indonesia, because they felt disgraced after a miserable interlude in the PRC. As one of the interviewees said: 'I returned to China regardless of the objection of my parents. How could I have the 'face' to ask them for help? I had to count on myself.'

In addition to this evasive stance, many of the Indonesian-Chinese found themselves in an unprivileged status in relation to their family members, due to their impoverished economic situation. In fact, we find many Indonesian-Chinese never had the chance to return to the family business in Indonesia; if they did return, they established their own businesses or became employees. Those who did resume business networks with their families had to wait five to ten years to accumulate enough economic strength to gain the same power status as their siblings. As Stack aptly points out, '[y]ou can go home. But you can't start from where you left. To fit in, you have to create another place in that place you left behind.' (Stack 1996: 199)

Therefore, when the interviewees were asked which place they regarded as home, we found their definitions of 'home' to be vague and contradictory. First, they regard Hong Kong as their current home in that they have settled down in Hong Kong as permanent residents for two decades. They acknowledge that they are more familiar with Hong Kong than with Indonesia and the PRC, but home in Hong Kong is for them no more than a 'dwelling house', a fixed spatial residence for their closest family or household. However, many of them do not really feel like being 'Hongkongnese', but prefer to remain as strangers in the city. One of the interviewees told us:

> After we arrived at Hong Kong, we did not think this was our place. Yes, we still have this feeling now. After all, we were new immigrants and not native to this place. If we were born here and grew up here, we might not have such a feeling.

This 'alien mentality' can be seen from the names of the associations set up by the Indonesian-Chinese, such as *'Qiao youshe'* [Society for Chinese Sojourners and Friends] or *'Qiao youhui'* [Association for Chinese Sojourners and Friends], and *'LüGang xiao youhui'* [Association for Chinese sojourning and Friends alumni in Hong Kong]. The terms of *'qiao'* (sojourn) and *'lüGang'* (travel to Hong Kong) both carry the connotation of living temporarily somewhere and reflect a self-image of the Indonesian-Chinese as sojourners in Hong Kong.

Second, the Indonesian-Chinese also speak of having a feeling of 'homeness' towards Indonesia, the place where they were born and grew up. Home in this sense is a place where they once felt at ease and were familiar culturally with. One interviewee told us that although he had left Indonesia forty years ago, he still feels his home is there.

> Whenever I returned to Indonesia, I really had a feeling of returning home. How nice it was! I was familiar with the geographical environment, the language and the customs. Whatever they talked to me I could understand immediately without any consideration. Entering that place was really like going home. If there were no turmoil in Indonesia, I even thought about going there to spend the rest of my life.

However, the interviewees did not have the option of returning to Indonesia after their long stay abroad and the resurgence of anti-Chinese repulsions in Indonesia, exemplified in the riot of May 1998 (see Chang and Mu 1998; Qiao and Hua 1998). When we asked a Palembang Chinese to locate his home, the immediate answer was 'Indonesia'. However, after a second thought, he added:

> How to say ... I am of course familiar with the customs and habits in Indonesia. But Indonesia is not a place for us? *huaqiao*. It is economically relatively backward and politically unstable. The Chinese living there have no guarantee of security. Whenever the political climate changes, the Chinese are always the most vulnerable ones to be hurt in Indonesia.

Finally, the Indonesian-Chinese still regard China as their home in the sense of the land of their ancestors and ethnic and cultural origins. This way of thinking is reflected in the mentality of some Indonesian-Chinese, who, shortly after they exited to Hong Kong, said to the press 'Don't forget us, motherland' (Ben 1986). However, the segregation and discrimination this group suffered in China still leave them with miserable memories and make them realize that China is not the place for them to live permanently. To them, China is more a cultural symbol than a concrete place of attachment. As one interviewee said:

> I am a Hainanese, but I have never joined any associations of the Hainanese in Hong Kong because the members there are really from Hainan, and I was born in Indonesia. There are some distances between us. For example, I cannot fully understand the language they use. I learned some Hainanese during my childhood in Indonesia. However, I have not used it for 30

years. It is really hard for me to pick them up again. In addition, although I returned to Hainan once, I know little about it except the name of my father's village. There are no common topics and emotional bonds between the real Hainanese and me.

As shown above, the Indonesian-Chinese have an inconsistent definition of what they consider as their 'home'. For them, 'home' is no longer defined by an ancestral attachment that they initially had longed for, but a split complexity that is not only separated into three spaces, but also into three meanings: Hong Kong is their 'functional home', Indonesia is their 'emotional home', and China is their 'ancestral home'. The notion of home is being pulled into these three directions and this 'unhealable rift' (Said 1984: 159) results in a strong sense of insecurity and a deep sub-consciousness for self-protection. The following quotation from an interviewee substantiates this kind of feeling:

> We love China, we love Hong Kong, and we love Indonesia. All of these places are our homes. We would be happy to see these places become rich and strong. To us, there are no differences between them. However, we learn from history that the state policies are always changing, and the results are not easy to predict. Therefore, we *huaqiao* do not want to count on anybody or any states, be it the Chinese government, the Indonesian government or the Hong Kong administration. It is better for us to count on and trust ourselves. We struggle by ourselves.

To overcome this predicament and secure a feeling of belonging and security in Hong Kong, the Indonesian-Chinese have attempted to seek a home because, as one of our interviewees said, 'The feeling of belonging is important, really important!' This feeling is based, as will be shown below, on a 'symbolic home' made up by the Indonesian-Chinese themselves.

MAKING A HOME

While the loss of home is often unavoidable in a world of mobility, many migrants also attempt to 'explore forms of healing, of taking new roots, and of finding new possibilities for growth' (Manuel 1997: 39) because 'to be rooted is perhaps the most important and least recognized need for the human soul' (Said 1984: 169) and 'our inclination to seek familiarity and identity is fundamental and basic' (Chan 1996: 48). This search for remedies for homelessness has also been undertaken by the Palembang Chinese mainly through two major strategies: establishing alumni associations and manipulating collective memory.

The Palembang Chinese Schools Alumni Association

Unlike most of the new immigrants from the PRC who can identify with others according to a shared geographic origin in Hong Kong by joining existing regional associations (*tongxianghui*) (Sinn 1997: 394–395; Sinn 2002: 4–8), the Palembang Chinese rarely joined these regional associations. They do not identify with the other sub-ethnic groups in Hong Kong, be they Cantonese, Fujianese, Hakkas, Chaozhounese or Hainanese, although these identities had been important to their parents in Palembang. Rather, they established a community of their own in the form of an alumni association, which is a new, adaptive genre of association in Hong Kong society and in the history of Chinese migration in general.

The Palembang Chinese Schools' Alumni Association (HK) was set up in 1987.[4] According to its bylaws, 'all teachers and students of the Palembang Chinese schools and their family members, as well as 'enthusiastic *qiaobao* [Overseas Chinese in Taiwan, Hong Kong and Macau] who support the schools' are eligible to become members (Journal of Palembang Chinese Schools' Alumni Association (JPCSAA) 1987: 12). The board of directors was elected after 'democratic negotiation' (JPCSAA 1997: 3). It was mainly composed of representatives of each grade of the Palembang Chinese schools, because such an arrangement was believed to 'represent broader sections, and can be easily accepted and trusted by the Palembang Chinese' (JPCSAA 1997: 3). It had 560 members by 2001 (Wang 2003: 220).

Significantly, while traditional Chinese associations make use of regional bonds and blood bonds as major principles of organization and organize themselves in either dialect groups or kinship associations, the Palembang Chinese in Hong Kong resort to classmate connections. However, this is not a complete departure from traditional Chinese organizational principles, but an innovative inheritance. In the first place, it borrows elements from traditional regional associations of ethnic Chinese. In particular, Palembang replaced their ancestral villages/towns in China as the new common place of origin, and Standard Chinese replaced their individual dialect as their new lingua franca. In addition, and more importantly, schoolmate connections in Indonesia came to serve as new blood ties by imitating the traditional lineage system. In his study of the Chinese in Sarawak,

T'ien (1953: 25–26) discovered that for the purpose of having a basis for joint economic actions, the two groups of ethnic Chinese both called by the surname T'ien but originating from different provinces of China and speaking different dialects, and having no demonstrable genealogical links, invented a common ancestor and addressed each other in kinship terms. Similarly, the Palembang Chinese have invented a fictive linage for the sake of re-establishing themselves since scattered schoolmate relations are too loose to construct a solid association. To overcome this difficulty, they have transformed loose schoolmate relations into a tight framework by imitating the Chinese lineage system by including all the key elements of a Chinese lineage system such as the usage of 'ancestor' [zuxian], 'generation' [shidai] and 'lineage property' [zuchan] (Freedman 1958: 126–133). Specifically, the school's headmaster, Mr Lai, is regarded as the symbolic 'ancestor' of the Palembang Chinese population; members of different grades constitute the layers of 'generation'; a common fund is their 'property' for the purpose of sustaining the community and enhancing the internal cohesion in the form of organizing community-wide activities; admirations for their common principal (Mr Lai) and commemorations of the mother school equate to the practice of ancestor worship.[5] It is obvious that this structure mirrors the lineage pedigree in traditional Chinese society and produces a fictive pedigree for the Palembang Chinese, based on which, they can easily locate their own positions in the community and define their mutual relations. This innovative schoolmate relation made the establishment of the Palembang Chinese community possible.

However, the establishment of the PCSAA is not a self-determining event, but is under constant regulation of both internal and external power relationships. Within the group, economic capital is the most visible power that heavily impacts on the community leadership. As to who was the founder of the PCSAA, we heard two different versions. One is the 'official one' recorded in the PCSAA journals. According to this version, the PCSAA was initiated by Mr Kang, who organized the preparatory committee in Shatin in August 1987, and finally arranged the founding meeting in October of the same year. He held the position of chairman for ten years. We learned another version from one of our Informants, one of the richest entrepreneurs in this community and a consultant of the PCSAA. According to him, it was another Palembang Chinese, a Mr Lin, who organized the first preparatory committee in Mei Foo. The principle, Mr Lai and our Informant were also present at that meeting. However, after having heard about this, Mr Kang rushed to call the funding meeting and claimed the establishment of the PCSAA. In this case, the others gave up their own plan. As this Informant said: 'How can one school have two alumni associations? We had to join the one set up by him for the interest of the whole community'. However, he pointed out that Mr Kang is not very popular among the Palembang Chinese, but a person who likes to be in the limelight. It is possible that this negative remark might be a result of his personal bias towards Mr Kang, but we think there is some truth in it, because in the several gatherings we have attended, we noticed that nobody listened to Mr Kang seriously when he delivered a speech on the stage.

We would like to view this dispute as a kind of competition between economic capital rather than a matter of personal contradictions. Mr Kang is one of the very few Palembang Chinese who has never been to China. He migrated to Hong Kong in the 1960s and entered the family business. In the late 1980s, when most of the newly immigrated Palembang Chinese were starting from scratch for survival in this strange place, he was already quite well off and had built many local connections. These advantages in economic strength and local knowledge provided him with an edge in the competition with other activists in the formation of the PCSAA. On the other hand, being new immigrants in Hong Kong, Mr Ling and Mr Lai were certainly weaker in terms of economic strength and local connections. This difference explains why a community dominated by former *guiqiao* was founded by a person who had never been to China, and was headed by him in the first ten years after its establishment.

In addition to disputes regarding the founding of the association, the re-election of association chairman and the purchasing of an Association Hall are other arenas to look into for the role of economic capital in the growth of this association. In 1999, Mr Kang resigned as chairman and Mr Ye, a middle-aged businessman, took over the position. The reason for this rearrangement, according to Mr Kang, was because of his bad health. However, according to our observations, there were more reasons behind it. Mr Yip was not merely younger and more energetic; more importantly, he is one of the most successful entrepreneurs in the Palembang Chinese community, whereas Mr Kang's business had been on the decline in the past ten years, and he correspondingly lost his influence in the community. This was highlighted in the matter of the purchase of a hall. In 1999, the PCSAA bought an association hall for the first time in its history that cost about two million HK dollars. This expense far exceeded the financial capital of the PCSAA. Obviously, additional donations were needed. This was unquestionably a duty for the chairman, who should take a lead in finding them. We cannot be sure if the re-election of the chairman had something to do with this investment plan, as it is not easy for outsiders to get details of such a subtle internal affair. However, the coincidence between these two matters hinted that economic capital mattered in this rearrangement. This conjecture is to some extent confirmed by later actions in the community. Soon after Mr Ye became chairman, he, together with three other entrepreneurs in the community, bought a flat in Mongkok costing HK$1,600,000, and provided it freely to the PCSAA as a permanent Association Hall. This action won Mr Ye respect and trust among the community, and once again suggested the importance of economic capital in the management of this Indonesian-Chinese community.

While economic power does play an important role, its influence is largely within the community and restricted to the area of leadership competition. The format of social grouping and the organizational principles adopted by the Indonesian-Chinese are not regulated by internal power relations but by larger external political and social forces. As indicated previously, when in the Mainland, the Indonesian-Chinese were 'Otherized' by mingled ideological, cultural and political forces into a separate category, suffering alienation and discrimination. Again, after exiting to Hong Kong, they were confronted with cultural barriers, structural disadvantages, misrecognitions and were given a periphery social status. Constrained in such power structures, they could neither identify with mainlander or 'Hongkongese', nor could they pick up any association form already adopted by them, but created a new form of social grouping, the alumni association, and made it into the base for homemaking.

To construct a collective memory

The primary basis for the Palembang Chinese community is a common origin and the memory of this origin. The expression, creation and circulation of a collective memory were therefore equally essential in the home-making exercise, which has served to produce a common history for members in this pseudo-family and helps to identify a new root. Memory, as we know, may be unreflective and latent, or it may be consciously recalled and mobilized to serve the present. Members of a group may be the bearers of memory, but they can also be prompted to *perform* the act of recollecting (Bal et al. 1999). Collective memory, the work of collective agency, can be created through a variety of devices. In the case of the Palembang Chinese, the devices include the generation and circulation of various forms of writing and photographs, the use of symbols and the organization of rituals.

Writings

The Association's journal is one of the most powerful vehicles for expressing, creating and circulating a collective memory. Except for the dry facts of association business (executive committee reports, financial reports, election results etc.), the major part of the journal is made up of materials that convey the 'memories and desires' of the community.[6] The memories can be divided into three categories.

The first category, consisting of creative writings that dwell on the reminiscences of their childhood and youth in Palembang, forms the majority of the journal's articles. They passionately recall the halcyon days at school: their academic accomplishments, the colourful extracurricular activities, the innocent friendships among peers as well as the deep affection between teachers and students. There are also warm descriptions of the folklore, food and natural beauty of Palembang City. It is impossible to allude to full texts here given the constraint of space; however, here are titles of some of these articles for illustration:

> 'The Moon in Palembang' (1989)
> 'A story of durian' (1991)
> 'Musi love warms my heart' (1995)
> 'Commemorate teachers and schoolmates' (1998)
> 'Commemorate mother school, cherish friendship' (2001)

No matter what form these works take – essays, poems or letters – they contribute in many ways to the construction of a history of the Palembang Chinese. Through the sentimental descriptions and fond recollections of the people and events in the past in Palembang, they stimulate and generate a collective memory among the members of this community, deliberately highlighting the strengths of friendship and the profound bonds with Palembang and ignoring any unpleasant happenings. The memory, in other words, is highly selective. This is best shown in the following poem celebrating the brotherhood of the Palembang Chinese based on their common past:

Though Palembang and Hong Kong are several thousand miles apart
The schoolmate bond is as close as that of brothers.
We are of the same root: we all drank from the River Musi.
We are of the same heart: impossible to forget the passion of the past.
(Ou 1988)

The Musi River, which is referred to with remarkable frequency in these writings, becomes the symbol of a cherished common origin, or, as one contributor claims, 'the root of the alumni of the Palembang Chinese School' (JPCSAA 1989: 12). Members talk of themselves as 'Musi people' or 'people who have drunken from the Musi River' as often as being past students of the schools. A number of poems pining for Palembang have Musi in their title, such as 'Where is the source of the Musi River?,' 'Musi Love is unchanged' (JPCSAA 1987: 6). 'Though the Musi is small, it can turn great wheels. Though the Musi is short, its friendship is everlasting', lines presented by Principal Lai at one of the gatherings, is used as the title of an article (JPCSAA 1991: 12). An editorial even points out that the association's 'only aim' is 'developing the refined tradition of we the Musi River people: namely, unity, mutual assistance and the spirit of friendship, and setting up our own alumni association' (JPCSAA 1989: 9).

While the Musi River marks the shared geographical origin, the cherished time is marked by their childhood and school days. What seems to matter more than an accurate retelling of historical events is the construction of a kind of mythic time in the past. The concern for shared origin has led this group of individuals, each with many layers of migration experience and years of misery and longing, to define a common pristine childhood/ youth.

The second group of materials consists of historical documents from the Palembang Chinese schools that are reprinted in the journal, especially in the special issues lavishly published to mark the fifth anniversary of the PCSAA (HK) in 1992 and the fiftieth anniversary of the Palembang Chinese School in 2001. They include the faculty and student roll of the school for each grade, the membership of the students' union for each year, articles written by former principals and the history of the school. These documents evoke latent memories of school days and reinforce identifications with their community. One of the readers recalls her reaction to the journal:

> The journal stirs nostalgic feelings and sentimental memories of the past ... Seeing the student roll, in particular, which consists of a list of over one

thousand names, I am lost in deep thought and reminiscence. In this list, I find the names of my classmates, my academic brothers and sisters, and many friends I was less familiar with or even never met before ... With each name, I see a lively young face. These faces then change into the faces of old men and old ladies. It is as if they are beckoning me, one by one, then chatting with me about ordinary, everyday matters, like members of a family ... Half a century has passed, yet our school days seem just like yesterday ... I would like to express my appreciation to the editors for their work, and to the schoolmate who has preserved this valuable document and is now sharing it with us. As our Chinese school in Indonesia does not exist any longer, this list provides us with a clue to seek old schoolmates and to commemorate our school. I cherish it very much. (JPCSAA 1993: 20)

The third group of materials consists of reports on the current situation of other Palembang Chinese living out of Hong Kong. These articles relate the recent situations of former teachers still in Palembang and news of former schoolmates scattered all over the world, and give accounts of the reunions of Palembang Chinese with their families and friends during their re-visits to Indonesia. Some of the correspondence among the Palembang Chinese is also published periodically. These writings have helped the Palembang Chinese to re-establish contacts with their former teachers, childhood friends and even separated siblings, and reconnect the past with the present. The Musi friendship is thus not merely an object of commemoration, but a vehicle for the reconstitution of a transnational community for the present.

Photographs and symbols

Photographs are also an important component of the journal. About 840 pictures of the Palembang Chinese have been published so far, greatly exceeding the number of articles. Apart from a small number printed along with articles, most of the photographs are printed in a separate photographic section. These photographs can also be divided into two categories. One category comprises pictures of gatherings, excursions, performances and other activities held by the Hong Kong association. The others are from their school days in Palembang, including photographs of the school campuses, group photos of a graduating grade or class, photos taken when seeing teachers and students off to China, and photos of various extracurricular activities. While the former group appears in the regular issues as a kind of record and report of current community activities, the latter are mainly published in the special issues to celebrate the shared history of the Palembang Chinese and authenticate the origin of their friendship and the origin of the group.

In addition to writings and photographs, graphic symbols are another community building block. Pictures or drawings of representative architecture in Palembang, such as the main building of the Palembang Chinese High School and the bridge over the Musi River, have been repeatedly put on the journal covers. In addition, such Indonesian-style architecture is graphically overlaid with some representative buildings in Hong Kong, such as the Bank of China Tower and the Convention Centre, to remind them of their shared migration experience, common origin and history.

Second, symbols of the Chinese Schools, such as the school motto, school badge, school song and the school's logo also regularly appear in the journal, especially in the special issues. The inclusion of these images of architecture, emblem or melody that symbolize the common history of the Palembang Chinese is clearly designed to foster group spirit and solidarity through evoking memory.

It is interesting to analyse the nature of this memory construction. In romanticizing their childhood/ youth, the group appears to be not only seeking solace in a happier time, and reinforcing the idea of origin as a basis for home-making. It is possibly also a way to forget the hard times experienced during the PRC years and the early days in Hong Kong. Other studies have demonstrated the difficulty of incorporating trauma into narrative memory (Bal et al. 1999: viii). If the periods in the PRC and in Hong Kong are indeed viewed by this cohort as the wasted years, to focus their memory on Palembang and see it through rose-tinted lenses, provides them a means of collective forgetting.

Rituals

Just as lineages hold ancestor worship rituals, which play a vital role in enhancing solidarity, the Palembang Chinese conduct rituals for a similar reason. Their rituals include parties organized to celebrate the anniversaries of the founding of PCSAA and funerals for their leaders or former teachers.

Every year since the establishment of the association, they have held parties on the anniversary of the PCSAA, with the fifth and tenth anniversary celebrations being the grandest. At each party, all the leaders, consultants and community members turned up. Sumptuous feasts were prepared, and colourful performances were put on. These community-wide gatherings were poignant occasions to remind the Palembang Chinese of the spirit of comradeship and cohesion in this community, and thus strengthened their shared identity.

In past years, several Palembang Chinese have passed away, including community leaders and former teachers. The association published memorial articles in the journal for each of them, and hosted funerals for the most respected ones. Since funerals are traditionally family affairs, it is significant that the PCSAA plays such an active role in funeral organization as a way to stress the tightly knit and pseudo-familial nature of the group. The first large-scale funeral was held in 1990 for one of the founders of the PCSAA, who was also a teacher in Palembang and vice-chairman of the association in Hong Kong. Over 300 community members, together with his relatives and colleagues, attended that funeral. The chairman of PCSAA, the school principal and his classmates gave speeches to extol his virtues as a teacher, a schoolmate and a friend, as well as his unselfish contribution to the establishment of PCSAA (JPCSAA 1990: 34–35). The death of their peers evoked reflections on their fate as part of a floating diaspora, reminding them of their status as homeless strangers in society and prompting cohesion within the community.

CONCLUSION

This chapter examines the question of 'home' for migrants through a case study of the Indonesian-Chinese in Hong Kong. It shows that in a world of movement, the romantic, unitary sort of home defined in the traditional way has been replaced by a more dynamic and fragmentary sort of home. The authors argue that whenever migrants leave their original home, unavoidable ruptures within home begin to appear along three dimensions, the dimensions of origin, emotion and function. Home thus is not any longer defined by the ancestral attachment that migrants had longed for, but becomes a split complexity that is separated into three spaces and also into three meanings. For the Indonesian-Chinese in Hong Kong, Hong Kong is their 'functional home', Indonesia is their 'emotional home' and China is their 'ancestral home'. The ruptures between these three dimensions deepen with the continuation of their migrant journey, producing deep insecurity and sub-consciousness need for self-protection in the hearts of migrants.

To overcome the psychic pain of homesickness and fulfil their deep quest for 'rootedness' and familiarity, migrants never stopped searching for and making up a home, and 'it is in and through the continuity of movement that human beings continue to make themselves at home' (Rapport and Dawson 1998: 33). Significantly, the migrants construct a new home by borrowing traditional social and cultural elements, without being regulated by internal and external power relations. In the case of the Indonesian-Chinese, the severed social connections and periphery status they have suffered deprive them from taking up conventional forms of social grouping, such as *tongxianghui*, adopted by most Chinese in Hong Kong, and force them to resort to alumni association, which is rather new in the history of Chinese migrants. In addition, it is through imitating the traditional Chinese lineage system and manipulating collective memories that it becomes possible for them to give meaning and solidity to the alumni association and construct a 'symbolic home' in Hong Kong.

As such, in a world of globalization, 'home' for Chinese migrants is a circular process with multiple dimensions. It starts from a 'consistent home', moves to a 'divided home' and returns to a 'consistent home in a symbolic sense', in which, migrants fulfil their innermost desire for a coherent home defined in the most traditional way by finding their ends in their beginnings. However, this consistency is only achieved symbolically, because unlike a traditional home where the three dimensions of home achieve consistency on a grounded and tangible territory, in this new home, the consistency is realized by relying on a subjectively constructed 'extra-territorial' space. This space that their home is based is a deliberate escape from the centre–periphery domination, which is 'not as a single space, but as a space which is comparable to any other, which may be found to be equivalent to any other. And, if so, it can be exchanged for other spaces; as a result, one can move in other spaces without losing one's identity' (Ma 1998: 38). Therefore, unlike their ancestors who sent their bones back to China for burial, we find the Indonesian-Chinese bury their peers in Hong Kong, a place not only geographically in the middle between China and Indonesia, but culturally hybrid (Siu 1999). Only by committing themselves to a subjectively constructed space free from any centre–periphery rule, could they transfer the feelings of loss and worry into more positive factors and really obtain a feeling of homecoming.

NOTES

[1] The classmate associations can be further divided into two subsets based on the location and nature of the school. The first subset, consisting of 23 out of a total of 32 classmate associations, is based on the Chinese-language high schools in Southeast Asia; the second, consisting of 9 schools, is based on the preparatory schools or tertiary institutions in mainland China. Among the former type of association, it is often the case that members are not only schoolmates, but also share the same place of birth (though not necessarily the same place of ancestral origin or dialect). These associations are predominant in number and show the greatest vitality.

[2] Due to the poverty and strict implementation of the socialist public ownership system in mainland China at that time, they had little savings or private property to bring with at the time of exit. In addition, as the state strictly restricted the outflow of foreign currency, the maximum amount of money that was allowed to be taken out of China was just several hundred Hong Kong dollars (Godley and Coppel 1990a: 97; Wang 2003: 293–294).

[3] This was related by a key member of one South-east Asian Chinese association based on his personal observations. This assertion is also supported by many articles in the publications of South-east Asian Chinese organizations.

[4] For a detailed study of the organization and activities of the Palembang Chinese alumni association see Wang, C. B. (1999).

[5] For example, they held parties for the birthday of the principal, gathered together to celebrate the anniversaries of the Chinese schools in Indonesia and published memorial articles to recall their school days. Among the 130 articles published in the first nine volumes of the PCSAA journals, 62 are on school history, campus life and teachers and students, which account for 48 per cent of the total sum.

[6] In March 2003, Wang Gungwu gave a keynote speech at the Second Conference of Institutes and Libraries for Chinese Overseas Studies, 13–15 March, 2003, at the Chinese University of Hong Kong entitled 'Mixing Memories and Desires', quoting T. S. Eliot's 'The Waste Land'. His point was that most of the materials researchers have collected on Chinese overseas focus on statistics, political activities, government policies and so forth, neglecting those that convey their feelings and aspirations. These elements, so far largely neglected by scholars in the field, are exciting concepts that can be used to guide future research.

REFERENCES

Bai, Ren (1983) 'Guiqiao rencai wailiu zai xianggang' [Outflows of returned overseas Chinese talent in Hong Kong], *Dipingxian* [Horizon], no. 30, pp. 22–23.

Bal, Mieke, Jonathan V. Crewe and Leo Spitzer (eds) (1999) *Acts of Memory: Cultural Recall in the Present.* Hanover, NH: Dartmouth College: University Press of New England.

Ben, Dian (1986) 'ZaiGang guiqiao de husheng: Zuguo, bie wangji women' [Cries from returned Overseas Chinese in Hong Kong: Motherland, don't forget us]. *Huaren yuekan* [Chinese Monthly], no. 1, pp. 28–30.

Bhabha, Homi K. (1994) *The Location of Culture*. London; New York: Routledge.

Burns, John P. (1987) 'Immigration from China and the Future of Hong Kong'. *Asian Survey*, vol. 27, no. 6, pp. 661–682.

Chambers, Iain (1994) *Migrancy, Culture, Identity*. London; New York: Routledge.

Chan, Wendy W. Y. (1996) *Home But Not Home: A Case Study of Some Canadian Returnees in Hong Kong*. M. Phil. thesis, Hong Kong University of Science and Technology.

Chang, C. Y. (1980) 'Overseas Chinese in China's policy'. *The China Quarterly*, no. 82, pp. 281–303.

Chang, Shenglin (2002) 'Transcultural home identity across the Pacific: a case study of High-tech Taiwanese transnational communities in Hsinchu, Taiwan, and Silicon Valley, USA'. In Aygen *Erdentug and Freek Colombijn* (eds), *Urban Ethnic Encounters: the Spatial Consequences*. London; New York: Routledge.

Chang, Song and Mu, Rong (eds) (1998) 'Heise de wuyue: Yinni baotu canhai huaren baoxing zhenxiang' [Black May: the truth of the atrocity committed against Indonesian Chinese in the riots of 1998]. Beijing: Zhongguo guangbo dianshi chubanshe.

Chin, James K. (2003a) 'The returned Overseas Chinese community in Hong Kong: some observations'. In Billy K. L. So et al. (eds), *Power and Identity in the Chinese World Order: Festschrift in Honour of Professor Wang Gungwu*. Hong Kong: Hong Kong University Press, pp. 291–310.

—— (2003b) 'Multiple identities among the returned Overseas Chinese in Hong Kong'. In Michael W. Charney et al. (eds), *Chinese Migrants Abroad: Cultural, Educational and Social Dimensions of the Chinese Diaspora*. Singapore: Singapore University Press, pp. 63–82.

Constable, Nicole (1999) 'At home but not at home: Filipina narratives of ambivalent returns', *Cultural Anthropology*, vol. 14, no. 2, pp. 203–238.

Davison, R. B. (1968) 'No place back home: a study of Jamaicans returning to Kingston'. *Race*, vol. 9, no. 4, pp. 499–509.

Espiritu, Yen Le (2003) *Home Bound: Filipino American Lives across Cultures, Communities, and Countries*. Berkeley: University of California Press.

Fei, Ling (1982) 'Wei "Lüyinzhe" bian' [Defending new Indonesian-Chinese migrants in Hong Kong] *Jing Bao*, July, pp. 42–43.

Fitzgerald, Steven (1972) *China and the Overseas Chinese: A Study of Peking's Changing Policy, 1949–1970*. Cambridge, UK: Cambridge University Press.

Fouron, Georges. (2003) 'Haitian immigrants in the United States: the imagining of where 'home' is in their transnational social fields'. In Brenda S. A. Yeoh et al. (eds), *Approaching Transnationalisms: Studies on Transnational Societies, Multicultural Contacts, and Imaginings of Home*. Boston: Kluwer Academic Publishers.

Freedman, Maurice (1958) *Lineage Organization in Southeastern China*. London: Athlone Press.

Godley, Michael R. (1989) 'The sojourner: returned Overseas Chinese in the People's Republic of China'. *Pacific Affairs*, vol. 62, issue 3, pp. 330–352.

Godley, Michael R. and C. A. Coppel (1990a) 'The Indonesian Chinese in Hong Kong: a preliminary report on a minority community in transition'. *Issues and Studies*, vol. 26, no. 7, pp. 94–127.

—— (1990b) 'The pied piper and the prodigal children: a report on the Indonesian Chinese students who went to Mao's China'. *Archipel*, no. 39, pp. 179–198.

Guldin, G.regory E. (1997) 'Hong Kong ethnicity: of folk models and change'. In Grant Evans and Maria Tam (eds), *Hong Kong: The Anthropology of a Chinese Metropolis*. Richmond, Surrey: Curzon Press, pp. 25–50.

Harman, Lesley D. (1988) *The Modern Stranger: On Language & Membership*. New York: Mouton de Gruyter.

Li, Haitian (1987) *Xianggang guiqiao de zhuangkuang* [The situation of the returned Overseas Chinese in Hong Kong]. In *The Fifth Anniversary of Chiao Yao Association Ltd*. Hong Kong: The Association, June 1987, p. 25.

Lu, Haiyun and Quan, Haosheng (eds) (2001) *Guiqiao quaojuan gaikuang* [A general account of returned Overseas Chinese and Overseas Chinese dependants]. Beijing: Zhongguo huaqiao chubanshe.

Ma Mung, Emmanuel (1998) 'Groundlessness and utopia: the Chinese diaspora and territory'. In Elisabeth Sinn (ed.), *The Last Half Century of Chinese Overseas*. Hong Kong: Hong Kong University Press, pp. 35–47.

Manuel, Dolores (1997) 'Imagined homecomings: strategies for reconnection in the writing of Asian exiles'. In Geoffrey Kain (ed.), *Ideas of Home: Literature of Asian Migration*. East Lansing: Michigan State University Press.

Mao, Qixiong and Xiaodong Lin (eds) (1993) *Zhongguo qiaowu zhengce gaishu* [A brief account of the Overseas Chinese work policies of the PRC]. Beijing: Zhongguo huaqiao chubanshe.

Mu, Cang (1979) 'Dalu laiGang guiqiao kule geyi' [All kinds of joy and sorrow of the returned Overseas Chinese in Hong Kog]. *Jing Bao*, July 1979, pp. 41–42.

—— (1980) 'Zuguo yinggai guanxin tamen' [The Motherland ought to care about them]. *Jing Bao*, Dec., pp. 26–27.

—— (1984) 'Xianggang yinni guiqiao de eyun' [Bad luck of the Indonesian returned Overseas Chinese in Hong Kong]. *Huaren yuekan* [Overseas Chinese Monthly], March, no. 2, pp. 26–27.

Ou, Bofen (1988) 'Unforgettable the passions of the past'. JPCSAA, p. 25.

Qiao, Yan and Hua Sheng (eds) (1998) *98 Yinni huaren caoyu* [A true record of the misfortunes encountered by the Indonesian-Chinese in the riots of 1998]. Guangzhou: Jinan daxue chubanshe.

Rapport, Nigel and Andrew Dawson (eds) (1998) *Migrants of Identity: Perceptions of Home in a World of Movement*. Oxford, UK: Berg.

Rushdie, Salman (1991) *Imaginary Homelands: Essays and Criticism, 1981–1991*. London: Granta Books.

Rutherford, Jonathon (1990) 'A place called home'. In Jonathon Rutherford (ed.), *Identity, Community, Culture, Difference*. London: Lawrence & Wishart, pp. 9–27.

Said, Edward (1984) 'Reflections on exile'. *Granta*, no. 13, pp. 159–172.

Sarup, Madan (edited by Tasneem Raja) (1996) *Identity, Culture and the Postmodern World*. Edinburgh: Edinburgh University Press.

Sinn, Elizabeth (1989) *Power and Charity: the Early History of the Tung Wah Hospital*. Hong Kong: Oxford University Press.

—— (1997) '*Xin xi guxiang*: a study of regional associations as a bonding mechanism in the Chinese diaspora: the Hong Kong experience', *Modern Asian Studies*, vol. 31, no. 2, pp. 375–397.

—— (2002) 'Tongxiang associations and the centering of Hong Kong in the Chinese diaspora world'. Paper presented at the *Repositioning Hong Kong and Shanghai in Modern Chinese History Conference*, University of Hong Kong, 11–12 June.

Siu, Helen (1999) 'Hong Kong: cultural kaleidoscope on a world landscape'. In Gary G. Hamilton (ed.), *Cosmopolitan Capitalists: Hong Kong and the Chinese Diaspora at the End of the Twentieth Century*. Seattle and London: University of Washington Press, pp. 100–117.

Somerville, Peter (1992) 'Homelessness and the meaning of home: rooflessness or rootlessness?' *International Journal of Urban & Regional Research*, vol. 16, no. 4: 529–539.

Stack, Carol (1996) *Call to Home: African Americans Reclaim the Rural South*. New York: Basic Books.

T'ien, Ju-Kang (1953) *The Chinese of Sarawak: A Study of Social Structure*. London: London School of Economics and Political Science.

Wang, Cangbai (1999) 'Xianggang guiqiao tuan'tiyanjiu: yi Jugang (Xianggang) xiaoyouhui wei li' [Study of the returned Overseas Chinese organization in Hong Kong: a case study of Palembang Alumni Association (HK)]. *Huaoqiao huaren lishi yanjiu* [Overseas Chinese history studies], no. 47, pp. 55–66.

—— (2004) 'Re-establishing networks: capital, power and identity in the making of an Indonesian-Chinese community in Hong Kong'. Unpublished PhD Thesis, Hong Kong: the University of Hong Kong.

Wang, G.ungwu (1981) *Community and Nation: Essays on Southeast Asia and the Chinese*. Singapore: Heinemann Educational Books (Asia).

Wong, Siu-lun (1999) 'Deciding to stay, deciding to move, deciding not to decide'. In Gary G. Hamilton (ed.), *Cosmopolitan Capitalists: Hong Kong and the Chinese Diaspora at the End of the Twentieth Century*. Seattle and London: University of Washington Press.

Zhang, L. (1998) *Stranger in the City: Space, Power, and Identity in China's 'Floating Population'*. Ph.D. dissertation, Department of Anthropology, Cornell University.

Zhongguo he shijie zazhishe [China and the world journal publisher] (ed.) (1998) *Huayi de beiqing: Yinni baotu jianta renquan shilu* [The tragedy of the ethnic Chinese: a record of the violation of human rights in Indonesia]. Hong Kong: China and the World Journal Publisher.

Zhuang, Guotu (2001) *Huaqiao huaren yu Zhongguo de guanxi* [Relationships between China and Overseas Chinese]. Guangzhou: Guangdong gaodeng jiaoyu chubanshe.

Chapter 10

Rethinking 'Home' in Diaspora
A Family Transnationalized?
A Place of Nostalgia?
A Commodity for Sale?

Maggi W.H. Leung

Home is probably the initial place with which we identify ourselves – an important place often taken for granted. A more critical rethinking of the concept of 'home' suggests that it is not simply a physical, well-defined place. Rather it is a complex idea acquiring multiple associations that change in time and space. The notion of home is particularly intriguing for those who are often en route, crossing borders either physically or mentally. Migrants, especially transmigrants, are examples *par excellence*. As these individuals' lived environment extends beyond national borders, they become embedded in webs of transforming social relations that stretch across geographical and cultural boundaries (Massey and Jess 1995). Consequently their feelings of home and sense of belonging can be anchored with respect to different places. This chapter offers a multi-layered understanding of 'home' in diaspora, drawing upon a broader research about the Chinese population in contemporary Germany conducted from 1999 to 2002 (Leung 2004) supplemented with some follow-up interviews conducted in Hong Kong in 2004.[1] More specifically, I shall illustrate the multiple meanings of home as understood by the participants of this study. Among the wide variety of the concepts of home, migrants' experience of a 'transnationalised home' will be highlighted. While transnational families and communities have existed for centuries, the increasingly affordable transportation and telecommunication technologies in the current age of globalization have enabled most migrants to stay better in touch with their families and friends in different parts of the world. The analysis of the transnationalized home will set the stage for an examination of a branch of migrant business, namely the travel agencies, which have commonly identified the 'homing desire' and 'sense of home' among their ethnic fellows as a business niche. Illustrations in the following demonstrate how the business strategies of Chinese travel agencies create and help sustain transnational communities and indeed redefine, to a certain extent, transnational ties to home among diaspora Chinese and what dutiful members of transnational families are doing. Before turning to explore these issues, a brief overview of the historical demographic development of the Chinese migrant communities in Germany is in order.

CHINESE IN GERMANY: AN OVERVIEW

Contrary to other major destinations for Chinese migration, Germany does not have a core history contributing to this population movement. Chinese sojourners arrived in Germany in the first half of the eighteenth century. Significant Chinese settlement in Germany began, however, only in the 1870s. These early settlers were mostly men, ranging from peddlers, labourers, seamen at one end of the social ladder, to diplomats and students at the other. Before the First World War, there were only a few hundred Chinese settlers. Between the two World Wars, there were a few thousand Chinese in Germany, who were concentrated in Hamburg and Berlin. The Second World War disrupted the Chinese populations in Germany, and most of them left. The current geography of Chinese settlement can be traced back to the end of the 1950s when larger numbers came from Hong Kong and Taiwan, most of whom entered the catering and restaurant business. In the 1960s and 1970s, a considerable number of ethnic Chinese from Indonesia, Vietnam, Laos and Cambodia arrived in Germany largely due to the anti-Chinese sentiment in their homelands. Since the late 1970s, there has been a sharp increase in the number of students and business people coming from Taiwan and more recently from the People's Republic of China (hereafter PRC). According to official census data, 77,309 individuals with Chinese and Taiwanese nationalities were living in Germany by the end of 2002 (Statistisches Bundesamt 2003: 40). These individuals make up, however, only a portion of the ethnic Chinese community. The Chairman of the European Federation of Chinese Organisations [*Ouhua lianhui*] (Personal communication, October 1999) estimates that there are currently 150,000 ethnic Chinese living in Germany, but this was often considered to be an over-estimate among my interviewees. As Giese (2003) observes, the new Chinese migration (from the early 1970s) to Germany is a highly heterogeneous process, forming (if at all) a loosely connected migration system. Community leaders sometimes categorize contemporary Chinese migrants into three groups: *laoqiao* (old sojourners) who arrived before the Second World War , *xinqiao* (new sojourners) who arrived in the 1960s and 1970s and *huayi* (people of Chinese descent) which comprises the ethnic Chinese migrants from South-east Asia arriving around the 1980s. Certainly one should add at least one important category, namely the new Chinese migrants arriving after the 1980s. This group of migrants is again highly heterogeneous. The new migration flow has also included an increasing proportion of business, professional and skilled migrants, many of whom having migrated as students. The diversity of the so-called Chinese community in Germany also accounts also for a plethora of the meanings of home and homeland among its members. Depending on the socio-economic background of individual migrant, his or her ability to establish and maintain ties with the different homes in transnational space would also vary.

MIGRATION, TRANSNATIONALISM AND 'HOME' IN DIASPORA

Transnationalism represents one of the most recent developments in the field of migration research in the past decade. Vertovec (1999: 447) defines transnationalism as 'multiple ties and interactions linking people or institutions across the borders of nation-states', where the dynamic ties, linkages or networks can be of an economic, socio-cultural and political nature. Transnationalism signifies therefore dynamic processes made up of dynamic and fluid relationships between people, states and capital that are increasingly geographically mobile and unfettered by national boundaries. Taking into consideration that research has also mapped out the transnational aspects of flows in capital, goods, information and population, Ma (2003:4) considers the study of migration to lie at the core of transnationalism when he notes that 'transmigration and diaspora are the most important constituent part of transnationalism'. The concept of transnationalism attained its position of importance in the migration discourse of the early 1990s. Instead of assuming migrants' journeys as permanent, linear and bipolar, advocates of the transnationalism underscore the cross-border circulation and multi-directional movements of people, materials and ideas. These frequent circulations and exchanges have created new or hybrid transnational cultures, identities and community spheres (Basch et al. 1994; Faist 1998; Rouse 1991). Whereas circular movements by migrants are not new,2 Portes et al.(1999), point out the historical distinctiveness of the contemporary phenomenon with the following observation (p. 217):

> While back and forth movements by immigrants have always existed, they have not acquired until recently the critical mass and complexity necessary to speak of an emergent social field. This field is composed of a growing number of persons who live dual lives: speaking two languages, having homes in two countries, and making a living through continuous regular contact across national borders.

Without a doubt, the revolutionary innovations in transportation technology and electronic communication have facilitated easier, more affordable and almost instantaneous, first-hand exchanges across great distances. To a large extent, one can argue that technologies and the consequential commonplace in long-distance travelling and telecommunication have redefined often taken-for-granted concepts such as home, family and the related duties, care and affections.

My exchanges with contemporary Chinese migrants also confirm the 'dual lives' (or even triple, quadruple lives) phenomenon observed by Portes and associates. As Wang and Wong (see Chapter 9 in this volume) contend in their contribution for this volume, home can be multiple, dynamic and fragmentary. While Chinese migrants in Germany, according to my interpretations, do not always conform to the 'circular process' in home-searching and home-making as experienced by the Indonesian Chinese in Hong Kong, their diverse conceptualizations of home is apparent. Most, if not all, of the migrants I have encountered share in their conceptualization of home as a place of multiplicity and fluidity. For some, home is the place where they were born. It is a place redolent in nostalgia, a place to which they can no longer return. Some consider home to be the lived experience of a locality, beginning when they first set their feet down; for others, home is a destination for which they have left or a prospect to which they have aspired. Home is not always anchored on stable, solid ground. While some leave their homes behind when they go on their journeys, others make home as part of their migration, bearing their 'mobile homes' with them in the manner of snails; some have multiple homes in different locales. Depending on the particular time/space context, a person's notion of home can also change, reflecting any of the above-mentioned perceptions.[3]

In her work *Cartographies of Diaspora*, Brah asserts that 'the double, triple, or multi-placedness of 'home' in the imagery of people in the diaspora does not mean that such groups do not feel anchored in their place of settlement' (Brah 1996: 194). Rather, participants of my research often consider themselves having a home being both 'here' and 'there'. The feeling of having multiple and transnationalized homes is not only found among first-generation migrants. In most cases the 1.5- (those who migrated when they were very young) or second-generation Chinese migrants interviewed also exhibited multiply located home identities. Michael (late 20s),[4] a Sinology and business student whose parents left Shanghai, first to make a home in Hong Kong where they stayed for a few years, and then to Hamburg 30 years ago, reflected on his sense of home:

> Sometimes I feel at home here in Hamburg, sometimes I feel at home in Asia... When? When I feel that it's too slow and quiet here, I miss Asia. And when I am sick of the crowds and hustle-bustle in Asia, then I feel at home in Germany... I am Chinese and I am German, I cannot deny either side of me. I am both and I want to have the best of both worlds. (Personal communication, November 1999)

Talking about his future plans, Michael aspired to a working life that would permit him to live in both worlds, touching home bases across transnational space.

Claiming home in different places, however, is not always merely an outcome of the migrants' intention. As Brah (1996:192) argues, 'The question of home ... is intrinsically linked with the way in which processes of inclusion and exclusion operate and are subjectively experienced under given circumstances'. Hegemonic ideas about belonging and not belonging in racial and cultural terms demarcate the socio-cultural space in which migrants and minority groups can lay claim to home. Many of the 1.5 or second-generation migrants interviewed commented on the fact that their physical appearance of 'not looking like Germans' hinders them from easily identifying Germany as home. While they feel at home in Germany in most cases, the social exclusion they experience tends to make a public acknowledgment of the place as home difficult. Pui Yee (late 20s), a Sinology and business student whose parents migrated from Hong Kong to Germany in the end of 1950s, regards herself as being 'Hong Kong Chinese' even though she was born and raised in Hamburg. She explained to me her feeling of being out of place in Germany (Personal communication, September 1999):

> Many people say that I am very German. But if you call yourself a German, they look at you funny and say, 'No'. You can't be German looking like me, right? At school I did not have many German friends. You will see who my friends are when they come. They are all, but one, atypical Germans. They [the 'Germans'] do not understand us. I don't feel that we are alike. It is strange, I don't know why.

Pui Yee had always aspired to 'return' to her other home, Hong Kong, after her university studies. Indeed, upon graduation, she began her new life in Hong Kong. While not being able to be physically near to her parents, she tries to be and is very present in all family affairs. She reflects regarding her and her siblings' relationship with their parents (Personal communication, November 2004):

> It's funny. I am so far away, but I am the one who talks to my mother the most. My sister lives in the same house with my parents, but they don't really talk. You know how my mom is. Sometimes she is very harsh. So my sister has adopted the strategy of not talking to her. I call mom quite often and talk for a long time, so I feel that I am the closest to my mother. I guess it's because I can hang up anytime if I can't stand it anymore. Haha. And my brother? He hardly calls. That is of course very hard for my mom. But what to do. His own family has become the centre of his universe.

One issue that lingers in the mind of most migrants who are away from the family is about caring for ageing parents. Pui Yee is also not an exception:

> My parents are still fit and young at heart. But yes, one of us has to be in Hamburg. No other choice. It's good that my sister wants to stay there, because I have always wanted to live in Asia. And my brother, though he did not really plan to, has now established a career in Beijing. I don't know if he wants to go home. Even he does, my sister-in-law [who comes from Malaysia where the couple met] might not want to. So we can't count on him.

As Pui Yee decided to materialize her dream to establish a new home in her ancestral homeland, she has to pay the price of being absent from her other home. Thanks to new components of transnational life such as e-mail and long distance telephone calls, the effect of physical distance between her two homes can be minimized. As a dutiful daughter, she has also renovated her father's village house which he left in the end of 1950s, so a longer-term return of her retired parents would be possible. Since her return to Hong Kong in 2001, Pui Yee has returned to Hamburg about twice a year, while both of her parents have visited over extended periods around important Chinese celebrations such as Ching Ming Festival (Tomb-Sweeping Day, *Qingmingjie*) and Chung Yeung Festival (Festival of the Dead Spirits, *Zhongyuanjie*),[5] her sister and brother's family have also spent holidays in Hong Kong. In today's world, transnational families are often 'frequent flyer families'. Despite the technological revolution in telecommunication, physical visits are still considered to be the best way to maintain concrete ties with one's kin members and friends in different homelands, and express one's love and care for them. Certainly, frequent flying is still difficult or unaffordable for most migrants; they do their utmost to save up to make their trip home whenever they can. Parents working overseas return to their families to make sure that 'home businesses' are in order; children and grandchildren make their ways to their ageing parents and grandparents to show their filial piety; and transnational grandparents, especially grandmothers, travel to grandchildren across distances to help their children out. Home visits are not only demand-driven. In the following section, I shall illustrate how a wide range of state agencies and private businesses have also identified the enticing power of 'home' in diaspora for their benefits.

DIASPORA AND TOURISM

The intensification of transnationalism is marked by, among other developments, an increase in international travel. For transnational families, visits – along with remittances, I would argue – are the most physical expression of familial obligations and care. Migrants' visits between different homes, as well as to other places where families, friends and relatives around the globe live, is one of the most cohesive forces that maintain transnational communities. Diaspora tourism has grown into a significant market niche in the tourism sector in recent years. While home can take on different forms and mean various places for each individual, a 'homing desire' (Brah 1996) is a heartfelt yearning common to almost all migrants. While this desire, coupled with a sense of nostalgia, might not lead them to stay in one home forever, it nevertheless serves as a potent force to entice migrants to make their journeys home again and again. The 'homing desire' of various diaspora (or so-called hyphenated communities, e.g. Asian-Americans) is the marketing target of many actors in the tourism industry, ranging from official tourist boards in the 'homeland' states to tourist agencies, restaurants and hotels in the private sector. The rapid development of this particular form of tourism has also attracted the attention in the academic community. In the call for papers at the Association of American Geographers Meeting held in 2002, the convenors of the session 'Travel to promised lands: tourism, space and diaspora' wrote:

> In recent years vacation products have been carefully designed, heavily marketed, and voraciously consumed by hyphenated communities driven by nostalgia for their perceived ancestral homes and the desire to experience authenticity. Diaspora is clearly a market niche...

Diaspora is more than only a market niche for private businesses. Perhaps as importantly, many nation-states are also eager to make use of this nostalgia among their 'sons and daughters' in diaspora for purposes which range from politics to economics. For example, the High Level Committee on Indian Diaspora, a major initiative set up by the Indian government to forge stronger ties with the Indian diaspora that is estimated to reach 15 million world-wide. Special tour packages, like pilgrim packages, have been developed and publicized to attract the so-called second generation PIOs (persons of Indian origin). The Bermuda Ministry of Tourism, citing another instance, has also been active in cultivating the African diasporic spirit through 'The African Diaspora Heritage Trail' project launched in 2001. The economic benefit of diaspora tourism can be reflected by the Armenian case. In 2001, hundreds of thousands of diaspora tourists visited Armenia to celebrate its 1,700[th] anniversary of the adoption of Christianity as the state religion, spending an estimated US$1,000 per person in the country.[6] The Armenian state strives to tap the estimated five million diaspora Armenians world-wide as potential visitors by improving the infrastructure needed to develop the tourism sector (Walters 2001).

Some other projects have been conducted for political reasons. A prime example is that of the Israeli state in promoting and sustaining the homing desire among Jews in diaspora. A significant segment of the Israeli tourist industry is designed to cater to Jews living throughout the world who pay visits to Israel for the purpose of pilgrimage. Cohen (2004) analyses a tour named 'Exodus', designed specifically for young Jews from North and South America, the UK and France, whose itinerary is arranged to first visit Holocaust sites, then includes a boat trip to re-enact their ancestors' flight to Palestine and finishes with several weeks spent in Israel. During the tour, powerful and emotional symbols are used to arouse or strengthen the image of Israel as a 'homeland' for these adolescent tourists. The Wales Tourist Board also pushes diaspora tourism with the slogan *'Mae'n Bryd I Ddod Adref* – It's Time to Come Home' – an initiative aiming to forge stronger links to the global Welsh community. The global Welsh community is important not only as a source of tourism earnings, but also as a key component of the political and cultural agenda of the newly established Welsh Assembly (Morgan and Pritchard 2004).

The significance of diaspora tourism can be clearly observed in the Chinese case. Official annual statistics show that Chinese from Hong Kong, Macau and Taiwan are by far the dominant source of visitors to the PRC. The figure reached 73.2 million in 2000 (87.7 percent of the country's official total arrivals) and is expected to increase.[7] It should be noted that this figure incorporates day excursions from Hong Kong and Macau, which have increased substantially in recent years due to the integration of the economies of the two Special Administration Regions with the mainland, especially that of the southern PRC, but fails to note that many making these trips are from South-east Asia and other world regions.

My research has confirmed that certain Chinese festivals, such as annual New Year, Mid-Autumn, Ching Ming and Chung Yeung Festival and special events such as weddings and funerals are important reasons for overseas Chinese to pay home visits. My communication with foreign exchange students with an ethnic Chinese family background at my university also verify the motivation of many young (1.5 to second-generation) ABC (American/Australian-born-Chinese), BBC (British-born-Chinese), CBC (Canadian-born-Chinese) etc. in getting to know their ancestral homes better.

Contrary to the studies mentioned earlier, my following analysis does not lay emphasis on state efforts towards propagating the homing desire among diaspora communities. Rather, my analysis will focus on the ways in which migrant entrepreneurs commodify 'home' and the 'homing desire' to produce business opportunity.

Chinese-owned travel agencies in Germany

A complete list of travel agencies operated by Chinese migrants in Germany is not available. Although estimates from my interviewees ranged from one to a few hundred travel agencies owned by ethnic Chinese in Germany, only the addresses of 35 such travel agencies were listed in the business directory *China-Branchenbuch* published in 1998. In addition, a few other firms that put advertisements in the monthly Chinese business newspaper *Chinesische Handelszeitung* and other Chinese language community publications were noted. The following analysis draws upon interviews with 11 travel agents in Hamburg, Frankfurt/Main and Mainz. The interviewees are migrants (or in one case, a descendent) from Taiwan, Hong Kong and the PRC.

Similar to many other 'classical' migrant businesses, the initial market opportunity for migrant-run travel agencies arises within ethnic communities. Migrant businesses generally find their niche in providing homey products and services. 'Ethnic consumer products' such as culinary items, music, videos and DVDs, entertainment (e.g. the popular karaoke clubs) newspapers, books and magazines, clothing and jewellery help produce and maintain ethnic identities, culture and traditions among migrant communities. Other service providers, such as legal and finacial consultants, translators, realtors and travel agencies, cater to co-ethnics who are unfamiliar with the language or bureaucratic procedures in the host countries. In a particularly concrete way, travel agencies perform a special function in constructing and maintaining community ties and identities across space. Unlike other ethnic goods and services which create a sense of home away from home, travel agencies foster the physical connections between family, friends and other community members in the transnational landscape. To facilitate their business in home-style, employers engage Chinese, or at least Chinese-speaking employees in higher proportion (ranging from 70 to 100 per cent of the personnel in the sampled agencies). Having said that, it is important to note that ethnic travel agencies are not restricted to providing diasporic services. As international travel became a commonly practised hobby, ethnic travel agencies have also availed themselves of a market place in which customers, migrants and non-migrants alike, seek pleasure by travel to destinations not related to their original migration history.

In spite of their modest scale (ranging from one to 18 employees in my sample), many of the travel agencies do not limit their services exclusively to selling plane tickets which shuttle their clients to and from European and Asian homes. Most of the agencies now also offer European travel arrangements and organize sightseeing tours and business excursions within Europe as well as to Asia. A few of the agencies also operate guest houses, sell international telephone cards, arrange health insurance, offer translation services or provide special assistance with visa applications and arrange invitation letters for clients interested in coming to Germany for studying, setting up businesses or even marrying.[8] Similar to other travel agencies, many of their business transactions are conducted via telephone, fax or email. A few of the Chinese travel agencies have also caught up with the web business trend, and have set up multi-lingual (German, Chinese and English) homepages from which customers can reserve their tickets via the internet. Unlike 'ordinary' travel agencies, some Chinese travel agencies provide 24-hour around-the-clock 'emergency' and weekend services via mobile phone. Extending work hours is only one of the strategies the Chinese, like other migrant-run agencies, have adopted to better their business potential. The following section will provide a close look at the special position many migrant entrepreneurs have identified in running their business: namely, presenting themselves as a comrade in diaspora.

Playing the Tongbao card

Chinese customers comprise from 50 to 90 per cent of the clientele of the Chinese travel agencies interviewed.[9] Chinese-speaking personnel and advertisements in Chinese language newspapers and community newsletters are key ways to capture the ethnic Chinese clientele. Word-of-mouth among customers also serves as a good advertising channel. Martin Chen, the owner of probably the oldest Chinese tourist agencies in Germany said, 'We don't need to do much advertising. The people who have lived in Hamburg for a while would know us anyway (Personal communication, January 2000)'. Their popularity is partially a result of his family's active involvement in the Chinese community ever since the 1920s.

Playing the ethnic card, that is, selling their Chinese identity to serve other Chinese sisters and brothers, marks the difference in marketing tactics between the Chinese-owned and non-Chinese-owned agencies. Ethnic camaraderie is effective, however, only when it is translated concretely into cheap fares and flexible service. It is, for instance, common that these agencies offer a different fare for ethnic Chinese customers. For a round-trip ticket from Frankfurt to Hong Kong that I bought in 2000, for instance, I received a DM100 discount from a DM900 fare merely because I was Chinese. Being surprised by this arguably discriminative price system, I asked for the reason for the discount. My travel agent explained, 'We have discounts for customers that are going home. So if you are from Hong Kong, you get the discount'. Among the life tips migrants pass on to their fellows, together with a good Chinese grocery store or a cheap long-distance telecom company, a reliable and cheap travel agency is frequently on the top of the list. Michelle (30s) from Hong Kong, who had lived in Hamburg for more than a decade, recommended her 'friendship' agency to me upon our very first encounter (Personal communication, September 1999):

> If you want to go home, you should call my travel agent. We have known each other for many years. They have good fares compared to other agencies. And they don't make a fuss when you change your plans. You know sometimes we have to change our plans last minute and it is always a trouble with agencies you don't know. You can reserve your tickets and they don't demand deposits. You can even pay the ticket the day before you fly. We trust each other. If you want to get tickets to go home, let me know, I will call them, or just say, you know me.

In order to display comradeship to their potential clients, travel agencies have to compete with price and take some risks such as prolonging the payment-free reservation period. Interviews with travel agencies show that the trust and friendship relationship between them and their clients functions reasonably well.

Another special service regularly offered by Chinese-owned travel agencies for their fellow brothers and sisters in diaspora is the cost-free upgrade in baggage allowance. Since migrants often travel heavily with gifts for family and relatives on the way 'home' on the hand, and with desired home products when they leave home on the other, the extra baggage allowance provides these agencies an important edge. When I saw Pui Yee's father off after his 2-month stay in Hong Kong, he was surprised how heavy his own luggage was (Personal communication, November 2004): 'Wow. 33 kg! Goodness. But good that I am allowed to carry 30 kg. So I am just a few kg over. Should be no problem. They will be nice to me, an old man bringing gifts to his family. Haha. They will make no fuss.'

Indeed, his personal belongings might only have weighed 2 kg. I did a quick survey of the content of his luggage. Not surprisingly, the other 31 kg comprised predominantly food, tea, herbs, magazines, newspapers and Hong Kong movies and TV soap opera series on VCDs. I teased him that he was carrying items that one could easily find in Hamburg. He gave me a mini-lecture in response:

> Aiya. How can you compare these with the stuff you get in Hamburg? For example, these sponge cakes are very special. Pui Yee's mother loves them. We call them 'Husband Cake'. That's what we used to eat when we were young. The shop is still there, after all these years. And I travelled all the way to Yuen Long to get these Chinese sausages. Have you not heard of this store? We village people consider the sausages there the best. A store with history, you know? And of course tea. You know, we have been in Germany for 40 years now, and we have never bought tea there. We always drink our tea from Hong Kong. And these fried tofu. They are so good. Pui Yee's mother has ordered them ...

Similar to his transport action upon departure, Pui Yee's father also completed the order from his daughter for his trip to Hong Kong and brought two bottles of German wine, a considerable amount of chocolate and cheeses, a loaf of German bread and a few magazines – things that Pui Yee misses the most from her other home.

In a very tangible way, Chinese travel agencies help fellow co-ethnics fulfil some of their obligations as responsible members of a transnational family. To a certain extent, one could consider that these travel agencies have redefined their customers' duties, or more appropriately, their capacity in transferring homey goods and memories to their transnational family. Readers might wonder how these agencies manage to provide these perks. According to the manager of the largest Chinese travel agency in Germany, they received special deals from the major airlines flying between Germany to the PRC, Hong Kong and Taiwan as they sell these tickets in large quantity. Small Chinese travel agencies would in turn sometimes buy up tickets from bigger agencies. Thus, even though these travel agencies are mostly competitors, a certain level of networking also exists when it works for mutual benefit.

As I mentioned earlier, speaking Chinese is another concrete way to show comradeship. Only being able to speak 'wrong' Chinese languages might restrict the agency's effort in offering a home-style service. Depending on the individual geographical backgrounds of the business-owners, their targeted clientele tends to differ. After having found out that I was from Hong Kong, Li Ning (40s), who is from the PRC, told me that he was in search of a Cantonese-speaking employee, as he hoped that the new colleague would contribute in expanding his business to a new 'sub-ethnic' terrain (Personal communication, November 1999):

> Like in Düsseldorf, there is one agent. The owner is from Hong Kong. Their target is the Cantonese-speaking customers. And there is another one that caters more for Hong Kong and Vietnamese customers. The Overseas Chinese from Vietnam, you know? They often speak Cantonese. Most of the restaurant-owners are Cantonese-speaking. There is a big market there. That's why I want to hire someone who speak or at least understand Cantonese.

Cultural affinity and proficiency in their customers' language and ways of thinking are clear advantages shared by Chinese agencies as compared to their non-Chinese counterparts. These advantages do not only bring them business opportunities from the Chinese migrant population in Germany and Europe at large, but also position them well in the expanding market for Chinese international tourism. The growing number of PRC tourists in the international landscape in the last few years has introduced remarkable changes to the tourist industry in Europe (and even more so in East and South-east Asia). Ever since the introduction of the Open Door Policy in the PRC in the late 1970s and the rising affluence of some Chinese people, it has been more convenient and popular for them to travel overseas, both for leisure or work purposes. The PRC recorded 16.6 million outbound tourists in 2002, surpassing Japan for the first time as Asia's largest source of outbound tourists (Scandinavian Tourist Board 2004). The World Tourism Organization predicts that China will become the biggest tourist destination and the fourth-largest source of outbound tourists by 2020 (Butler 2003). Travel and tourism operators all over the world are eyeing the PRC as a huge source of potential travellers.

In Germany, visitors from the PRC and Hong Kong now represent the third largest group of international hotel guests outside of Europe (only guests from the USA and Japan exceeded this total), having spent a total of 800,000 overnight stays in 2004 (Deutsche Zentrale für Tourismus e.V., 2005).[10] The importance of the Chinese tourist market is not only reflected by the increase in body count. According to the Chinese statistics (Zhang 2004), a Chinese tourist spends an average of 3,000 Euro while visiting Germany, which is much above the figure for an average international tourist. An example illustrates the increasing importance of PRC visitors in the German tourism market-place: the Mayor of Füssen (a popular tourist location in the state of Bavaria in southern Germany) announced the city's new plan to build more hotels and strengthen the tourist industry; its advertising focus would be oriented toward Chinese tourists (*Süddeutsche Zeitung* 2001). The intensifying connections of the Chinese state and nationals in global socio-economic webs are the seed of the golden dream of many Chinese travel agents. The entry of the PRC into the World Trade Organization in 2001 is also perceived as a great opportunity for those, like the travel agencies in my study, who are building bridges of goods, services and people between the PRC and the wider world. The increasing mobility of the PRC Chinese contributes directly to the expansion of Chinese-owned tourist agencies. The observations of O' Loughlin (40s), an Irish tourist guide who has worked for a German agency for over 10 years recalls the development in this economic sector (Personal communication, February 2002):

> When I first started working in Germany [ten years ago], I toured American and Japanese tourists around mostly. And then more and more Taiwanese came. And now there are a lot more tourists from China and India coming to Europe. I can't smell Chinese food anymore after doing one of those [Chinese] tours, I tell you! [laugh] Our agent used to have bus tours for the [PR] Chinese. But now there is no more. They are now all organized by the Chinese tourist agencies and usually they don't hire a normal tourist bus, but just one of these 9-seaters. For a few people, they hire a Chinese driver who serves at the same time as the tourist guide. So the driver must be Chinese, you know? Basically this part of our business is gone. Practically, we don't have any more Chinese clients, neither bus rentals, nor tours.

As a matter of fact, offering tours for as few as a single tourist is a common service offered by Chinese travel agents. Mei (20s), a student in Heidelberg from Chengdu organized a tour for her parents during their short visit (Personal communication, February 2002):

> When my parents came to visit, of course they wanted to tour around. But I could not bring them around myself as I had classes. And they couldn't go around by themselves without any German [or English]. So I called one of these travel agencies and asked if they had tours. They advertise it in the [Chinese business] newspaper. I called and they said they did not have any tours then, but they could organize one for my parents, only for my parents. And it was not that expensive. So I did that. Basically you hire a car and a driver who is also the guide. It worked out fine.

Being able to provide service flexibly and cater to the special needs of Chinese clients is the market edge Chinese travel agents have found. 'I am Chinese, I know what they need' captures the general belief among Chinese travel agencies, an asset that non-Chinese travel agencies lack. In the following section, more details will be given on the ways these businesses have commodified the sense of home, both for their Chinese clients leaving Germany to go home, or leaving home to visit Europe.

Marketing the homing desire, feeling of home and comradeship

Among the different migrant businesses, travel agencies facilitate migrants' life overseas, providing spaces where migrants can 'get things done the way like at home' in the form on last-minute changes and payments. They are particularly 'close to heart' since they help pave their journeys home, bringing them physically, among other destinations, to their (ancestral) homes. Hence, Chinese tourist agencies find their niche beyond simply selling far-flung destinations through promoting 'Fernweh' ('distance-sickness'), as travel agencies usually do, but just as intensively, by marketing Heimweh (home-sickness) among their fellow co-ethnics in diaspora. The 'homing desire' is the main item making the sales pitch in this advertisement placed by a travel agency in Düsseldorf:

> The great Yangtze, the Great Wall,
> Yellow Mountain, the Yellow River;
> Weigh like a thousand stone in my heart.
> At any time, at any place, as close as my heart.

Here, by painting a beautiful, romanticized (stereo)typical landscape in the readers' mind, the travel agent evokes nostalgic sentiments, and even almost a sense of duty to return home. During our interview at his travel agency, Li Kai (40s), who had studied German language and literature and worked in the tourism branch in the PRC before he migrated to Germany in the late 1980s, pointed out more explicitly the importance of the 'homing desire' in his very successful and expanding business. In answering a question about the opportunity structure in the travel agency sector, he said,

> How should I say? Put it this way. Among German people, they might not once think of going away. But among Chinese, may they be from Hong Kong or China, they want to go home. So I believe that every single Chinese

who is running on the street here could potentially become my customer (Personal communication, December 1999).

With a confident smile, he continued to explain his philosophy for business success:

> That was my thinking when I set up my firm [in 1993]. I am cultivating that. Who does not want to go home? If they have the money, when they have holidays, they want to go home. They are there, [the market is] stable. It all depends on how you operate, how you run your business. There are also Chinese travel agents that closed down. So I say, theoretically the business is stable, because the clientele is stable. The point how you get these people who want to go home, that is another question. The stabling factor is that these people are here, and they want to go home (Personal communication, December 1999).

Indeed as world tourism in general suffered from serious disruption after the terrorist attacks in the USA on 11 September 2001, homeward travel was the least affected portion of tourism. As Hsien (40s) observes, 'Business trips have been cancelled. But for those who need to go home, nothing can scare them away' (Personal communication, January 2002). As one would logically expect, the rousing of homing desire is particularly noticeable prior to important Chinese festivals. Advertisements in the newspapers and on the Internet reminding readers of the coming of Chinese New Year or Mid-Autumn Festival – these are two special occasions when (transnationalized or translocalized) families get together.

Most of the Chinese travel agencies do not only bring sojourners 'home', they also provide services to bring the sojourners' families to Europe as Mei's experience in the last section points out. Another travel agency in Aachen, which also has a branch office in Beijing, advertises in the Chinese business newspaper:

> Do your parents, brothers, sisters, family and friends want to visit Europe?
>
> Choose two of the short-term tours here.
>
> We will apply for the tourist visa for you!

Tour organizers act, to a certain extent, almost as a member of the transnational families, easing the burden on their fellows in bringing their families and friends to visit them. After their arrival, these tour agencies also make them feel comfortable and 'at home' while in Europe. To achieve this hominess, there is a presumption that Chinese tour operators are better equipped to satisfy the wishes of their co-ethnic tourists. As Li Kai stated with a perplexed tone, 'Chinese understand the wishes of Chinese more. Europeans don't understand. The people from China are sometimes quite strange (*qiguai*) (Personal communication, December 1999)'. Linkages among Chinese travel agencies across space within Europe are hence a valuable resource to ensure that their customers will be served in an acceptable-to-Chinese manner. In order to satisfy the desire of tourists who come to visit Europe on '7-day, 7-country' tours, transnational inter-firm networks come in handy, especially for smaller-scale agencies which do not have branch offices where their tours visit. Concrete arrangements made to create hominess include hiring Chinese-speaking tour guides, hosting visitors in Chinese-run hotels, and having a few meals taken during their tour in Chinese restaurants.

Compared to other branches of Chinese businesses, one observes a stronger tendency for travel agencies to be more than just service providers, but also personal friends, a brother or a sister who is there to help. One of the advertisements in the Chinese community newspapers stands out in its effort to market the sense of brother- and sisterhood. This particular enterprise offers a wide range of services beyond typical travel arrangements, including sales of telephone cards, health insurance and the provision of translation services. Its almost full-fare service was advertised with the following 'touching' wordings in their advertisements:

> Listening to your heart's desires, respecting your treasured privacy,
>
> Freely offering all types of living, work, and residency consultation and advice,
>
> Enthusiastically calming your worries and resolving your difficulties.

This oath may sound rather exaggerated and over-sentimental, but the frequent use of this kind of language by travel agents is striking when compared to advertisements of other Chinese migrant businesses. Travel agencies present themselves as much more than a sales agent. Rather, they hope to be perceived as a trusted family member, who is ready around-the-clock to help out with any issues that transnational families and communities have to deal with, both 'at home here and there'. Another example can be cited from an advertisement by an agency in Mainz:

Gladly willing to share the burdens of Chinese travelling to Germany, and provide service to Chinese worldwide.

Again, the pledge seems a bit bombastic when compared with what travel agencies usually offer. But, at least for the one who designed the motto, arousing or acknowledging comradeship with tens of thousands or millions of 'sisters and brothers', not only in Germany but in the global horizon, is one of the tactics which draws potential clients. These advertisements also reflect the special significance travel agencies hold, or at least try to achieve, for the creation and maintenance of diaspora community identity and solidarity when compared to other sorts of migrant businesses. The stirring of homing desire and feelings of home and comradeship has, of course, no guarantee of success. To most of those interviewed, price is still the trump card. Other than reasonable fares, the provision of tailored and flexible service to fulfil clients' travel needs, which is a provision not always supplied by ordinary travel agencies, is also crucial. Nevertheless, a touch of understanding and solidarity as comrades or family members together in diaspora does not hurt.

CONCLUSIONS

The question of 'home' is particularly intriguing among those whose life-worlds stretches borders. Reflections from informants in this research illustrate the need to rethink and redefine the traditional notion of 'home' as only a piece of grounded and material territory existing in singularity. 'Homemaking' can or should be conceptualized as complex and fluid psychological, cultural, social, economic and political processes. Transnational migrants commonly identify multiple places as home, due to their own and their families' migration biographies on the one hand, and the social space offered by 'host' societies to allow migrants to claim them as home on the other. Depending on circumstances, migrants maintain their multiple homes using different means, ranging from nostalgic reminiscence in their minds, to writing letters or emails, calling, to travelling back for home visits. While migrants have always expressed their multiple identities and allegiances through communication, visits and remittances, ever-more accessible and affordable air transport and telecommunication technology have redefined lives of many transnational migrants. This chapter focuses on the role of migrant-owned travel agencies in establishing and maintaining the linkages among members of transnational families and communities. More specifically, I have illustrated from the case of Chinese-owned travel agencies in Germany, how the concept of 'home' and 'homing desire' are being commodified in the tourism business. By presenting their customers' homeland as a place of nostalgia and reminding sojourners of coming family festivals, travel agencies create and refresh *Heimweh* in their business, more than *Fernweh* which is the main sentiment being marketed by 'ordinary' travel agencies. As brothers and sisters in diaspora, these ethnic Chinese travel agents foreground their cultural affinity and knowledge of China to appeal to co-ethnics. By commodifying China as 'home at heart' and festival celebrations as required events for a Chinese person, these marketing tactics help reinforce the meaning of a 'genuine home' as located in China, and the 'need to return' among 'dutiful sojourners'.

In addition to bringing migrants home, tour operators also create a home for visitors. Travel agencies participate actively, from applying for visas to offering reasonably priced tickets that originate from Asia to Europe and fending off 'unnecessary cultural shocks' such as 'bad food' or 'uncomfortable accommodation' from their Chinese visitors. Often working in regional networks, small-to-medium-scale tour operators shuttle hundreds of Chinese tourists in a 'home-like cultural bubble' across Europe, creating of the feeling of 'home-away-from-home' for them. As more PRC are allowed and can afford to join the troop of world trampers, tourism-related Chinese migrant businesses can be expected to further boom. Nevertheless, they are by no means immune to the competition from other non-Chinese travel agencies. Convinced of the massive growth market, a number of big German tourism companies, such as the joint venture TUI China set up in 2003, have launched Chinese ventures and pledging to 'create the prerequisites Chinese tourists need to spend a high-quality holiday in Germany' (TUI AG 2003). German hoteliers have also studied and adapted their service to suit the 'Chinese taste', such as their preference for Chinese food and the expectation of a kettle in the hotel room (Deutsche Welle 2003).

Like different turns of a kaleidoscope, I have shed some light on the different facades of the fluid notion of 'home' in transnationalism. Meanings of home, nostalgia and homesickness have been topics in the diaspora research explored by cultural geographers, anthropologists and scholars in cultural studies. However, connections between this realm of literature and other areas, such as the studies on migrant businesses, are rarely made. This chapter represents a modest effort to underline the constructiveness in transcending the all-too-stubborn disciplinary borders that exist within the social sciences. Interviewees and observations in this study have shown how cultural sentiments and psychological desire can be turned to marketing tactics for businesses, and how business strategies can in turn redefine the meaning and nature of transnational families and communities. By actively and sensibly entwining the economic, political, social and cultural aspects of transnationalism, one can decipher the complexity of the dynamic and contextualized phenomenon.

ACKNOWLEDGMENTS

This chapter draws upon findings from my doctoral research conducted from 1999 to 2002, funded by the German Academic Exchange Service. I thank all my interviewees who were generous to share their valuable time, experiences and ideas with me. I would also like to acknowledge the financial support given by the Chinese University of Hong Kong to present an earlier version of this chapter at the Fifth Conference of the International Society for the Study of Chinese Overseas held in May 2004.

NOTES

[1] Throughout this chapter, unless otherwise noted, 'Chinese' refers to ethnic Chinese, rather than nationals of the People's Republic of China or Taiwan.

[2] Glick Schiller (1999), for example, notes that transnationalism can be observed in the migration waves to North America that occurred as early as 1880. The strong transnational linkages among early Chinese migrants in South-east Asia centuries ago also provide a good example of 'early transnationalism'.

[3] For a more detailed discussion of the conceptualization of home among Chinese migrants in Germany, see Leung (2004).

[4] All informants have been given pseudonyms.

[5] Ching Ming and Chung Yeung Festivals are important dates when families make journeys to the graves of their ancestors to perform cleansing rites and pay their respects. For many natives from Hong Kong villages, these two festivals are more important than the Chinese New Year – contrary to the general perception of Hong Kong people.

[6] Approximations of visitors for the event range from 150,000 (Chatinian 2001) to 500,000 (Walters 2001).

[7] In 2000, the number of tourists visiting the PRC was 83.4 million, up more than 14.5 per cent in 1999. Of that, foreign tourists numbered 10.16 million, an increase of 20.5 per cent. Visitors from Hong Kong numbered 58,56 million, while those from Macau were 11,54 million, a rise of 10.73 per cent and 31.38 per cent respectively. Taiwan visitors numbered 3.109 million, an increase of over 20 per cent (CNTA 2004).

[8] Invitations were required for the application of visas (of an education or business nature) before the PRC granted Approved Destination Status (ADS) to Germany in 2002. Only countries with ADS are allowed to promote their tours in the PRC.

[9] The sample is not necessarily statistically representative. The list of interviewees was generated from a Chinese business directory and advertisements in Chinese newspapers and community publications. It can be assumed that ethnic Chinese are the targeted clientele for these businesses.

[10] The figure is expected by the German National Tourist Board to reach one million by 2009 (Chen 2004).

REFERENCES

Basch, Linda, Nina Glick Schiller and Cristina Blanc-Szanton (1994) *Nations Unbound: Transnational Projects, Postcolonial Predicaments, and Deterritorized Nation-States.* Langhorne PA: Gordon and Breach.

Brah, Avtar (1996) *Cartographies of Diaspora: Contesting Identities.* London, New York: Routledge.

Butler, Tom (2003) 'Europe woos China's tourists'. BBC News online UK edition, 14 November. URL: http://news.bbc.co.uk/1/hi/world/asia-pacific/3269937.stm (accessed April 2004).

Chatinian, Zara (2001) 'Staying away: tourism to Armenia suffers effects of tragedy in America'. *ArmeniaWeek*, September. URL: http://www.armeniaweek.com/sept282001/cancellation.html (accessed April 2004)

Chen, Wen (2004) 'Chinese tourists eye European vacations'. *Beijing Review.* URL: http://www.bjreview.com.cn/200402/Nation-200402(E).htm (accessed April 2004).

China National Tourism Administration (CNTA) (2004) 'Review of China's tourism industry'. URL: http://www.cnta.com/lyen/2fact/inbound%20tourism.htm (accessed April 2004).

Cohen, Erik (2004) 'To stand in the shoes of my ancestors: Tourism and genealogy'. In Tim Coles and Dallen J. Timothy (eds), *Tourism, Diasporas and Space.* London, New York: Routledge, pp. 139–152.

Deutsche Welle (Online) (2003) 'Chinese tourists in Germany: Castles and the Autobahn'. 16 November. URL: http://www.dw-world.de/dw/article/0,,1029315,00.html (accessed April 2004).

Deutsche Zentrale für Tourismus e.V (2005) *Incoming – Tourismus Deutschland. Zahlen – Fakten – Daten 2004. Edition 2005*. Frankfurt: Deutsche Zentrale für Tourismus e.V.

Faist, Thomas (1998) 'Transnational social spaces out of international migration: Evolution, significance, and future prospects'. *Archives Européennes de Sociologie*, vol. 39, no. 2, pp. 213–247.

Giese, Karsten (2003) 'New Chinese migration to Germany: Historical consistencies and new patterns of diversification within a globalized migration regime'. *International Migration*, vol. 41, no. 3, pp. 155–184.

Glick Schiller, Nina (1999) 'Transmigrants and nation-states: Something old and something new in the U.S. Immigrant experience'. In Charles Hirschman, Philip Kasinitz and Josh DeWind (eds), *The Handbook of International Migration: The American Experience*. New York: Russell Sage Foundation, pp. 94-119.

Leung, Maggi (2004) *Chinese Migration in Germany: Making Home in Transnational Space*. Frankfurt/Main: IKO Verlag.

Ma, Laurence (2003) 'Space, place and transnationalism: The Chinese diaspora as a geographic system'. In Laurence Ma and Carolyn Cartier (eds), *The Chinese Diaspora: Space, Place, Mobility and Identity*. Lanham, MD: Rowman and Littlefield, pp. 1–49.

Massey, Doreen and Pat Jess (eds) (1995) *A Place in the World? Places, Culture and Globalization*. London: Oxford University Press.

Morgan, Nigel and Annette Pritchard (2004) 'Mae'n Bryd I Ddod Adref – It's time to come home. Exploring the contested emotional geographies of Wales'. In Tim Coles and Dallen J. Timothy (eds), *Tourism, Diasporas and Space*. London, New York: Routledge, pp. 233–245.

Portes, Alejandro, Luis Guarnizo and Patricia Landolt (1999) 'The study of transnationalism: pitfalls and promise of an emergent research field'. *Ethnic and Racial Studies*, vol. 22, no. 2, pp. 217–237.

Rouse, Roger (1991) 'Mexican migration and the social space of postmodernism'. *Diaspora*, vol. 1, pp. 8-23.

Scandinavian Tourist Board (2004) *Chinese Outbound Travel Market – 2004 Update*. Tokyo, Japan: Scandinavian Tourist Board. URL: http://www.visitscandinavia.or.jp/en/Corporate/intelligence/ChinaReport/Chinese%20Outbound%20Travel%20Market%202004.pdf(accessed April 2004).

Statistisches Bundesamt (2003) *Statistisches Jahrbuch für die Bundesrepublik Deutschland*. Wiesbaden: Statistisches Bundesamt.

Süddeutsche Zeitung (2001) 'Chinesen sollen Füssener Betten füllen', 20 April, p. 37.

TUI AG (2003) 'TUI: Expansion on the Chinese market goes into the next round'. Press release, 4 April. URL: http://www.tui.com/en/pressemedien/press_releases/2003/pm20030404a_china.html (accessed April 2004)

Vertovec, Steven (1999) 'Conceiving and researching transnationalism'. *Ethnic and Racial Studies*, vol. 22, no. 2, pp. 447–462.

Walters, Melissa (2001) 'Armenia's tourism sector develops'. BISNIS Bulletin, May, http://www.bisnis.doc.gov/bisnis/bulletin/015Bull1.htm (accessed April 2004).

Zhang, Di (2004) 'Mingnian Beijing youke ke "Ouzhou ziyouxing". Shoutui Deguo yidiyou xianlu'. [Beijing tourists allowed to go on 'European individual travel" next year. First offers: German routes]. *Beijing China News, 20 December.* URL: http://www.bj.chinanews.com.cn/news/2004/2004-12-20/1/65.html (accessed April 2004).

Chapter 11

The Sinwa of Reunion:
Searching for a Chinese Identity in a Multicultural World*

Live Yu-Sion

This chapter approaches the question of 'returning to the roots', which the descendants of the Chinese on Reunion Island increasingly are searching for as China rises on the global scene. Today, the great majority of the descendants of the Chinese, or of the Sino-Reunionese, no longer speak their ancestral languages – Cantonese or Hakka – and they have lost the essential cultural elements of their parents or grandparents, but recently they have taken up the search for their cultural origins. What might be the motives for this wish to 'return to the roots' for these persons who call, consider and perceive themselves as culturally Chinese? What historical and political circumstances have favoured the re-emergence of movements for identity assertion among the Chinese descendants? The case of the Chinese descendants offers a unique chance to analyse the reconstruction of ethnic identities under the influence of a waning colonial power such as France and a rising global power such as China.

In this chapter, it is argued that as the 'frenchification' process on Reunion Island of the early French colonial period has changed to permit more individual cultural identification, the descendants of Chinese migrants have begun to reshape their ethnic identity. Simultaneously, the People's

---

* Translated from French by Camilla S.K. Christensen.

Republic of China (PRC) has emerged as an economic power in the world that takes advantage of the presence of descendants of Chinese migrants to dispatch numerous diplomatic, cultural and trade delegations to Reunion Island. It is concluded that co-operation at state level within various fields has initiated a 'resinification' process, although it is still in its infancy.

HISTORICAL BACKGROUND AND SOCIAL ORGANIZATION OF THE CHINESE IN REUNION

Reunion is an island in the south-western zone of the Indian Ocean, 880 kilometres east of Madagascar. The island became a French possession in 1642, and first called Bourbon Island, its name was changed to Reunion in 1793. In 1946, its legal status changed and the island became a French overseas territory (*département*).

From the very beginning Reunion has been a multiethnic and multicultural island, characterized by the ability of people from five continents to live together. Inhabited since 1663 by successive waves of slaves, enlisted men from Madagascar, the Comoro Islands, Africa and Tamil Nadu; 'French settlers'; European and Chinese migrants; Indian traders from Gujarat, etc., the island is today characterized by a great ethnic and racial heterogeneity. The biological and cultural mix of three and a half centuries is often mentioned as one of the elements permitting different groups to live in peaceful coexistence and in mutual tolerance. Today, Reunion has more than 720.000 inhabitants.

The history of the Chinese on Reunion Island is well researched in its broad outlines (Helly 1976; Durand and Hin-Tung 1981; Wong 1996; Live 1999). It was characterized by two kinds of immigration: indentured and/or contract labour migration and so-called voluntary migration. The former began in 1840 just a few years before the abolition of slavery on Reunion. The turn to foreign labour to replace slaves in the plantations was the main motive behind the recruitment of indentured Chinese workers. The first contingent of these workers arrived in 1844 from Malaya, not directly from China. These men were intended to work in farming and build dykes and banks, but two years later the French colonial government halted the recruitment of Chinese, since they were considered 'bad workers' following a number of revolts and other acts of violence due to insufficient food rations, beatings, long working hours, salary cuts, etc. Living and working conditions on the plantations were hardly any different from those borne by the Malagasy and African slaves, since the main motives of the plantation owners were profits at any price.

In 1901, a second attempt to employ a shipment of 808 Chinese from the provincial capital of Fuzhou in Fujian Province in China met with the same failure as the first. The Chinese refused to accept the conditions of virtual slavery. Nearly all of them left the island in 1907, as a consequence of the disturbances which they caused on various plantations (strikes, protest marches to the capital Saint-Denis, mutinies in 1906 in Saint-Louis and in Saint-Suzanne). In the end, they were repatriated to China by the colonial authorities.

The so-called voluntary Chinese immigration to Reunion began after a law was passed in 1862, which allowed any foreigner to take up employment in the colony. This legal decision was complemented, about 20 years later, by a law 1882, which specified that any migrant could place a request with the governor at the end of his contract, if he wanted to reside on the island. It also allowed for the immigration of women and for the reunification of families. Furthermore, from 1898 onwards, the establishment of a shipping route between Hong Kong and the Mascarene islands of Madagascar, Mauritius and Reunion made it possible to go directly to Reunion, without first going through Mauritius (Ly-Tio-Fane 1981). Subsequently, every year several hundred Chinese from the southern province of Guangdong left their home villages for Reunion. Between 1920 and 1940, their numbers steadily rose to more than several thousands. Some arrived to reunite with their families, while others were driven by local events.

In 1946, the laws and regulations concerning immigration into France also became applicable to Reunion when the island became an overseas French *département*. After 1950, Chinese immigration practically ceased, because of the closure of the PRC borders. It was not until 1964, the year when diplomatic relations between the PRC and France were re-established, that a renewal of the Chinese migratory movement to Reunion could be hoped for, but actually it was not until the 1980s, after the reopening of China, that a limited migration wave resumed between Reunion and China. At present, the great majority of Chinese on the island are thus descendants of the voluntary migrants of the early twentieth century, not from the indentured workers of the nineteenth century.

Language and ethnic groups

Since the majority of Chinese migrants came from Guangdong Province, there are only two Chinese dialects represented on the island: Cantonese and Hakka. The Cantonese-speaking Chinese were the first to arrive in 1880s from the villages around the city of Guangzhou – Nanhai, Shunde, Shajiao. They generally settled in the northern part of the island, in Saint-Paul, Le Port, Saint-Denis, Saint-André, and Saint-Benoît, because Le Port was the arrival harbour of the newcomers, and Saint-Denis is the capital of Réunion.

The first Hakka-speaking Chinese arrived from Meixian County in Guangdong Province or by way of Mauritius from the latter part of the 1880s. A few years later, more Hakka-speaking settled in the south of the island (Saint-Pierre, and Le Tampon), probably due to the commercial rivalry and long-standing divisions between them and the Cantonese.

Scarcely more than 20 years ago, the Cantonese-speaking Chinese from Reunion referred to themselves as *Punti* (*bendi* in Standard Chinese), which means 'a local inhabitant' or 'a native' in their dialect, and to the Hakkas as Hakka (*kejia* in Standard Chinese), which means 'a guest', 'the Other'. Today, these labels have tended to gradually disappear with the new generations. In the past, the division between the Cantonese speakers and the Hakka speakers was a consequence of the Hakka migration towards the southern provinces of Fujian and Guangdong, and from 1730 more specifically towards the villages of Xinhui, Haoshan, Enping, Kaiping, as a consequence of political measures by the Qing Dynasty. The settlements of the Hakka gradually threatened the Cantonese and generated rivalry between the two ethnic groups. These rivalries were aggravated with the uprising of the Red Turbans in 1854 against the local authorities. Some Hakka were enrolled in the militias defending the villages and towns against the Cantonese. Bloody conflicts broke out between the two ethnic communities, and the Hakka ended up being legally expelled from Cantonese territories (Wan 1966). The prejudices and stereotypes used about the Hakka – mean, austere, thrifty, hard-working, destitute, masterful – were born from these antagonisms and brought to Reunion with overseas migration.

Population size

Today, ethnic Chinese represent a very small percentage of the overall population on Reunion. In the nineteenth century, there were fewer than a thousand ethnic Chinese, but between 1900 and 1950 the figures increased from 1,000 to 4,000 (see Table 11.1). However, the frequency of migratory movements between Mauritius, Reunion, the Seychelles, and Madagascar prevents any precise assessment. Currently the ethnic Chinese population of the island is reckoned at between 20,000–25,000 – but exactly who counts as an ethnic Chinese in Reunion? In France, census made on the basis of ethnicity or religion is prohibited and that makes any evaluation of the population of Chinese descendants difficult and complex.

Table 11.1. Number of Chinese in Reunion (1902–1941)

Year	1902	1907	1911	1921	1926	1931	1936	1941
Number	1,378	810	884	1,052	1,626	2,242	2,845	3,853

Sources: 1848–1860: Archives Départementales de la Réunion 6M, *Population et statistiques*; De la Barre de Nanteuil, *Législation de la Réunion, Éditions Donnaud, Paris*, 1861; 1865–1896: *Annuaire de l'île de la Réunion*; 1902-1941 : Archives Départementales de la Réunion, 6 M. *Population et statistiques*.

Different groups of Chinese descent

The historical record of Chinese immigration to Reunion enables us to make a current distinction between four separate groups[1] of Chinese and Sinwa.[2] The word 'Chinese' covers persons who speak the language and identify themselves as Chinese, whereas the word 'Sinwa' designates those who have not mastered any Chinese language or dialect and do not identify themselves as Chinese.

The first group consists of immigrants who were born in China. They still speak a Chinese dialect, with a bit of Creole and a smattering of French. They form a small minority of immigrants who have been in Reunion since the inter-war years (1920–1940). They are mostly restaurant owners and shopkeepers, because commerce was at that time one of the quickest means of economic and social integration.

The second group consists of Chinese descendants born before 1945, who were educated and brought up in Reunion society, but with little exposure to the French educational system. In many cases, they attended a local Chinese school, and they have assimilated some aspects of Chinese and Creole culture, but little by way of French culture. They have a poor command of French, but they speak Chinese and Creole fluently and do not experience any deep sense of crisis in cultural identity. Some of them have taken over the family businesses and gradually turned them into more spacious and modern businesses like self-service operations or mini-marts, while others have entered various firms on the island as salaried employees or workers. Since the 1970s, the social and economic changes on Reunion have led to a rise in their standard of living.

The third group is made up of persons born after the 1950s and educated in the local French educational system. They no longer speak Chinese, apart from a few phrases, and may only use Creole to talk to their parents and friends. In the 1960s and 1970s most of them underwent higher education in France and have entered liberal professions (as doctors, dentists, architects, lawyers etc.), large private firms (as accountancy experts, engineers, traders), or the public sector (as administrators, and teachers). Their feelings of belonging to the Chinese community remain relatively strong. This generation is to a great extent assimilated into French culture, but for about 20 years they have been making efforts to 'get back to their roots' through an attempted reappropriation of selected salient aspects of Chinese culture (Chinese language, calligraphy, *taiji quan* [Chinese gymnastics], *qigong* [vital energy gymnastics] and Chinese food and gastronomy). This group is now experiencing some moments of identity crisis.

The last group consists of persons of mixed descent who no longer have any knowledge of the Chinese language or culture. This 'métissage' [hybridity], recent or not, of a fringe sector of the Chinese population is noticeable above all in the physical appearance of different individuals. In some cases their dominant physical features do not correspond to their Chinese surnames. A person from Reunion with a Chinese surname may look like a Creole, a Malagasy, a Tamil, or a Caucasian. Quite a number within this group, at a certain point in their lives, try to rediscover their Chinese origins (by setting up associations, travelling to their ancestral villages, organizing or joining in traditional feasts, visiting pagodas regularly, reading Chinese stories in Creole translation etc.).

CONSTRUCTION AND REMOULDING OF A MULTICULTURAL IDENTITY

The analysis of the creation of the Sinwa identity only concerns the generations born in Reunion. This identity creation takes place in two phases:

- absorbing different cultural elements of Creole, Chinese and French origin. This primary identity proves to be multiethnic and multicultural.

- attempting to restructure a mixed identity into a more narrowly defined Chinese identity.

The cultural identity developed by generations of Chinese born on the island must be seen in its particular social and economic context of a relatively long period of isolation when Reunion from 1663 to 1965 was somewhat 'forgotten' by France. Until the late 1960s, Reunion remained economically underdeveloped, with few schools, hospitals or public housing and a poor infrastructure. The health institutions were limited, and infectious diseases like malaria continued to afflict a considerable portion of the population. From the 1970s onwards, this situation began to improve with the introduction of free medical care, social security, and the establishment of the Departmental Directorate for Health and Social Affairs.

The long isolation provided a context in which different cultures from all over the world met, exchanged, and intermingled. This interpenetration of languages, religions, and philosophies gave birth to a 'métissage' which nowadays has acquired its own identity (See Alber 1990; Baggioni 1985; Barat 1989; Benoist 1975; Chaudenson 1979). The island's Creole language is the outcome of a linguistic brew of French with African, Asian, and Malagasy languages. It has become the *lingua franca* of a large majority of the population, with the exception of new arrivals from France. As a result, all ethnic Chinese born on the island are socialized in Creole culture, but simultaneously identify themselves as Chinese.

In short, the individual is caught up in the dialectic of self and other. The development of Chinese identities has followed a path of progressively moulding and modifying, and adopting different forms throughout its existence, responding to the events and disruptions in the social, political, cultural, or economic life of the island. In short, the Sinwa cultural identity has developed in accordance with the transformations affecting Reunion society.

French cultural influence is among the pertinent factors with an evident impact on Reunion society, but it was only after Michel Debré, a native of France, was elected as deputy in 1963 that a policy of assimilation tending to eliminate the Creole language and culture had an effect. Schooling was one of the instruments of this 'Frenchifying' policy. The elite had already established a *lycée* for their children, and for a long time this institution was the only means of social advancement for the youth of the island. For the rest of the population, the authorities had set up junior colleges and technical schools. There were also private schools run by religious orders. At present Reunion possesses a large number of junior colleges and *lycées*, and one university serving 12,000 students.

In addition, the introduction of television brought the island into contact with the rest of the world, and lifted the inhabitants' insular outlook. The island can now receive several satellite channels and this has brought profound changes into daily life and transformed the islanders' ways of thinking. One consequence of this inflow of images from overseas has been the identification with modern ways of living in a consumer society such as that of France (Live 1997).

In this multicultural context, a Chinese way of life has developed with specific Chinese social and cultural organizations, such as community institutions, professional associations, places of worship and schools. The first Chinese cultural associations based on clan or regional affiliation were set up by the Cantonese in 1877 in the capital of Reunion. (Wong 1996: 93). Formerly, these associations played a role in preserving and disseminating a Chinese cultural heritage by organizing language, calligraphy or cookery courses, traditional festivities, or encouraging people to get together through sports like table tennis, football, basketball, or through group outings, dances and banquets.

The first Chinese school was founded in 1927 in the capital of Saint-Denis (Huaqiao zhi bianzuan weiyuanhui 1966), and schools established later all came under the responsibility and organization of the Chinese Chamber of Commerce, which financed them through contributions from merchants. The Chinese Chamber paid teachers from Mauritius or China to teach the Chinese children in Reunion. The language of instruction was Hakka in the Hakka schools, and Cantonese in the Cantonese schools. After the Second World War, however, these Chinese schools set up in the interwar period were dissolved by the French colonial authorities who were trying to eradicate all cultural characteristics other than French. The colonial administration saw in such schools elements of cultural separation, and set out to control them by demanding that there should be less time spent on Chinese- than on French-language teaching. In order to comply with the new regulations, the Chinese set up bilingual Franco-Chinese schools (Durand and Hin-Tung 1981; Wong 1996).

After the Second World War, with Reunion becoming a French overseas *département*, children's education in French schools became compulsory. In addition, Chinese parents, having abandoned all hope of returning to

China, no longer saw any point in Chinese education for their children. The generation born of Chinese parents in the 1950s thus went to French primary and secondary schools.

This assimilation of different Creole, Chinese, and French cultural components confronts the generation of the Sinwa with an identity problem. Its intensity varies with the individual involved, but the post-war youth are concerned about their cultural identity. They are living out a paradoxical situation – acknowledging themselves as Chinese, or as being of Chinese descent, and they are considered as such by the society of the island at large – but they do not master any Chinese language, nor do they integrate any Chinese cultural elements into their daily lives. Their *lingua franca* is Creole, but they do not feel themselves to be Creole or French, and they hardly participate in any Creole or French cultural activities. Faced with that situation, they have begun to restructure their mixed identities and have started to incorporate elements of Chinese culture into their cultural identities. Among the factors influencing the return to Chinese cultural roots are the discrepancy between the legal and cultural designation of personal names as well as confronting differences in phenotypes.

The matter of assigning personal names creates problems regarding personal and social identities among the Sinwa. In France, the law enforces the rule of paternal filiation according to feudal traditions of patrilinity. The family name, being a sign and symbol of affiliations, locates and ties an individual to both a lineage and a personal history. It is at the same time a marker and a classifier of the individual's identity that is linked to the identity of generations, to a region or to a country, and eventually to a social status. Hence, a male Sinwa from Reunion who inherits the family name of his father also takes at the same time the first name of his father as part of his family name. The French administration, however, does not allow any modification of family names from one generation to the next.

What complicates this situation even more is that in general Chinese families give their children both a French-sounding and a Chinese first name; the latter is not used in official documents but commonly used in the family and among friends. Another aberration in the allocation of family names is the custom from southern China of creating a social name by adding the prefix 'Ah' to the first name. It seems that at the end of the nineteenth century and the beginning of the twentieth, French colonial officials wrote down these social names as family names for the Chinese who entered Reunion. Once written down as official family names, the

Sinwa still bear them from generation to generation, although they know that their 'real' family names are quite different. In conclusion, from an early age a Sinwa has a plural identity.

A fairly recent event might even intensify the possession of a family name in the light of the desire of the Sinwa to go back to their roots. With the generalization of the teaching of Standard Chinese in Reunion since the 1980s, some Sinwa have discovered through studying Standard Chinese how their family name and first names are written and pronounced in China. Since then, in their correspondence with friends, they have signed their letters or their e-mails using the transcription of their name and first name in Standard Chinese.

The complexity and aberrations in the transmission of family names may become even more confused with the application in France of the law of January 2005, allowing the French to give children either the family name of their father and/or that of their mother. If some Chinese parents decide to adopt the principles of this new law, a Sinwa child will be able to have many names.

Thus the Sinwa*s* simultaneously have different family names and first names (French and Chinese) that are used according to the circumstances or situations of their daily lives. This means that they navigate between several identities, which are ruptured, inappropriate or confused, and this plural identity may cause them psychological identification problems.

The second factor of phenotype is even more at the heart of the ethnic and cultural identity of the Sinwa*s*. Since the 1960s when young Sinwa*s* first went to France to study, they encountered ethnic differences in French society. They met racism as part of everyday life in France and because of their Chinese features, they were not considered as French, but as Chinese. The way others looked at them made them realize that they were in fact Chinese, something they had not been conscious of as part of Reunion society. This phenomenon shows that in general the problem of the individual identity is raised when the notion of difference appears.

Once they finished their studies, the young Sinwa*s* returned to Reunion and started looking back at their ancestral origins. They created cultural associations with activities involving Chinese language classes for children and adults, classes of traditional dances, classes of calligraphy or Chinese cooking, trips to learn languages or sightseeing tours in China, etc. In the words of one of my informants,

On their return from their higher education in France in the 1980s, the second- and third-generation Chinese believed that their own language and culture had been distorted by the pressure to become French. In order to counteract this assimilation, they went back to their 'roots', visiting their ancestral villages to meet up with members of their family and rediscover some traditional Chinese cultural values. People of the third generation, whose parents had rejected their 'Chineseness', turned back to Chinese culture. Many have that aspiration.

The problem raised by phenotypes – the colour of eyes or skin, the type of hair, etc. – suddenly became an element of national group adherence for the young Sinwas in France. In Reunion, however, society is not structured by colour prejudice, but by social distinction based on phenotype, which remains a social criterion for ethnical differentiation and for identity attributions. It is through the phenotype that people from Reunion determine to which ethno-cultural group an individual belongs. In the field of social representation, the stereotypes and prejudices based on physical features are used as instruments for ethnic division. Subsequently, the phenotypes of second- or third-generation ethnic Chinese defined the Sinwas in Reunion according to the stereotypes, prejudices and normative expectations defined by Reunion society and primarily as different from other ethnic groups such as the Chinese from China, the Tamils, the Indians, the French and so on. In France, they simply became part of the larger ethnic denomination of Chinese from China.

THE CHINESE STATE: KEY TO 'RESINIFICATION'?

The recognition of being defined as Chinese when studying in France occurred in Reunion simultaneously with French decentralization policies begun when François Mitterrand took office in May 1981. The law on decentralization passed in December 1982 gave in Reunion some decision-making power to locally elected people and facilitated changes in political, economic, and social life such as independent radio stations, the commemoration of the abolition of slavery in 1848, the creation of Reunion Academy and the University of Reunion, etc.[3] This new policy also encouraged the expression of ethnic identities and ethnic movements for roots recovery started in the mid-1980s. Tamil, Chinese, Gujarat, Malagasy or African ethnic and cultural associations quickly emerged, proclaiming their rights to assert distinct ethnic identities. These associations typically teach ethnic customs and habits, arrange for travel to ancestral countries and invite artists, intellectuals and other cultural agents with the object of restoring an ancestral culture to members in Reunion.

As for the Sinwas, the elements or the signs which illustrate their endeavours to return to their roots appear in the cultural events that they set up for traditional festivals. Annual festivals like those for Guandi (a warrior of the Eastern Han dynasty, 25–220 A.C., who was deified in the sixteenth century) or the Chinese Lunar New Year have been organized for several decades. Artistic groups from China are regularly on tour at Reunion (acrobats, jugglers, dancers, traditional musicians, calligraphers, painters, etc). This wish for a 'resinification' by way of cultural activities is, however, illusory, since these traditional festivals are only occasional and take place within a short period of time (a few days distributed throughout the year). The reality is that the Sinwas do not live in a Chinese social and cultural context, but in a context which is Creole. What exists for them is the feeling of belonging to a Chinese unit that is part of China and its diaspora.

Part of the distance encountered among the Sinwas to China and Chinese culture may also be attributed to the relationship between the two countries in question: the PRC and France. Neither the PRC (nor Taiwan) succeeded in establishing a consulate, an embassy, or an economic representation on Reunion territory. The reason most often mentioned by the public authorities is that the Sinwas are French, and so, there is no need to establish a diplomatic delegation in a French *département*. Thus, China has not played any direct role in the construction of the Sinwa identity. Moreover, from 1950 to the late-1970s, there was a period of a nearly total rupture of the bonds between the Sinwas and their relatives in the PRC, due to the China closed-door policies. Only since the 1980s, with the opening of China, the bonds have been strengthened by family visits and tourism.

In the economic and commercial fields, trade between China and Reunion has not been important, either, but has been developing gradually since the mid-1980s. From 1951 to 1985, the quantum of Chinese imports to Reunion went from 120 to 520 tons, which corresponds only to a value of 3,364 to 15,050 million Francs (Gerard 1989: 148). In 1986, China for the first time organized a three-day trade fair in Saint-Denis, but this was not followed up. In 1991, the municipality of Foshan in Guangdong Province, represented by the deputy mayor, carried out a display and sale of local products (textiles, domestic appliances, silk fabrics, clothes and various plastic products) in the Parc des Expositions in Saint-Denis. Some Sinwa tradesmen, however, go to the International Trade Fair in Guangdong every year to buy Chinese products. In 1991, a twinning between the cities of Foshan and La Possession was realized.

Official and diplomatic relations, on the other hand, have developed intensely since 2003. Frequent visits by Chinese state delegations have been undertaken to Reunion, and draft treaties have been signed between Chinese and Reunion political representatives. In January 2003, for the first time in the history of the relations between Reunion and China, the Chinese ambassador in Paris visited Reunion. The Chinese diplomat came, as he declared, in order to 'open a door on the sea route connecting his country to this strategic region in the Southern hemisphere, a passage in particular to South Africa ... and to establish contacts to fill a vacuum never filled in the 39 years of Chinese–French relations'.[4] He was received by the mayor of the district of Tampon, who is of Chinese origin, and by representatives of the Chinese community. Until then, the Chinese delegations on official trips to Reunion were received by presidents or those in charge of the Chinese associations, but this was the first time that a Sinwa politician received a Chinese high dignitary. During that visit, the PRC ambassador was also greeted by representatives from the most important Reunion institutions, in particular by the president of the 'Région-Réunion'. During that visit, three draft treaties on education, research and sports, on technology exchange and on private initiatives within fishing industries were signed between the PRC and Reunion. Another important decision taken on this occasion was that official procedures were begun with the French government in Paris to establish a Chinese consulate in Reunion.

Right after the PRC ambassador's visit, another Chinese delegation of 120 people landed on Reunion for a two-day stay. Lead by a Chinese vice-premier, accompanied by three ministers, economists and cultural officials, the delegation was met by the Prefect of Reunion, the president of the 'Région-Réunion', the deputy and mayor of Tampon, as well as by the representatives of about 15 Chinese cultural associations. This short stay by the Chinese delegation in Reunion was not followed by the signing of any draft treaty, but some co-operative projects were set up, in particular the export to the island of Chinese semi-finished products, a partnership in the study of Chinese and Western medicine and the possible arrival of Chinese tourists in Reunion.

The mayor of the Tampon district André Tien Ah Koon[5] requested on this occasion that the Chinese vice-premier send four Chinese language teachers and also open a Chinese consulate in Reunion. He declared: 'There is nothing worse than loosing your roots. This [Sino-Reunion] coming together is of benefit for the Chinese community of the island'. In his response, the vice-premier accepted the request for teachers, but the question of the accreditation of a consulate was 'in the hands of the Chinese government'.[6] A few months later in June 2003, André Thien Ah Koon was appointed a negotiator of the Ministry of Foreign Affairs in charge of the development of relations with China.

In September 2003, Reunion received a visit from a new Chinese delegation consisting of 18 Chinese experts from the municipality of Tianjin. The object of this trip was to reinforce the bonds of co-operation between Reunion and China. The Chinese were experts within higher education, training, the processing of products, the study of medicinal plants, fishing, aquaculture, industry, tourism, the promotion of culture, language and sport, etc. Among the envisaged projects were the establishment of a research centre for traditional Chinese medicine, a luxury hotel on Reunion's west coast, a unit for sea food processing, a factory to make television sets and the creation of a representative Chinese office in Reunion. As a consequence, in November 2003, a managerial convention aiming at 'the establishment of exchange and co-development relations' was signed between Reunion and the PRC.

In 2004, a cultural year celebrating China in France became the occasion for Reunion to push for projects for economic and cultural co-operation with the PRC. In March 2004, a delegation of Chinese investors arrived in Reunion. The delegation was in keeping with the preceding missions. The 12 Chinese officials had discussions with Reunion business managers and a working session was organized at the Institut Universitaire de Technologie in Saint-Pierre between the Chinese officials and the officials of Reunion and of the Regional Agency of Reunion Energy in order to develop co-operation in the field of solar energy. Most importantly, however, was the inauguration of an economic bureau of Chinese representation in Saint-Denis. On that occasion, a local paper ran this headline: 'China opens its "embassy" in Reunion on Wednesday'.[7] Under the principle of reciprocity, Reunion would open a similar bureau in the PRC.[8]

In April 2004, another form of exchange was initiated by the PRC when the Hôpital de Saint-Pierre (a hospital complex of in southern Reunion) received representatives from the University Hospital of the city of Tianjin with the aim of establishing co-operation between the two institutions. The project aimed at training Reunion practitioners in acupuncture, while the Hôpital de Saint-Pierre would provide technical assistance to the Chinese hospital regarding neurology and other advanced technologies.[9]

In July 2004, for the second time within a year and a half, the PRC ambassador in Paris, visited Reunion, such an event had never before occurred within such a short time span, since the resumption of the relations between France and China in 1965. The Chinese diplomat had come to open an exhibition of Chinese writings, initiated by the Association of Reunionese of Chinese origin and by Saint-Denis city hall. At the preview of this exposition, he said in response to a request to open an air route between China and Reunion, 'If I am here, it is in order to strengthen the co-operation between China and Reunion'.[10] During his stay, he also signed two agreements aiming at more co-operation between the PRC and Reunion with regard to education and the media.

The former stated that The Regional Education Authority of Reunion agreed to receive a teacher of Chinese from the PRC to work in the Oriental sections of Reunion Schools. Recently, the Chinese language has attracted more and more students. In 2004, the Regional Education Authority listed 402 students studying Chinese, distributed in seven schools (three secondary schools and four high schools); 109 had Chinese as their first language, 191 as their second language and 102 as their third language.[11]

The second agreement, relating to media, allowed a local chain of satellite networks to transmit the cultural, sporting and educational programmes of China Central Television (CCTV4) to Reunion. This project materialized, in December 2004 with the effective launch of CCTV on the Reunion network. Reunion thus became the first French overseas *département* to broadcast programmes from the PRC.

In October 2004, delegates from the Association of the Chinese People for Friendship with Foreign Countries were received by the official Reunion authorities, by the Association of Tradesmen, company managers and Chinese executives in Reunion. This time, the members of the delegation were from Shandong Province and Zhejiang Province. Their spokesperson declared: 'We have come here to get to know Reunion, and to see the possibilities of co-operation in the commercial and economic field ... To see is to believe ... seen once is better than heard a hundred times'.[12]

The Sinwa of Reunion: Searching for a Chinese Identity in a Multicultural World

In November 2004 the International Fair of the Mascarene, which is held every year in the city of Port showcased arts, craftsmanship and technical know-how. The fair of 2004 was largely devoted to the skills and traditional culture of China. Because of the bonds between Reunion and the municipality of Tianjin that had been established during the past few years, the latter sent an important delegation of about one hundred persons. The presence of China at the international fair was not just a commercial and cultural occassion, but it also aimed at 'tightening the bonds between the peoples who contributed to populate Reunion,' according to the manager of the fair. For ten days, a Chinese village of 1000 square metres sheltered about 40 artists who gave shows of martial arts, traditional Chinese songs and dances to the visitors as well as demonstrations in calligraphy, stone engraving, ceramics (pottery and chinaware), embroidery and Chinese massage. A pavilion of Chinese gastronomy, spread out over 200 square metres was enlivened by 11 great chefs, representing the four main Chinese cuisines (Beijing, Shanghai, Sichuan, Guangdong). Finally, Chinese tradesmen also exhibited different manufactured products (from electric appliances to a jumble of various articles).

For the ethnic Chinese and Sinwas of Reunion, the year 2004 was also marked by another major event: the festival to honour Guandi. On that day, the three temples dedicated to him (two in Saint-Denis and one in Saint-Pierre) experience a particular liveliness. The Chinese, Sinwas, Creole and often mixed families come to meditate, to make offerings and wishes, burn incense, etc. and in 2004 the participants could for the first time celebrate in Saint-Denis for four entire days. On the programme was conferences, Chinese music, traditional dances, demonstrations of *taiqi quan*, lion and dragon dances, juggling and Cantonese opera performances by Chinese from the PRC. Stands were installed on the pavements for demonstrations of calligraphy, paintings, silk embroidery, gastronomy and genealogy.

The public authorities (the Saint-Denis city hall, the Regional Council, the Regional Board of elected representatives) and Reunion enterprises, mostly of Chinese origin, had contributed to the financing by the Chinese cultural associations of this Guandi festival of 2004. The day it opened, the Mayor of Saint-Denis, who was accompanied by his Deputy Mayors, the representatives of the local communities, the Deputy and Mayor of the city of Tampon, the Chinese Ambassador from Mauritius, the Minister of Justice (of Chinese origin) and the Mayor of the Republic of Mauritius, declared in his speech that 'the Chinese community have known how to assert themselves without losing their roots. They have taken up their place in our pluralist culture. This is why the celebration of Guandi is a festival for all people from Reunion'.[13] People from Reunion of all origins kept going to Rue Sainte-Anne for four days in order to view the two Chinese community temples and Chinese culture imported from China. On this occasion, the Department Council also for the first time opened the gates to the garden of its colonial villa, and invited the Chinese community to an evening related to the festivities of Guandi.

It is too early to predict the impact on the ethnic Chinese and the Sinwas of these ongoing and intense exchanges and cultural, economic[14] and political actions taking place between the PRC and Reunion . The PRC hopes to make Reunion an 'aircraft carrier to Europe in the Indian Ocean', that is to say an economic springboard for investing there and to getting into the European Market. As to Reunion, because of its economic ambitions, it is important to China as an ultra-peripheral region of Europe and steppig stone to Africa. With one foot in Africa and another in Asia, Reunion positions itself as the future place for Chinese entrepreneurial investments. However, major obstacles still have to be surmounted such as French and European legislations, entry visas for Chinese tourists remain thorny and labour costs and high custom rates that make Reunion uncompetitive for investments.

As a consequence, in spite of the optimism shown by the economic and political agents in Reunion, the projects and agreements concluded between China and Reunion are far from being realised. As for the impact of the PRC, however, cultural and ethnic ties seem to have been partly revived by these new Sino-Reunion relations giving the people in charge of the associations the hope of a 'resinification' of the younger Sinwa generations.

CONCLUSION

The historical, social, economical and cultural development of the Chinese immigration to Reunion reflects a high degree of integration of the Chinese and their descendants, but the question which worries the Sinwas most is still their cultural identity. After having been through a de-culturalization period with the 'frenchification' and 'creolization' of Reunion, as French colonial policies permitted ethnic identification, the Sinwas expressed a strong interest in belonging to a Chinese universe and to differentiating themselves from other ethnic groups. What they are experiencing is an identity construction in which they cannot find themselves and which is not anchored to the centre of their personality but lies on the fringe of it.

As the possibilities for a renegotiation of their identity were permitted by the French administration, young Sinwas were exposed to French ethnic perceptions of them as being Chinese as a consequence of their physical appearance, but when China emerged as a global economic power and became increasingly present on Reunion, a process of redefinition of what ir means ro be Sinwa has begun For some, the Creole culture is no longer considered as bringing high standing and prestige as compared to the Chinese culture that is now perceived as having remarkable depth and seniority. By trying to recover elements of Chinese culture, they appear to hope to collect fractured elements of a cultural identity. Whether or not the version of Chinese culture that is at their disposal at the moment as a sponsored PRC interpretation of Chinese culture is what the Sinwas are longing for only time will tell, but China's new global economic and political presence clearly contributes to raising the ethnic awareness of being of Chinese descent in Reunion and thus strengthens the identity construction even among creolized Chinese migrants.

NOTES

[1] I prefer to use the idea of a 'group' rather than a 'generation'. The former designates a collection of individuals with certain socio-cultural characteristics in common, while the latter is only useful insofar as one generation of immigrants engenders a second or third one – whose parents no longer share the same cultural background.

[2] *Sinwa* is a Creole word with a pronunciation being close to the French word *chinois* for Chinese.

[3] In 1983, Reunion became a mono-départemental region (Région-Réunion) in accordance with the Law of 22 July 1982 on politics of decentralization. This law transfers the regional executive from the Préfet to the president of the elected assembly. The regional council should promote the economic, social, medical, scientific and cultural development and the regional development.

[4] *Le Journal de l'Île de La Réunion*, 13 January 2003, p. 13.

[5] André Thien-Ah-Koon is a Hakka of the 'second generation' born in 1940 at Tampon. His was elected as mayor at the commune in 1983, and deputy in 1986. Since then he has been re-elected for his respective mandates.

[6] *Le Journal de l'Île de La Réunion*, 19 January 2003, p. 7.

[7] *Le Journal de l'Île de La Réunion,* 9 March 2004, p. 6.

[8] According to Article V of the Convention signed on the 12 November, 2003 between China and the Région-Réunion: 'in each of the regions, a representation office will be used as a supporting point in the implementation of the co-operation between the two parties'. The Reunion office joined the representation offices of the French cities, regions and departments in China. The Alsace, Bretagne or PACA (Provence-Alpes-Côte d'Azur) regions, the department of the Hauts de Seine and the cities of Lyon and Toulouse have had offices of representation in China for years.

[9] *Le Quotidien,* 16 April 2004, p. 8.

[10] *Le Journal de l'Île de La Réunion,* 16 July 2004, p. 10.

[11] *Le Quotidien,* 17 April 2004, p. 3.

[12] *Le Quotidien,* 29 October 2004, p. 20.

[13] Ibid.

[14] Let us take the following example: in 2001 12,200 tons of goods are imported from China to Reunion with a value of 37.7 million euros, that is to say a growth of 21 per cent compared to 2000. The principal imported products are electrical supplies, toys, furniture, electrical water heaters, fitness machines ... Reunion, for their part, exports 874 tons of goods to China with a value of 5.2 million euros. The exported products are 99 per cent frozen fish. China is Reunion's 10th partner country for imports and the 7th partner country for exports. *Le Journal de l'Ile de la Réunion,* 16 January 2003, pp. 12–13.

REFERENCES

Archives Départementales de la Réunion 6M, *Population et statistiques* 1848–1860 and 1902–1941 *Annuaire de l'île de la Réunion* 1865–1896.

Alber, Jean-Luc (ed.) (1990) *Vivre au pluriel. La production sociale des identités à l'île Maurice et à l'île de La Réunion.* Saint-Denis: Université de La Réunion.

Baggioni, Daniel (1985) 'Marqueurs d'ethnicité et identité culturelle: problèmes de définition à La Réunion'. In *Culture(s) empiriques(s) et identité(s) culturelle(s) à la Réunion.* Saint-Denis: Université de La Réunion.

Barat, Christian (1989) *Nargoulan: culture et rites malbars à La Réunion.* Saint-Denis: Editions du Tramail.

Benoist, Jean (1975, reprinted 1983) *Un développement ambigu.* Saint-Denis: Fondation pour la Recherche et le Développement dans l'Océan Indien. Nouvelle edition.

Chaudenson, Robert (1979) *Les créoles français.* Paris : F. Nathan.

Durand, Dominique and Hin-tung, Jean (1981) *Les Chinois de la Réunion.* Capetown: Australes Éditions.

Filliot, J-M (1974) *La traite des esclaves vers les Mascareignes au XVIIIe siècle.* Paris: Orstom.

Gerbeau, Hubert (1995) 'Regard et discours sur les "races" de La Réunion'. In Pascal Blanchard et al. (eds) , *L'Autre et Nous: scènes et types.* Paris: Syros, pp. 97–102.

Ghasarian, Christian (1991) *Honneur, chance et destin.* Paris: L'Harmattan.

Gérard, Gilles (1989) 'Les Réunionnais d'origine chinoise. Mémoire de Maîtrise de chinois'. MA diss. Bordeaux: Université de Bordeaux III.

Helly, Denise (1976) 'Des immigrants chinois aux Mascareignes'. In *Annuaire des Pays de l'Océan Indien*, vol. III, pp. 103–124.

Huaqiao zhi bianzuan weiyuanhui (ed.) (1966) *Liuniwangdao huaqiao zhi* . Taibei: Huaqiao zhi bianzuan weiyuanhui.

Live, Yu-Sion (1997) 'Sociologie de la Réunion: mutations, paradoxes, représentations, migrations'. In Bernard Chérubini (eds), *La recherche anthropologique à La Réunion : vingt années de travaux et de coopération régionale,* Saint-Denis, Université de la Réunion and L'Harmattan.

Live, Yu-Sion (1999) 'The Overseas Chinese in Reunion Island'. In Lynn Pan (ed.), *Encyclopedia of Chinese Overseas.* Singapore: Chinese Heritage Center Publications, pp. 356–359.

Ly-Tio-Fane, Huguette (1981) *La diaspora Chinoise dans l'Océan Indien Occidental.* Aix-en-Provence: Greco-Océan Indien.

Wan, Lo (1966) 'Communal strife in midnineteenth century Kwangtung', *Papers on China*, vol. 19 (East Asian Research Centre, Harvard University).

Wong, Édith Hee-Kam (1996) *La diaspora Chinoise aux Mascareignes: Le cas de la Réunion.* Saint-Denis: Université de la Réunion and L'Harmattan.

Chapter 12

Altered States:
Indigenous Australian and Chinese Diasporic Alliances

Peta Stephenson

This chapter examines the impact of globalization on the formation of new cross-cultural alliances. It is less concerned with the economic ramifications of changing labour and capital patterns than with the new networks for meeting that have emerged as a consequence of these shifts. Recent discourse on globalization has focused on the material outcomes of new commercial developments and innovations in technology at the expense of recognizing how the growing internationalization of the world impacts upon those at the community level –particularly on those who are minority group members. In the context of a multitude of international examples of alternative community formations, this chapter focuses on one particular trans-national partnership forged by individuals and community groups. It uncovers new forms of hybrid political, cultural and social alliances initiated by Chinese diasporic and Indigenous peoples in Australia, and contemplates the significance of these for dominant understandings of the Australian nation-state.

'Altered states' in the title of the chapter does not refer to Ken Russell's critically acclaimed 1980 film. It alludes, instead, to the *alterity* or 'Otherness' of the communities under discussion. Both Indigenous and Chinese Australians are minorities in Australia who share similar but also profoundly different experiences of marginalization within so-called mainstream Anglo-Australian society. Separately, Aboriginal and Chinese diasporic peoples constitute minority populations and those who have forged cross-cultural networks of meeting are, in effect, a minority within a minority. The number of Indigenous and Chinese Australians engaged in cross-cultural partnerships is relatively small but, as this chapter shows, the significance of these cultural, political and emotional unions reaches far beyond the number of people involved. As we will see, these cross-cultural and trans-national engagements bespeak a new network of meeting that challenges the sustaining myths of nationalism and calls for an altered imagining of the nation-state.

Cross-cultural partnerships between Chinese migrant and Indigenous communities in Australia take a variety of forms. Some are based on shared cultural and artistic expression, others stem from a common political agenda, some are the result of shared genealogies and histories, while others have arisen as a consequence of romantic love and companionship. In almost all cases, however, these alliances emerge from an awareness of the related experiences of struggle by marginalized minorities against the homogenizing tendencies of nationalist constructions. My intention is not to suggest that Indigenous and Chinese Australians share the same experience of oppression and exclusion, nor to imply that this is the only way in which these minority groups experience Australia. But in registering the connections between a wide range of subaltern minorities, the fostering of common platforms for future struggles can be initiated and promoted. Moreover, Indigenous/Chinese political and social alliances indicate, as Indigenous academic Marcia Langton asserts, that the 'now toxic relationship between many Australians of British background and indigenous people must cease to be the only litmus test for cultural relations' in Australia (cited in Perera 2000: 12).

The Chinese-Australians discussed in this chapter reflect some of the divergent histories and experiences of the Chinese diaspora in Australia. The immense variety among different Chinese diasporic communities in Australia rules out the possibility of locating a singular or coherent notion of the typical 'Chinese-Australian experience'. These people are simply 'too different, socially and culturally, to constitute anything like a homogeneous group' (Ommundsen 2000: 90). The personal and family trajectories of William Yang and Zhou Xiaoping, two Chinese-Australians profiled in this chapter, are emblematic of the heterogeneity of the Chinese migrant experience in Australia. Yang is a third-generation Chinese-Australian descended from Chinese sojourners who made their way to Australia in search of gold in the late 1800s. While Chinese indentured labourers or so-called coolies had earlier migrated to Australia to relieve severe labour shortages in the agricultural and pastoral industries, they did not arrive in large numbers until the discovery of gold in New South Wales and Victoria in the 1850s. News of the discovery of gold spread quickly and the Chinese presence grew from the first arrivals in 1848 (small numbers of Chinese were present in Australia from the 1820s) to some 30,000 by 1901.

In certain areas the Chinese vastly outnumbered their European counterparts. By 1888 in Darwin (formerly Palmerston) in the Northern Territory, there were 6,000 Chinese compared with just 1,000 white settlers (Sham-Ho 2003: 166). The Chinese constituted the largest non-Anglo and non-Indigenous population in Australia and their presence soon aroused the jealousy of the Europeans, who resented what they saw as 'unfair competition'. Chinese and other Asian workers encountered a vast array of restrictive and discriminatory legislation designed to impede their economic success. White resistance to the employment of Chinese labour was first voiced in opposition to Chinese coolies or indentured labourers, then to Chinese diggers on the gold mines and subsequently to 'free' labourers after the alluvial gold deposits petered out. White labourers, trade unionists and other agitators for the exclusion of the Chinese were largely successful in persuading political and legislative bodies to enact laws to restrict Chinese immigration in order to undermine their economic endeavours. 'Yellow peril' discourse in Australia was a critical catalyst of the unification of the separate colonies into a federated Australia in 1901 and of the introduction of the Immigration Restriction Act (commonly known as the 'White Australia Policy').

Those Chinese who remained in Australia after the decline in alluvial gold yields found a limited range of work prospects available to them. The lucky ones who were fortunate enough to find gold relied on their own social networks and contacts to start their own businesses. The influx of Chinese diggers onto the goldfields had generated a great demand for Chinese goods such as rice, tea, silk, porcelain, ginger and other delicacies. Even after the alluvial gold mining petered out and the majority of Chinese left the goldfields, Chinese storekeepers were still able to supply the increasingly urban Chinese populations with these necessities. Yang's maternal grandfather Chun Wing was a See Yup from the Canton region of Guangdong province (Yang 1996: 42). With the gold he found near Pine Creek (about 200 kilometres south of Darwin), he started his own shop and, after establishing his business, sent for a wife from China. Yang's paternal grandfather Ah Young was another Chinese sojourner who came to Australia in search of gold. Also from the south of China, Ah Young was of the Hukka clan. When gold ran out at the Palmer River diggings in North Queensland, he bought a cane farm near Cairns before also sending back to China for a wife.

Yang's grandfathers were in a position to marry Chinese women, but many other Chinese men in Australia married Aboriginal women. In 1861 there were only ten Chinese women in the whole of Australia – two in New South Wales and eight in Victoria (Sham-Ho 2003: 166). Given the shortage of Chinese women, and the fact that the majority of white women shunned the Chinese, inter-marriage between Chinese men and Aboriginal women was relatively common. Even when Chinese women began migrating to Australia in larger numbers, Aboriginal/Chinese marriages were not unusual. Indigenous and Chinese communities were thrown together for economic and social reasons. Aboriginal people dispossessed of their lands often welcomed the outsiders to establish reciprocal relations and new food supplies away from ration stations. The Chinese, who were also (but very differently) ostracized from the broader Australian community, sought companionship, solidarity and labourers among the local Indigenous people. In short, these were alliances of survival forged between groups excluded by the dominant culture politically, socially and culturally (Martinello 2003: 27). Chinese and Indigenous communities have also been historically bound together by racist and restrictive legislation outlawing their working, social and sexual partnerships. Discriminatory policies introduced in Queensland, Western Australia and the Northern Territory sought to prevent Aborigines and 'Asiatics' from 'cohabitation' and to stop the Chinese from employing Aborigines (thereby denying Europeans a valuable labour supply).

Yang had a 'completely assimilated upbringing' and was raised in Australia 'in the western way' (1996: 21). Partly because his father spoke Mandarin and his mother Cantonese, Yang and his siblings grew up speaking only English. Zhou, however, had no English-language skills before coming to Australia from Hefei as an adult in 1988. Zhou belongs to what some people have called 'new migrants' or the 'Tiananmen Square generation' of migrants. In the late 1980s and 1990s over 40,000 immigrants came to Australia from the People's Republic of China (PRC) (Ommundsen 2000: 89). Sometimes called the 'second goldrush', this large influx of Chinese has given rise to comparisons with the only other period of mass Chinese migration to Australia – the early gold diggers of the mid to late 1800s. Most of the recent wave of 'Tiananmen Square' migrants were young, urban and well educated. Many came to Australia to enrol in short-term English language classes to take advantage of the Australian government's 'education for export' policy. The opportunity offered by the ELICOS (English Language Intensive Courses for Overseas Students) scheme, by which Australia hoped to tap the Asian market for education dollars, meant that large numbers of Chinese were able to enter Australia on student visas (Ommundsen 2000: 90).

The events of 4 June 1989 in Tiananmen Square left this group stranded in Australia. Many were allowed to overstay their visas because of fear of persecution by the Chinese government if they returned to the PRC. The Australian government granted the students refugee status and eventually approved their permanent residency in Australia. Not all of the Chinese immigrants were English-language students. Many had come as postgraduate students, academics, artists and professionals, while others gained entry through family reunion programmes. Nor were all of the Chinese who entered Australia during this period from Mainland China. They came to Australia from Singapore, Hong Kong, Taiwan and other parts of the vast Chinese diaspora in Asia.

Separated by a roughly one-hundred-year gap, the largely illiterate Chinese sojourners who arrived in Australia in the late nineteenth century might appear, at first glace, to have little in common with the relatively well-educated Chinese who came to Australia in the late twentieth century. But some similarities between the first and second 'gold rushes' do exist. In each case, the immigrants were motivated by dreams of freedom, and by hopes of prosperity and greater opportunities (Ommundsen 2000: 90). The multicultural Australia the 'Tiananmen Square generation' of migrants encountered differed dramatically from the 'White Australia' the early Chinese endured, but economic imperatives played a major role in each wave of migration. Global shifts in supply and demand, changing labour patterns and the internationalization of world markets were common to each period. In other words, the first and second waves of Chinese migration to Australia emerged in the context of what we now know as globalization.

CROSS-CULTURAL ARTISTIC PRODUCTION

A growing number of Indigenous and Chinese Australian visual artists, playwrights, musicians and performers are working collaboratively to produce challenging and innovative forms of cultural expression. Indigenous and migrant communities are increasingly articulating what Suvendrini Perera has called a new 'cultural script' (cited in Shen and Edwards 2000: 5) that refuses essentialist notions of the nation-state and calls into question the Australian social and geographic imaginary. In reinterpreting and recasting the available repertoire of national narratives in their collaborative artistic, literary and theatrical endeavours, Aboriginal and Chinese Australians legitimize alternative histories and subjectivities, while simultaneously claiming a 'voice' in the public arena. This nascent form of trans-national story-telling not only resists the constraints of white nation rhetoric, it exposes the rather parochial nature of Australian national culture.

The problematics of identity and representation, and of who is authorized to speak for/about whom, are contested issues that more Chinese-Australians are grappling with in their work. Such vexed questions are especially pertinent when the person or community being represented is Indigenous. Aboriginal and Torres Strait Islander people are among the most researched, studied and analysed 'subjects' in the world. The vast majority of accounts have been undertaken by non-Indigenous people, and predominantly by dominant group members. But what if the individual collaborating with or representing Indigenous people is non-Indigenous and non-white? Does our perception of their work change if we learn that the artist is not white but Chinese? Should Chinese-Australians' representations of Aborigines be 'read' differently because they are not part of dominant white culture and therefore not racist (or not racist in the same way) (Murray 1996: 26-27)? A case in point is artist Zhou Xiaoping, whose 'right' to choose Aboriginal portraits as subjects has been contested by white Australian critics. Diana Giese notes that Zhou's paintings of his Aboriginal friends are not always well received: '[t]here are those who would deny Zhou, as a Chinese man ... the right to paint Aborigines at all' (Giese 1997: 69).

As Tseen Khoo suggests, the essentialism implied in such a judgement warrants closer attention. It seems that critics are opposed to Zhou's paintings of Aboriginal people because he is a *Chinese* man: '[i]n these arguments Zhou is, and always will be, "not-Australian"' (Khoo 2001: 100). Ironically, Zhou's establishment of a network of Chinese migrant and

Indigenous knowledges could be characterized as 'not-Australian'. Zhou has spent years living with and painting Aboriginal people in remote areas of Arnhem Land, the Kimberley region and north Queensland, 'sit[ting] close to them as friends' (cited in Giese 1997: 71). His attempts at '[r]eally understanding these people ... Understanding them from the inside, not just the outside' (cited in Giese 1997: 69) are illustrative of his negotiation of a cross-cultural alliance with Aboriginal people that (perhaps inadvertently) contests the quarantining of Indigenous politics and identities from migrant political and cultural identities. This cross-cultural union not only challenges the usual bifurcation of Indigenous and diasporic discourses, it simultaneously undermines the notion of Australia as a territorial zone with distinct and sovereign borders, replacing it with a porous inter-cultural and inter-racial political space. In traversing national boundaries and establishing a coalition of minority knowledges and politics that does not heed the sovereignty of the nation-state, Zhou's relationship with his Aboriginal friends could indeed be construed as 'not-Australian'.

Like their Anglo-Celtic counterparts it is incumbent on Chinese-Australians, as non-Indigenous people, to be alive to the complexities in-

Figure 12.1: Zhou Xiaoping, 'Land', 1998

Source: *Through the Eyes of Two Cultures* (Exhibition Catalogue) (1999). Beijing: National Gallery of China, no page.

volved in representing or depicting Aborigines in their work. But silencing their attempts to portray Aboriginal people by invoking spurious notions of one's 'right' or 'qualification' to do so might be counter-productive. After all, who is positioned to decide if Zhou has served a sufficient 'apprenticeship' as a friend of Aborigines to paint them? White art critics or Aboriginal people themselves? As a graduate student of Charles Darwin University in the Northern Territory, Zhou's (Anglo-Celtic) supervisors and others questioned not only whether or not he was eligible to paint Aboriginal people, but the particular way in which he depicted them (see Figure 12.1).

Zhou does not shy away from representing the harder social and economic realities that Aboriginal communities confront. Many (non-Indigenous) viewers prefer softer, more picturesque depictions of Aboriginal people: '[t]hey like little children with big smiles' (Zhou cited in Khoo 2001: 70). The fact that non-Indigenous art critics find Zhou's depictions too brutal, and the misguided liberal response of attempting to defend the 'poor Aborigines' from Zhou's representations, are signs of 'white guilt' (Khoo 2001: 100). Such reactions are an indication of how uncomfortable Anglo-Celtic Australians feel when reminded of the living conditions many rural Aboriginal communities endure.

Zhou often takes his paintings and drawings of his Aboriginal friends (or photographs of his portraits if they are too big) back to the communities. He is conscious of his moral and ethical duty to his friends and during the past 15 years has made many return visits to the various Aboriginal communities he has painted. He has even been given a 'skin' name that ties him to particular Aboriginal people, giving him both rights and responsibilities in relation to them. He has also been entrusted with particular 'Dreamtime' or creation stories, information only bestowed upon those deemed ready and responsible enough to receive it. Importantly, Zhou understands the critical difference between public and private knowledge. Some knowledge is sacred and not to be shared with 'outsiders', and certainly not to be painted for public viewing.

Zhou, now based in Melbourne, regularly shows his paintings that have been inspired by the Aboriginal people he has met on his journeys throughout the country. He is conscious that he not only has an important duty to his Aboriginal friends, he wants to promote Aboriginal culture more generally (personal communication 12 August 2004). Zhou's pieces have been exhibited from Beijing and Taiwan to Darwin, at the Museum of Chinese Australian History and the National Gallery of Victoria (Giese

1997: 73). At the Ballarat Fine Art Gallery in 2002 (in regional Victoria), Zhou showed his paintings at the From China to Arnhem Land and Beyond exhibition. Zhou also worked closely with the late Indigenous artist Jimmy Pike, whose work has been exhibited in France, Germany, the UK, Japan and China (see Figure 12.2).

Figure 12.2: Photographer unknown, 'Jimmy Pike and Zhou Xiaoping in China', 1996
Source: *Through the Eyes of Two Cultures* (Exhibition Catalogue) (1999). Beijing: National Gallery of China, no page.

In 1996, Zhou and Pike held a joint exhibition in Zhou's home town, Hefei, and in 1999 Through the Eyes of Two Cultures, another collaborative exhibition (including their drawings of each other) was held at the National Gallery of China. Considering that the Gallery had never shown an Australian artist before, the exhibition was an important forum in bringing Aboriginal, and Australian culture more generally, to the attention of Chinese audiences (see Figure 12.3).

Prominent Chinese-Australian photographer and performer William Yang's portrayal of Indigenous people also challenges the dominant style of representing Aboriginality (Byrne 2004). His 2002 photo documentary

Altered States: Indigenous Australian and Chinese Diasporic Alliances

周小平　杰米・派克
互画像(一)　1995
Zhou Xiaoping & Jimmy Pike
Drew each other (1)　1995
Charcoal on paper
64cm x 100cm

周小平　杰米・派克
互画像(二)　1995
Zhou Xiaoping & Jimmy Pike
Drew each other (2)　1995
Charcoal on paper
100cm x 64cm

Figure 12.3: Zhou Xiaoping and Jimmy Pike, 'Drew each other' (1 and 2), 1995
Source: *Through the Eyes of Two Cultures* (Exhibition Catalogue) (1999). Beijing: National Gallery of China, no page.

Shadows recounts a moving story of dispossession and reconciliation through a series of monologues accompanied by music and hundreds of slides projected from multiple projectors. Unlike the overly picturesque depictions of Indigenous people favoured by white Australians, Yang's imagery is frank and uncompromising. Far from the softer and more complementary imagery of smiling Aborigines (often children) used in government sponsored publications and posters, Yang depicts the harder truths confronting Indigenous communities including alcohol use and abuse at Enngonia, an Aboriginal settlement in north-western New South Wales. In his respectful, but nonetheless confronting documentation of the Aboriginal community's disintegration, Yang leaves the viewer in no doubt that the shadows of the past continue to haunt the present. Yang's performance not only challenges the audience to confront the harsh realities that many Indigenous communities face, it acknowledges that they are the result of an enduring colonial legacy.

For a descendent of the Chinese diaspora to challenge white Australians to acknowledge the ongoing ramifications of colonization and their agency in it, is to contest white national rhetoric that migrants should be forever 'grateful' and not criticize their adopted country. In *Shadows* Yang compares the story of an alleged massacre of Aborigines at Enngonia with the Nazi's attempted extermination of Jews by contrasting imagery of the alleged site of the Aboriginal massacre with that of a concentration camp in former East Germany. In narrating the story in this way, Yang suggests that both communities are holocaust survivors who bear the scars of attempted genocide. When one considers that the Report of the National Inquiry into the Separation of Aboriginal and Torres Strait Islander Children from their Families found that the Australian government's removal of so-called 'half-caste' children from their families coincided with one of the United Nation's definitions of genocide, Yang's drawing of a link between the two is not unfounded. In the wake of white Australia's historical amnesia, Indigenous Australians are often forced to do 'our' remembering for 'us'. In solidarity with their Indigenous counterparts, Zhou Xiaoping, William Yang and other members of the Chinese diaspora are increasingly bearing witness to a history and a colonial legacy that white Australians have still not confronted.

As a 'new migrant' to Australia, Zhou was unprepared for the white Australian criticism of his depictions of Aboriginal people. Soon after his arrival he met and painted various Aboriginal communities without any real knowledge of the white settler anxiety his work would incite.

Yang, who grew up in Australia on the other hand, was well versed in the politics of cross-cultural representation. In the 1980s and 1990s Yang was uneasy with the idea of photographing Aboriginal people: 'Of course I was interested in Indigenous culture, and why shouldn't all Australians be interested in Indigenous culture, but I didn't feel that I should photograph Aboriginal people in the 80s because, in some ways I felt that their emerging photographers should be doing that, that it was their story' (personal communication 2 September 2004). By the year 2002, when Yang was performing his photographic monologue *Shadows*, he 'felt comfortable telling an Aboriginal story' (Ibid.).

There were a number of contributing factors. For one thing, Yang had established lasting friendships with Aboriginal people at Enngonia. He was not using the images of nameless Aborigines, but photographing and telling the stories of his friends. Yang had also spent time researching his own family history. He recovered stories of oppression and marginalization from the broader Anglo-Australian community. He understood that the pressure on his family to relinquish their cultural and social traits to become 'Australian' was not an isolated experience. The fact that Yang was not taught to speak Chinese was a legacy of the pressure that migrants *and* Aborigines faced to conform and assimilate to white Australian norms: 'Because I'd gone into my own history, which is a history of marginalization, then I could empathize with the Aboriginal culture' (Ibid.).

Far from challenging his credentials to represent Aboriginal people, Yang was commissioned by the organizers of the 2002 Adelaide Festival to do a photographic piece with Aborigines. This interest in Yang's images of Aboriginal people marks a point of departure from some of the negative responses to Zhou's work, but Yang's initial brief was to portray Aboriginal children. As we have seen, white Australian audiences often favour images of smiling Aboriginal children because they are less challenging than pictures representing the social and economic hardships faced by Aboriginal communities. When the Festival organizers approached Yang to do a photographic essay, they did not have a particular Aboriginal language group in mind (Ibid.). Rather than depict anonymous Aborigines as nameless representatives of their race, Yang portrayed the experiences of Aboriginal people he knew personally. Again, the vexed issues of representation and appropriation reveal themselves. Are images of unidentified and unknown Aborigines examples of a dehumanizing iconism, or of a sensitive reluctance to identify individuals? (Murray 1996: 26)

Not all cross-cultural artistic, theatrical and literary production initiated by Indigenous and Chinese Australian communities is celebratory. The trans-national dialogue between these groups also alludes to the difficulties and ambiguities that affect their fraught yet potentially productive relations. The Chinese characters in recent novels by Indigenous authors Melissa Lucashenko (1999), Kim Scott (1999) and Alexis Wright (1997), for example, are portrayed as both the allies of Aboriginal people *and* as the beneficiaries of colonization. Chinese protagonists are simultaneously portrayed as sharing with their Indigenous counterparts a mutual sense of exclusion from the broader Australian community, and as colonizers or invaders who exploit Indigenous labour, land and waters for personal profit. Minoru Hokari suggests that narratives that emphasize migrants' contribution to the nation are welcomed by contemporary historiography as an example of the multicultural dimensions of Australia's past. However, this type of narrative lacks the historical imagination necessary to regard such economic endeavours as having been built on the exploitation of Indigenous people's land and waters (Hokari 2003b: 93). The Aboriginal/Chinese-Australian artistic and literary production explored here testifies to an honest and sincere attempt to embrace these relationships in their entirety, that is, to recognize that Chinese immigration 'furthered both the colonizing and decolonizing processes on the Australian continent' (Curthoys 2001: 172).

THE POLITICS OF INDIGENOUS/CHINESE ALLIANCES

A willingness to embrace the colonial as well as the potentially emancipatory aspects of Aboriginal/Chinese relationships is an important precondition for a shared political agenda. A perhaps unanticipated result of former Member of Parliament Pauline Hanson's[1] racism against Aboriginal and Asian Australians was the formation of new political alliances by Indigenous and Chinese Australian community groups. With Hanson's victory in the 1996 Federal election, race-based discourses reclaimed a central place in Australian nationalism. Prior to Hanson's re-racialization of Australian identity, the discourse of race had been almost entirely expunged from a public and political debate preoccupied with multiculturalism and ethnicity. 'Asians' were condemned by Hanson for taking jobs that rightfully belonged to white Australians, while Aborigines, on the other hand, were rebuked for not working hard enough, and thereby constituting a cost to the hardworking taxpayer (Povinelli 2002: 40). Hanson not only decried the access of Aborigines and Asians to the nation's economic assets, she was also anxious about their claims to the nation itself. In her insistence that the nation was in danger of being 'swamped' by Asians, she reinvoked notions of the 'yellow peril' and the 'Asian menace' that debarred Asians from entering the newly federated nation in 1901. Hanson also objected to Indigenous land rights on the basis that such 'benefits' were only available to Aboriginal people 'no matter how minute the indigenous blood'. In both cases, Hanson sought to deny Asian and Aboriginal Australians resources to which whites claim sole entitlement. Hanson's rhetoric reminds us that the white Australian national consciousness is still anxious about maintaining racial supremacy and cultural and economic dominance.

Hanson's objectification of Aboriginal and Asian Australians, and her attempts to undermine their claims to 'Australianness', assisted many Chinese-Australians to comprehend that they share with Aboriginal people the search for a sense of belonging to Australia. An acknowledgement of the experiences that Indigenous and Chinese Australian people share was integral to the initial formation of their closer political and social ties, but the potential for these alliances to strengthen and mature depended on Chinese-Australians' ability to reflect on their agency in the Australian post/colonial endeavour. In his assessment of Chinese language media in Australia, Edwin Tsung-Rong Yang has noted a high consciousness among Chinese-Australian commentators of the need for Chinese communities to participate in Reconciliation.[2] Notwithstanding their support of Reconciliation, however, Chinese-Australians simultaneously constructed themselves as 'new migrants' who bore no responsibility for past injustices (despite benefiting from them indirectly in the present) (Edwards 2001: 23).

Other members of the Chinese diaspora clearly acknowledge that they are implicated in Australia's colonial past and present. In a published interview with Peter Read, Elsie Chan, for instance, claimed that despite sometimes feeling rejected from Anglo-Australian society, she did not disassociate herself, though of Chinese descent, from the past misdeeds of white settler Australians, claiming: '[i]t was a bad thing we did, as a community' (cited in Read 2000: 66). Perhaps Jen Tsen Kwok's words provide the best summary of Chinese-Australians' ambiguous social location as both the victims and beneficiaries of white Australian racism:

> We have all inherited the consequences of [Aboriginal] oppression, because we are enjoying the fruits of 200 years of dispossession of the Aboriginal people, the labour and sweat of underpaid Aboriginal pastoral workers, and the virtually unpaid labour of the 'stolen generation' ... For the ... Chinese community – as Australians who understand the acts and attitudes of the past from the point of view of a downtrodden minority, or as newcomers free of cultural ties to Aboriginal oppression – it is a unique opportunity to assist in making restitution. (Kwok 2001: 200–201)

To ensure that Reconciliation moves beyond a 'closed national ritual' centred only on Indigenous and Anglo-Celtic Australians, Hokari calls for what he labels 'open Reconciliation' (Hokari 2003b: 96–98). This alternative mode of Reconciliation acknowledges that groups other than Anglo-Australians are implicated in the colonizing mission. Recent Chinese arrivals, or so-called 'new migrants' who have no genealogical ties to earlier Chinese pioneers are not directly accountable for the actions of their countrymen and women, but they do share responsibility with other Australians for the ongoing ramifications of past injustices. Indeed, even Chinese nationals who have never been to Australia but who purchase goods made or grown there indirectly benefit from the appropriation of Aboriginal and Torres Strait Islander land and waters. In this context Australian colonization has global implications, and Aboriginal Reconciliation must therefore cross national boundaries (Hokari 2003b: 95).

As Tessa Morris-Suzuki reminds us:

> We who live in the present did not create the violence and hatred of the past. But the violence and hatred of the past, to some degree, created us. It formed the material world and the ideas with which we live, and will continue to do so unless we take active steps to unmake their consequences. (Cited in Hokari 2003b: 98)

BEYOND THE NATION-STATE

Cross-cultural alliances between Indigenous Australians and their Chinese diasporic counterparts exist beyond national configurations of race and identity. Indigenous/Chinese partnerships challenge the quarantining of Aboriginal discourses and identities from those of the diaspora. The partitioning of 'the Indigenous' and 'the immigrant' in dominant Australian ideologies and discourses is evident in Australian historiography, in the university environment and in much public and political debate. Discussion on Reconciliation and Native Title[3] centres largely on a dialogue between 'black' and 'white' Australians, while debates on multiculturalism, immigration and asylum seekers rarely include any consideration of Aboriginal issues, centring instead on 'settlers' and 'migrants'.

But nationalist constructions based on the binary oppositions of 'black/white' and 'migrant/settler' blind us to two important realities. First, diasporic communities are engaged in a relationship with Indigenous people whether they know an Aboriginal person or not. This is because immigration, 'whether British or non-British, European or non-European, lies within rather than *after* a history of colonization, *within* the history of relations between Indigenous and non-Indigenous peoples' (Curthoys 2001: 172). Regardless of the racism and other forms of discrimination and prejudice migrant communities have encountered in Australia, *all* immigrants remain the beneficiaries of the dispossession of Aboriginal and Torres Strait Islander people. Second, 'black/white' and 'migrant/settler' dichotomies obscure the fact that Indigenous and various non-white migrant communities have engaged in complex networks of meeting on a range of levels, both historically and in the contemporary era. These cross-cultural meetings suggest an adaptive resilience to diversity that is lacking in the wider Australian community.

By focusing on the complex entanglements between Aboriginal and Chinese Australian communities, the Australian nation becomes incidental. It is at the point of conjunction between Indigenous and (Chinese) diasporic subjectivities that the framework of 'Australia' or any other 'nation' loses hold (Hokari 2003a: 94). Our challenge then, is not so much to see across cultures, but to think without centres (Hokari 2003a: 96). According to Dipesh Chakrabarty, it is important to 'unfocus' the nation by focusing on what is fragmentary and episodic 'precisely because that which is fragmentary and episodic does not, cannot, dream of the whole called the state and therefore must be suggestive of knowledge forms that are not tied to the will that produce the state' (Chakrabarty 1995: 757). By decentring or 'deprovincializing' the nation, we can pay homage to the very rich, complex and multifaceted flow of inter-ethnic, racial and cultural exchanges between Indigenous and diasporic peoples without being entrapped by limited and essentialist notions of nationhood. In other words, by focusing on people and places, we unfocus the nation.

CONCLUSION

This chapter has illustrated that one's identity as an Australian does not necessarily have to emerge through a recognition of (white) Australian mythologies and national narratives. It has documented an alternative sense of 'Australianness', one that emerges creatively and imaginatively, without buying into dominant national rhetoric. In telling their own stories, histories and experiences, Chinese-Australian and Indigenous communities are emancipating subjectivity from an identification with the nation-state. It is not so much that the two Chinese-Australians profiled here, William Yang and Zhou Xiaoping, have set out purposefully to oppose or refute white Australian mythologies of nation. Rather, they have creatively sidestepped them. They have maintained traditions of remembering, of community and of shared genealogies that ignore dates like 1788[4] and the coastal boundaries written on the map of Australia. Their identities and cross-cultural alliances with Indigenous people have artfully bypassed the sustaining myths of white Australian nationhood such as the Anzac legend[5], Ned Kelly[6], the Eureka Stockade[7] (and other white male triumphalist narratives of nation). In a sense, Indigenous and Chinese Australian communities have been obliged to circumvent dominant national narratives because they do not see their own experiences represented in them. Yang describes how, what he calls 'alternative histories of Australia' expose the gaps and fissures in 'mainstream' Australian historiography:

> I'm trying to give a personal story to history, because I think that history– history if you're just doing generalisations and statistics – really doesn't have any meaning ... The way I think that history could be told is to find an engaging story set in that period and then allude to larger events – contextualize that story in a larger historical event. And, in some ways the pieces I do are like alternative histories of Australia, in that they're not really the mainstream history, but they're stories of marginalized groups alluding to a larger history – mainstream history – which people know. (Personal communication 2 September 2004)

Dominant narratives of nations cannot speak for these new hybrid communities that cross cultures and transcend national boundaries. These new networks of meeting refuse to be contained by national borders or the universalizing tendencies of national imaginaries. In the absence of a meta-narrative capable of 'explaining' the complex entanglements between Indigenous and diasporic communities in national terms, our emphasis must shift to individuals and communities, to the local, the specific and the contingent. Thinking beyond the nation requires a whole new way of thinking. According to Deborah Bird Rose, we need look no further than the Indigenous Australian epistemology to develop this alternative worldview, because

> knowledge, in all Aboriginal systems of information, is specific to the place and to the people. To put it another way: one of the most important aspects of Aboriginal knowledge systems is that they do not universalize. Moreover, the fact that knowledge is localized and specific is one of the keys to its value. (Rose 1996: 97)

In borrowing a more decentralized, partial and particular system of knowledge from Australian Indigenous epistemology, we not only 'unfocus' the nation, we pay homage to conjunction, to intricate webs of human and cultural connections. Aboriginal/Chinese diasporic relations can thus be a course to deprovincializing the Australian nation and to emancipating Anglo-Celtic Australians from our rather narrow and reductive imagining of it. These historical and contemporary cross-cultural engagements expose the gaps in white Australian historiography and identity. In voicing these 'alternative histories of Australia' the Chinese-Australians profiled in this chapter point to the need for an altered imagining of the Australian nation-state.

Aboriginal/Chinese cross-cultural encounters have a very long history in Australia. Established initially by Aboriginal people and Chinese indentured or coolie labourers (or 'free' settlers lured overseas by the prospect of accumulating wealth), today they are being brokered by the descendents of these early Chinese migrants (William Yang) and 'new migrants' (Zhou Xiaoping) alike. 'New Chinese migrants', those who since the early 1980s have left China to settle elsewhere – regardless of their purpose, legal status and citizenship – differ from the early Chinese arrivals in terms of education, income, gender and English language proficiency. But, like their forebears, some Chinese-Australians – including those discussed in this chapter – are engaging in social, cultural and artistic alliances with Aboriginal communities. In doing so, they are continuing the long tradition of Aboriginal/Chinese cross-cultural engagement established more than a century ago.

NOTES

1. Pauline Hanson was the owner of a 'fish 'n' chip' shop in Ipswich (near Brisbane, Queensland) who was pre-selected by the Liberal Party to stand in the safe Labor seat of Oxley at the March 1996 election. She was subsequently disendorsed by the Liberal Party, but gained election as the independent member for Oxley following an electoral swing of 22 per cent, the largest against the government of any seat in the country. In her maiden speech to Parliament (URL: http://www.zipworld.com.au/~rocket/hanson/hanson1.htm) she called for the abolition of multiculturalism, special benefits for Aboriginal people and the halting of Asian immigration. The Queensland election of June 1998 was the first test of the electoral appeal of her newly established One Nation Party, and it won an amazing 22.7 per cent of the primary vote. One Nation won 11 of 89 seats in the one-house Queensland Parliament, outvoting the previously governing National Party. But Hanson enjoyed much greater popularity and electoral support when her rhetoric consisted of populist simplicities than when attempting to formulate detailed policies. In October 1998, Hanson lost her re-election campaign, and by mid-February 1999, support for One Nation had dropped to two per cent of the national electorate, with a number of One Nation's Queensland MPs resigning from the party. One Nation eventually lost official party status in Queensland due to an insufficient number of MPs.

2. Reconciliation promotes recognition of prior Aboriginal ownership and occupancy of the land as a precondition for reaching an agreement between Indigenous and non-Indigenous Australians about the foundations and future of Australian society. It was, until recently, an officially sanctioned government objective. In 1991 the Council for Aboriginal Reconciliation was established. It was given 10 years to research the conditions in which Indigenous people lived, and to try to raise awareness in the broader community about Aboriginal issues. It was hoped that by 2001, or the Centenary of Federation, that the nation would be reconciled. Reconciliation means different things to Indigenous and non-Indigenous Australians. From an Indigenous perspective, the precondition for Reconciliation is a recognition of land rights, while from the perspective of the current government, Reconciliation is predicated on their 'extinguishment'.

3. After 204 years, the false doctrine of *terra nullius* was thrown out by the High Court of Australia in the landmark Mabo case of 1992. The High Court recognized Aboriginal and Torres Strait Islander people's common law rights to land, that is, it recognized their Native Title. According to the Native Title Act of 1993, the High Court found that Native Title covered the whole continent in 1788, but that it had been extinguished by Crown grants of 'freehold' or ordinary title. This effectively left only government or Crown land open to Aboriginal and Torres Strait Islander land rights claims. Native Title survived on vacant Crown lands, state forests, national parks, beaches and foreshores. In 1996 the High Court found in favour of the Wik people of Cape York Peninsula, confirming that not all colonial tenures fully extinguished Native Title, and that Native Title may also exist on Crown land covered by pastoral leases. In the Wik decision, the High Court found that the rights of Native Title holders and pastoralists could coexist. The rights of Indigenous people, including the rights to visit sacred sites, hold ceremonies and collect 'bush tucker', could continue alongside a pastoral lease but, in the case of a dispute, the pastoralists' interests would prevail.

⁴ 1788 marks the date of the first white settlement in Australia.

⁵ ANZAC stands for Australian and New Zealand Army Corps. The Anzac legend developed around the deeds of Australian soldiers at Gallipoli and on the Western Front in the First World War. In *The Anzac Book* (1916), war correspondent C.E.W. Bean played a pivotal role in the evolution of the Anzac legend. In an attempt to salvage something from the appalling waste of life, Bean sought to show Australians that, even in defeat, their soldiers should be a source of pride.

⁶ Ned Kelly, one of Australia's most famous bush rangers is revered as a hero, even though he was the leader of a gang of outlaws (that operated in northern and central Victoria) who shot and killed police officers. An Irish immigrant, Kelly is widely remembered as the victim of harassment from the police and other authorities, as a man who was fighting to protect the rights of his family and people like him.

⁷ In response to attempts by authorities to regulate the goldfields around Ballarat, Victoria in the 1850s and to raise revenue by imposing a very high licence fee, protestors constructed a defensive fortification at the Eureka Lead. Using the Eureka Stockade and with a flag of their design (the 'Southern Cross' flag), protestors pledged to defend the rights and liberties of 'common' folk against greedy authorities. On 3 December 1854 they were overrun by more than 270 troops who killed between 20 and 30 men. By the time the leaders of the revolt were taken to court, public sentiment against the authorities was so strong that they could not find a jury to convict the men, and the leader of the rebellion was elected to Parliament within a year.

REFERENCES

Bean, C.E.W. (1916) *The Anzac Book: written and illustrated in Gallipoli by the men of Anzac*. London; Melbourne: Cassell.

Byrne, Matt. 'Shadows of the past haunt the present'. URL: http://www.messenger.net.au/Pulse/htm/shad06.html (accessed 9 February 2004).

Chakrabarty, Dipesh (1995) 'Radical histories and question of enlightenment rationalism: some recent critiques of subaltern studies', *Economic and Political Weekly*, vol. 30, no.14, pp. 751–759.

Curthoys, Ann (2001) 'Immigration and colonisation: new histories', *UTS Review*, vol. 7, no.1, pp. 170–179.

Davidson, Alistair (2003) 'The politics of exclusion in an era of globalisation'. In Laksiri Jayasuriya et al. (eds), *Legacies of White Australia: Race, Culture and Nation*. Perth: University of Western Australia Press, pp. 129–144.

Edwards, Penny (2001) *Lost in the Whitewash: Colloquium Report*. Canberra: The Centre for Cross–Cultural Research, Australian National University.

Giese, Diana (ed.) (1997) *Astronauts, Lost Souls and Dragons: Voices of Today's Chinese Australians*. St. Lucia: University of Queensland Press.

Hokari, Minoru (2003a) 'Anti–minorities history: perspectives on Aboriginal–Asian relations'. In Penny Edwards and Shen Yuanfang (eds), *Lost in the Whitewash: Aboriginal–Asian Encounters in Australia, 1901–2001*. Canberra: Humanities Research Centre, Australian National University, pp. 85–101.

—— (2003b) 'Globalising Aboriginal reconciliation: Indigenous Australians and Asian (Japanese) migrants', *Cultural Studies Review*, vol. 9, no. 2, pp. 84–101.

Khoo, Tseen (2001) 'Re–siting Australian identity: configuring the Chinese citizen in Diana Giese's astronauts, lost souls and dragons and William Yang's sadness'. In Wenche Ommundsen (ed.), *Bastard Moon: Essays on Chinese–Australian Writing*. Melbourne: Deakin University, pp. 95–109.

Kwok, Jen Tsen (2001) 'To be a great nation'. In Chek Ling (ed.), *Plantings in a New Land: Stories of Survival, Endurance and Emancipation*. Brisbane: Society of Chinese Australian Academics of Queensland, pp. 199–201.

Lucashenko, Melissa (1999) *Hard Yards*. St. Lucia: University of Queensland Press.

Martinello, Jennifer (2003) 'As strands of plaited music: my Chinese-Aboriginal-Anglo heritage'. In Penny Edwards and Shen Yuanfang (eds), *Lost in the Whitewash: Aboriginal-Asian Encounters in Australia, 1901–2001*. Canberra: Humanities Research Centre, Australian National University, pp. 23–35.

Murray, Dawn (1996) 'Wijay na...?', *Art Monthly Australia*, no. 92, pp. 26–27.

Ommundsen, Wenche (2000) 'Birds of passage? the new generation of Chinese-Australian writers'. In Ien Ang et al. (eds), *Alter/Asians: Asian-Australian Identities in Art, Media and Popular Culture*. Annandale: Pluto Press, pp. 89–106.

Perera, Suvendrini (2000) 'Futures imperfect'. In Ien Ang et al. (eds), *Alter/Asians: Asian-Australian Identities in Art, Media and Popular Culture*. Annandale: Pluto Press, pp. 3–24.

Povinelli, Elizabeth A. (2002) *The Cunning of Recognition: Indigenous Alterities and the Making of Australian Multiculturalism*. Durham and London: Duke University Press.

Read, Peter (2000) *Belonging: Australians, Place and Aboriginal Ownership*. Cambridge: Cambridge University Press.

Rose, Deborah Bird (1996) *Nourishing Terrains: Australian Aboriginal Views of Landscape and Wilderness*. Canberra: Australian Heritage Commission.

Scott, Kim (1999) *Benang: From the Heart*. North Fremantle: Fremantle Arts Centre Press.

Sham-Ho, Helen (2003) 'Lost in the whitewash concluding comments'. In Penny Edwards and Shen Yuanfang (eds), *Lost in the Whitewash: Aboriginal-Asian Encounters in Australia, 1901–2001*. Canberra: Humanities Research Centre, Australian National University, pp. 163–167.

Shen, Yuan-fang and Penny Edwards (2000) 'United by the sweep of a tarnished brush', *Panorama*, 18 November, pp. 4–5.

Wright, Alexis (1997) *Plains of Promise*. St. Lucia: University of Queensland Press.

Yang, William (1996) *Sadness*. St Leonards: Allen and Unwin.

—— (2004) interview with the author, 2 September, Melbourne, Australia (unpublished transcript in the possession of the author).

Zhou, Xiaoping (2004) interview with the author, 12 August, Melbourne, Australia (unpublished transcript in the possession of the author).

Index

Aborigines, *see* Indigenous Australians
All-China Federation of Returned Overseas Chinese (*Qiaolian*), 54, 68, 85, 159
amnesty, 115, 141–144, 160
Anti-Chinese legislation, 7; sentiments, 156, 193, 211
associations, 237, 239. *See also* Palembang Chinese Schools Alumni Association
    Chinese alumni, 20–21, 186, 188, 195, 197–198, 204
    Chinese classmate, 205
    Chinese clan, 241
    Chinese cultural, 243–244, 246, 249
    ethnic Chinese, 72–73, 158, 159n9, 186
    ethnic Chinese in Reunion (France), 2, 245–246, 248
    Filippino-Chinese, 159n10
    Indonesian-Chinese, 173, 186, 192
    kinship, 195
    native-place, 191, 195
    Overseas Chinese, 54, 61
    Panyu, 104
    Qingtian Chinese, 72–73, 78
    South-east Asian-Chinese, 187
Australia, 23, 40–46, 70, 95, 108, 110, 113, 114, 154–156, 165, 172–173, 188, 218, 254–271. *See also* Chinese-Australians
Australasia, 6–7, 26n13, 37, 45, 46, 47, 102, 165, 175

Beijing, 4–6, 25, 46, 48, 53, 108, 187, 215, 226, 249, 261
Brazil, 41, 98, 110
Budapest, Hungary, 15, 116, 128, 131. *See also* Hungary

Canada, 7, 38, 39, 40–46, 94, 110, 113, 156, 172, 183
Canton, *see* Guangzhou
Central and Eastern Europe, 13, 71, 72
chain migration, *see* migration, chain
China, People's Republic of (PRC),
    and economic investments from Hong Kong, 12, 76, 84, 88, 91, 93–95, 97–99
    and economic investments from Macau, 75, 76, 91, 98
    and economic reforms, 5, 8, 12, 13, 37, 49, 51, 52, 57, 61, 70, 76, 84, 94, 137
    as an economic superpower, 1, 108
    and foreign direct investment (FDI), 9, 40, 56, 78
    Great Power status, 9, 57–59
    Greater China, 52
    Super Power, 53
China, Republic of, *see* Taiwan (Republic of China)
Chinatown, 1, 2, 7, 23, 146
Chinese associations, *see* associations
Chinese-Australians, 255–260, 262, 267, 270, 271. *See also* Australia
Chinese Communist Party (CCP), 3, 61n7, 61n9, 68, 173
Chinese coolie workers, *see* migrants, coolie labour

275

Chinese diaspora, *see* diaspora, Chinese
Chinese entrepreneurs, *see* migrants, entrepreneurs
Chinese identity, *see* identity. *See also* 'Chineseness'
Chinese language, *see* Standard Chinese (Mandarin) (*putonghua*). *See also* dialects, Chinese
Chinese migrants, *see* migrants
Chinese migration, *see* migration
Chinese Nationality Law 1980, *see* migration policies
Chinese students, *see* students abroad
Chinese tourists, *see* tourism
'Chineseness', 45, 244
citizenship, 143, 271
    Chinese, 3–4, 61, 158
    dual, 4, 59
    Filipino, 141, 143, 153
    nationality, 55, 58, 59, 60
class, 23, 93, 191
    intellectual, 155, 175, 245
compatriot (*tongbao*), 57, 76, 85, 88, 93, 95, 112, 127
contract labour, *see* migrants, contract labour
coolie, *see* migrants, coolie labour
Creole culture, 238–240, 242, 245, 247
Creole language, 21, 238–240, 242, 251n2
cross-cultural alliances, 23, 254, 255, 259, 260, 268, 270

Deng, Xiaoping, 57, 58
département, 235, 236, 241, 245, 248, 251
dialects. *See also* Standard Chinese (Mandarin) (*putonghua*)
    Chinese, 153, 195, 196, 205n1, 222, 237, 238, 240
    Hakka, 21, 234, 237, 241, 251
    Minnan, 191,
    United States, 37
diaspora
    Armenian, 217
    Chinese, 46, 99, 103n7, 104n19, 203, 210–214, 216, 217, 228, 245, 255, 258, 264, 267–268
    concept of, 23, 45–47
    Indian, 217
    Jewish, 218

tourism, 20, 216–219, 221, 229
donations, *see* migrants, and donations. *See also* remittances
dual citizenship, *see* citizenship, dual

East Asia, 44, 167
economic activities of migrants, *see* migrants, economic activities; migrants, investments by migrants
economic reforms, *see* China, economic reforms
education, 5, 11, 44, 74–76, 94, 141, 155, 165, 169, 170, 172, 188, 189, 231, 246, 247, 248, 258, 271. *See also* students abroad
    Chinese, 186, 242
    French, 239, 241, 244
emigrants, *see* migrants
emigration, *see* migration
emigration policies, *see* migration, policies
employment, 12, 92, 116–119, 139, 173, 183, 236, 256
entrepreneurs, *see* migrants, entrepreneurs
ethnic Chinese (*huaren, huay*i), 3, 8, 9, 11, 16, 17, 22, 42, 43, 53–56, 59, 62n9, 84–85, 93–94, 218. *See also* migrants
    in Germany, 211, 212, 219–221
    in Indonesia, 187, 188, 195–196
    in Italy, 117
    in North America, 102
    in Reunion (France), 19, 21–22, 237, 238, 240, 244, 249–250
    in Southeast Asia, 186, 211
    in the Philippines, 137–138, 140, 142, 147, 152, 153, 158
ethnicity, 23, 266
    Chinese, 21, 173
    data on, 238
exploitation, 266
European Commission, 17
European Union, 129

family, 45, 59, 86, 87, 92, 100, 191, 192, 203, 213, 215, 216, 218–220, 227, 228
    enterprises, 92, 121, 123, 192, 197, 238
    family members of Chinese migrants in the PRC (*qiaojuan*), 85, 91, 96, 100
    and name, 242–243

remittances, 79
reunion, 5, 20, 79, 88, 92, 221, 258
transnational, 222
female, *see* gender
fertility, 40–41, 44, 46
foreign direct investment (FDI) in China, *see* China, People's Republic of (PRC), and foreign direct investment (FDI); *see also* migrants, investments
France, 22, 38, 39, 68, 71, 72, 73, 92, 98, 111, 124, 126, 170, 172, 188, 218, 234, 236, 238–245, 247, 248, 262
'frenchification', 21, 234, 240
Fujian, China, 4, 6, 11, 14, 36, 46, 56, 88, 91, 95, 114, 125, 137, 138, 139, 153, 154, 188, 191, 236, 237

gender, 271
 and migration, 2, 4, 23, 39, 46, 86, 142, 187, 242, 270
 patrilineality, 242
Germany, 20, 38, 39, 72, 73, 110, 124, 126, 170, 210, 211–220, 222–225, 228, 229
globalization, 2, 15, 17, 19, 38, 60, 83, 99, 100, 116, 121, 125, 128, 133, 158, 171, 176, 177, 183, 184, 185, 204, 211, 254, 258
 global capitalism, 2, 5, 13, 17, 21, 23, 83, 102, 116
 global cities, 6, 7, 23
'Great Migration', 36
Greater China, *see* China, People's Republic of (PRC), Greater China
Guangdong, China, 4, 11, 56, 83–102, 114, 125, 138, 154, 168, 187, 236, 237, 245–246, 256
Guangzhou (Canton), China, 4, 6, 88, 96, 114, 237
guiguo fuwu (return to serve the country), *see* students abroad

Hakka Chinese, *see* dialects, Hakka
Hansson, Pauline, 266–267
Heilongjiang, China, 5
'home'
 concept of, 2, 18–21, 178, 182–185, 210–211

 making a, 194–203, 210, 212, 214, 216, 219, 225–226, 228–229
 homeland, 47, 86, 93, 96, 114, 155, 183, 211–212, 216–218, 229
Hong Kong and economic investments in the PRC, *see* China, People's Republic of (PRC), and economic investments from Hong Kong. *See also* migrants, in Hong Kong; compatriot; students abroad, from Hong Kong
host-country response to migrants, 9, 60
huaqiao, *see* migrants, *huaqiao* status
huaqiao huaren yanjiu, *see* migration studies
huaren, *see* ethnic Chinese
huayi, *see* ethnic Chinese
human traffickers, 92
Hungary, 125. *See also* Budapest, Hungary

identity, 18, 19, 21, 185, 242, 259. *See also* 'Chineseness'; transnational, and identity
 diasporic, 22, 228, 234
 ethnic, 2, 22, 234. See also ethnicity
 of ethnic Chinese, 22, 139, 190, 203, 220, 240–244, 251
 multicultural, 239–244
illegal migration, *see* migration, illegal
immigrants, *see* migrants
immigration, *see* migration
indentured labour, *see* migrants, indentured labour
Indian migration, 4, 44–45, 145, 217, 235, 244
 and dual citizenship, 4
 and migrant investments, 4, 9, 40
 and remittances, 26n14
indigenous Australians, 23, 254–255, 257, 259–262, 264–272
indigenous Indonesians, 190
Indonesia. *See also* migrants, from Indonesia in Hong Kong; students abroad, from Indonesia
Indonesian-Chinese, 62, 211
integration of migrants, 3, 46, 53, 139, 238, 250
intellectuals, *see* class, intellectual
international migration, *see* migration

International Society for the Study of Chinese Overseas, 3, 108, 230
investments by migrants, *see* migrants, economic activities
irregular migrants, *see* migrants, irregular, undocumented; migration, irregular, illegal
Italy, 15, 38, 39, 94, 125, 133. *See also* migrants, in Italy
and Chinese migration, 17, 38, 123, 125, 129–131, 133
and fashion industry, 121, 130
Made in Italy, 115, 116, 117, 120, 121, 128, 131, 132

Japan, 38, 39, 40, 41, 98, 166. *See also* migrants, in Japan; students, in Japan
Jilin, China, 5

Kaisa Para Sa Kaunlaran, 142, 147

labour migration, *see* migration, labour
languages, *see* Standard Chinese; dialects
Latin America, 9, 14, 45, 145, 155
Liaoning, China, 5, 138
liuxue, *see* students abroad

Macau, China and economic investments in the PRC, *see* China, People's Republic of (PRC), and economic investments from Macau. *See also* compatriots
Macao, *see* Macau
Made in Italy, see Italy, *Made in Italy*
Mandarin, *see* Standard Chinese (*putonghua*)
Manila, the Philippines, 14, 146,
Marcos, Ferdinand E., 137, 141
market reforms, China, *see* China, People's Republic of (PRC), and economic reforms
marriage, 257
memory, 101, 195, 198, 199, 202
men, *see* gender
Mexico, 38, 44
migrants, *see also* economic activity; ethnicity, Chinese; China, People's Republic of (PRC), and foreign direct investment (FDI); *yimin* (migrant), concept of; migration
Chinese concept of, 3, 84, 85, 103n8, 166–170
contract labour, 2, 4, 8, 39, 235
coolie labour, 4, 14, 24, 90, 256, 271
and cultural attachments, 8, 53
and donations, 9–12, 57, 67, 74–78, 86, 88–89, 94–95, 101–103
economic activities,
entrepreneurs, 2, 16, 20–21, 219, 220
and ethnic economy, 117, 132, 219–228
and family dependants in the PRC of Chinese migrants (*qiaojuan*), 56, 85, 86, 87, 96, 100, 101, 190
and foreign direct investments, *see* China, People's Republic of (PRC), and foreign direct investment (FDI)
from Hong Kong, 211, 215, 216, 222, 258
in Hong Kong, 20, 38, 40, 45, 47, 50, 56, 88, 90, 92, 112, 113, 147, 165, 169, 174, 175, 183, 186, 187, 191–192, 194, 195, 197–198, 201, 202–204
and *huaqiao* status, 142, 150
and identity, *see* identity; 'Chineseness'
and import-export business, 124–126, 128, 150
indentured labour, 2, 235, 236, 256, 271
from Indonesia in Hong Kong, 20, 182–204, 213
investments, 9, 12, 78
irregular, 1, 2, 16, 25
in Italy, 15, 45, 71–73, 75, 92, 115–122, 124, 126–128
in Japan, 69, 110, 113, 114, 168, 170
in Macau, 90, 92
new Chinese, 3, 8, 9, 15, 19, 60, 115–122, 132, 137–140, 142, 144, 145, 151, 153, 173, 212, 247, 271
and number of Chinese in Italy, 115
and number of Chinese in Reunion (France), 237–238
and number of Chinese in the Philippines, 140
and political system, 53–56

278

skilled, 2, 7, 16, 19, 31, 36, 45–47, 60, 176, 212
in Spain, 45, 68, 71, 92, 124, 126, 130, 132, 133
and trading, 2, 7, 13, 14–17, 45, 71, 72, 102, 147, 155
undocumented, 7, 17, 123, 139, 140, 144, 145, 153
and work/employment permits, 147, 173
migration, *see also* migrants
British, 36, 49
chain, 92
distinctiveness of Chinese, 2, 7–9, 35–37, 47, 49, 51–61
and economic development, 6, 8–12, 15–16, 58, 73, 78, 94, 101
and entrepreneurship, 14–16, 116–122, 124–128, 150, 219–228
European, 7–8, 36, 37
and globalization, 13, 17, 38, 116, 133
history from China, 2, 14, 76, 151–152, 157, 169–175
history from China to Australia, 256–258
history from China to Germany, 211–212
history from China to Reunion (France), 235–236, 241–244
history of Indonesian-Chinese, 188–189
illegal, 139–140, 143, 154, 159
India, *see* Indian migration
irregular, 1, 16, 30, 44
labour, 39–40, 235
trading, 2, 7, 13, 14–17, 71–72, 102, 147, 155
undocumented, 6, 16
migration policies, 44, 92, 177, 186, 257
See also *see* All-China Federation of Returned Overseas Chinese; Australia; Italy and Chinese migration; Overseas Chinese Affairs Office (PRC)
Chinese Nationality Law 1980, 4
Law for the protection of the rights and interests of the People's Republic of China's returned overseas Chinese and their relatives, 55

of the PRC, 12–13, 24, 55–60, 99, 186, 189–190, 245–250
'migranthood', 19–20, 165–177
migration studies, 2, 18, 23, 49–53, 60–61. See also Overseas and Ethnic Chinese Studies
migration theory, 7, 13
multicultural identity, *see* identity
multiculturalism, 21, 44, 266, 269

Naples, Italy, 110, 131
nationalism, 255
in Australia, 266
in China, 170, 186
nationality, *see* citizenship
Nationality Law, *see* migration policies, Chinese Nationality Law 1980
native place association (*tongxianghui*), 72, 73, 191, 195, 204
native village of sojourning Chinese (*qiaoxiang*),13, 52, 83–102
new Chinese migrants, *see* migrants, new Chinese
New York, 7. *See also* globalization, global cities
North Eastern China, 5, 6, 46

open-door policies, *see* China, Republic of (PRC), economic reforms
Overseas Chinese, *see* migrants, new Chinese; migrants, *huaqiao* status
Overseas Chinese Affairs Office (PRC), 54
Overseas and Ethnic Chinese Studies, 8

Palembang Chinese Schools Alumni Association, 186, 188, 195–203. *See also* Indonesia; migrants, from Indonesia in Hong Kong
Panyu, Guangdong, China, 11–12, 83–84, 88–96, 99–102, 110–114
patriotic, 57
People's Republic of China (PRC), *see* China, People's Republic of (PRC)
Peru, 41, 110
Philippines, the, 15, 16, 17, 40, 110, 137–158, 172, 183
Pike, Jimmy, 262–263
Prato, Italy, 92, 120, 122, 123, 126, 127
PRC, *see* China, People's Republic of (PRC)

279

qiaojuan, see migrants, and family dependants in the PRC of Chinese migrants (*qiaojuan*)
Qiaolian, see All-China Federation of Returned Overseas Chinese (*Qiaolian*)
qiaoxiang, see native village of sojourning Chinese. *See also* native place association (*tongxianghui*)
Qing government, 55, 58
Qingtian, Zhejiang, China, 10–12, 67–80
and migration history 70–72, 92
See also Wenzhou, Zhejiang, China; native village of sojourning Chinese

racial exclusion and discrimination, 190, 193, 198, 266, 269
of Chinese migrants, 7, 17, 18,
religion, 216, 238, 240, 245, 249
remittances, 2, 9, 10–12, 39–40; 56–57, 64–80, 84, 100, 102, 190, 216, 228
Reunion (France), 21–23, 234–236, 244–245
and China, 245–250
ROC, see Taiwan (Republic of China)
Rome, Italy, 7, 15–16, 118, 124, 126, 128–131
Russia, 5, 6, 45,
Russian Far East 45, 69, 127

Second World War, 11, 21, 50, 60, 71, 87, 92, 100, 166, 170, 173, 176, 211, 241
Shanghai, China, 4, 5, 6, 46, 95, 114, 174, 249
Singapore, 38, 39, 40, 47, 88, 92, 94, 95, 98, 169, 175, 188, 256. *See also* students abroad, in Singapore
Sinwa, 234, 238–251
skilled migrant, *see* migrans, skilled
sojourner, 18, 36, 44, 47, 84, 168–170, 173, 183, 192, 211, 212, 226, 229, 255, 257, 258
Spain, 15, 39, 45, 98
and migrants from China, 132–133
See also migrants, in Spain
Standard Chinese (Mandarin) (*putonghua*), 187, 191, 195, 243, 248, 257. *See also* dialects
stereotypes, 244

about Hakka, 237
students abroad, 5, 19–20, 43, 155–177, 186
becoming migrants, 53, 165, 176
and *guiguo fuwu* (return to serve the country), 19
from Hong Kong, 165, 168
from India, 172
from Indonesia, 172, 173
in Japan, 5, 166
from Macau, 165, 169
in Singapore, 169, 175
in United States, 5, 165, 169–172
and *weiguo fuwu* (serve the country), 19
Sun Yat-sen, 55

Taiwan (Republic of China), 38, 40, 43, 45, 55, 76, 94, 95, 98, 113, 114, 147, 174–176, 183, 211, 218, 219, 224
tongbao (compatriot from Hong Kong, Macau and Taiwan), *see* compatriot
tongxianghui, see native place association (*tongxianghui*)
tourism, 20–21, 223–225, 248. *See also* diaspora, tourism
traders, *see* migrants, and trading
transformation societies, 7, 14
translocalism, 24
transnational families, *see* family, transnational
transnationalism, 18, 100–101, 212–213
and communities, 211
and identity, 183
and nation-states 22, 24
See also family, transnational
Tsinoy, 139–158

undocumented migration, *see* migration, undocumented; migration, illegal; migration, irregular
United States, 11, 36, 37–40, 43, 44, 45, 94, 95, 98, 100, 110, 113, 114, 172, 175, 183. *See also* students abroad, in the United States

values, of Chinese culture, 244
visas and passports, 45, 144, 220, 231, 229, 250, 258

weiguo fuwu (serve the country), *see* students abroad and *weiguo fuwu*
Wenzhou, Zhejiang, China, 12, 13, 68, 83, 84, 89–92, 100–102, 124–126. *See also* native village of sojourning Chinese
   and economic development, 96–100
   and migration, 13, 88, 90–93, 96–102
women, *see* gender
work permits, *see* migrants, and work/employment permits

Xiamen, China, 11, 103, 155

Yang, William, 262–265
yimin (migrant), concept of, 140, 165–168, 170, 178n6. *See also* migrants; migration
youth, 199, 200, 202, 240, 242
Yunnan, China, 6, 154, 188

Zhejiang, China, 6, 10, 11, 36, 46, 67, 68, 74, 79, 83, 84, 89, 127, 153, 248
Zhou, Wangsen, 67
Zhou, Xiaoping, 259–266